State-Corporate Crime

Critical Issues in Crime and Society
Raymond J. Michalowski, Series Editor

Critical Issues in Crime and Society is oriented toward critical analysis of contemporary problems in crime and justice. The series is open to a broad range of topics including specific types of crime, wrongful behavior by economically or politically powerful actors, controversies over justice system practices, and issues related to the intersection of identity, crime, and justice. It is committed to offering thoughtful works that will be accessible to scholars and professional criminologists, general readers, and students.

Mary Bosworth and Jeanne Flavin, eds., *Race, Gender, and Punishment: From Colonialism to the War on Terror*

Raymond J. Michalowski and Ronald C. Kramer, eds., *State-Corporate Crime: Wrongdoing at the Intersection of Business and Government*

Susan L. Miller, *Victims as Offenders: The Paradox of Women's Violence in Relationships*

Susan F. Sharp, *Hidden Victims: The Effects of the Death Penalty on Families of the Accused*

Robert H. Tillman and Michael L. Indergaard, *Pump and Dump: The Rancid Rules of the New Economy*

Marina Valverde, *Law and Order: Images, Meanings, Myths*

Michael Welch, *Scapegoats of September 11th: Hate Crimes and State Crimes in the War on Terror*

State-Corporate Crime

WRONGDOING AT THE INTERSECTION OF BUSINESS AND GOVERNMENT

EDITED BY
RAYMOND J. MICHALOWSKI
RONALD C. KRAMER

RUTGERS UNIVERSITY PRESS
New Brunswick, New Jersey, and London

LIBRARY OF CONGRESS CATALOGING-IN-PUBLICATION DATA

State-corporate crime : wrongdoing at the intersection of business and
government / edited by Raymond J. Michalowski and Ronald C. Kramer.
     p. cm.—(Critical issues in crime and society)
   Includes bibliographical references and index.
   ISBN-13: 978-0-8135-3888-4 (hardcover : alk. paper)
   ISBN-13: 978-0-8135-3889-1 (pbk. : alk. paper)
  1. Corporations—Corrupt practices—United States.   2. Political corruption—
United States.   3. Social ethics—United States.   4. United States—Politics
and government.   I. Michalowski, Raymond J.   II. Kramer, Ronald C.
III. Series.
   HV6769.S72   2006
   364.16 80973—dc22   2006013275

A British Cataloging-in-Publication record for this book is available
from the British Library

Manufactured in the United States of America

For the victims of Hurricane Katrina, who have vividly demonstrated the human cost of elite power games,

And for Jill and Jane

Contents

State-Corporate Crime

to military units, CIA operatives, and clandestine "assets" charged with designing and carrying out tactical missions in support of the strategic goals (Kennan 1967).

The front-line cold warriors who helped agent provocateurs plant bombs in third-world countries, trained foreign police in the use of torture, helped plan and fund counterrevolutions against developing socialist nations, carried out assassinations of leaders who seemed to threaten U.S. Cold War interests, or fought in what came to be known as "low intensity warfare" against governments that did not support the U.S. were far removed from the leaders whose policies they were carrying out (Blum 2004; Herman 1982; Klare and Kornbluh 1989). If anything questionable or illegal came to light, leaders could always claim "plausible deniability," saying they had not ordered the specific crimes in question. Indeed, they may not have meant that some specific, heinous crime be committed in the name of freedom and democracy. Nevertheless, they created a political culture and organizational frameworks that ultimately led to heinous acts that would not have occurred without that culture and those frameworks.

We find a similar chain-of-command issue in the more recent scandals involving the torture of U.S. captives in the "war on terror." There is substantial evidence that in Afghanistan, in Camp X-Ray in Cuba's Guantanamo Bay, and in Iraq—most notably in the Abu Ghraib prison—members of the U.S. armed forces and privately contracted interrogators were enmeshed in a system where criminal abuse of so-called enemy combatants had become routine (Danner 2004; Hersh 2004; N. A. Lewis 2005; Ratner and Ray 2004). The Bush administration, however, was successful in claiming plausible deniability, thus protecting both its inner circle and its military leaders by limiting prosecutions to the lowest levels of involvement (Schmitt 2005).

It is probably true that no high-level U.S. official specifically ordered torture. Yet it is also true that the Bush administration appointed an attorney general who had previously drafted legal opinions justifying torture on narrow legal technicalities such as the fact that Al Qaeda is not a nation and has not signed the Geneva Convention (Danner 2004; Greenberg and Dratel 2005). Decisions of this sort at the top of the political pyramid go a long way toward creating an organizational climate in which the torture of suspected terrorists—regardless of how minimal the evidence against them—can easily be interpreted as heroic duty.

Similarly, when corporate managers mandate accelerated production, increased worker output, or reduced costs, they are not specifically ordering increases in injuries due to assembly-line speedups, intensification of repetitive-motion tasks, or reductions in expenditures for safety equipment or worker training, even though such outcomes are predictable (Aulette and Michalowski 1993). As with political leaders, plausible deniability means that those who issue such orders will normally not be seen as guilty for the causal chain leading to the harms those orders cause. When it comes to widely disbursed harms such as environmental damage or consumer injuries, the insulation between elites and the causal process leading to harm becomes even thicker. The ability of Union Carbide Corporation to isolate its managerial chain from responsibility for the deadly 1984 leak of methyl iso cynante gas in Bhopal, India, that killed over fifteen thousand people is a particularly vivid case of plausible deniability in operation (Moro and Lapierre 2002).

Contemporary narratives of harm resulting from decisions by economic and political elites lack clear villains. This is perhaps appropriate, since many of these harms are the products of complex organizational arrangements, not the mendacity of specific individuals (Kramer 1984). Without straightforward causal chains leading from criminal to victim, however, these crimes fit poorly within the dominant consciousness of criminology, and therefore receive less attention from criminology than the harms they cause would seem to warrant.

Fifth, criminology is an academic discipline. This means that criminologists are disciplined by the organizational demands of higher education. The ability to survive and advance in a university setting requires that criminologists not only teach but also conduct research and publish research findings. As Tombs and Whyte (2003) have noted, governments provide little or no funding for research into wrongdoing by political leaders or their allies in business, industry, or the military. When governments provide money for criminological research—and governments are the primary source of criminological research dollars—these monies are primarily designated for research into the causes and control of crimes and vices associated with poor and less powerful segments of society (National Institute of Justice 2005).

The structure of research financing plays a significant role in determining what the majority of criminologists will investigate. Well-funded areas of study attract scholars anxious to advance their careers. Government-sponsored research also funds graduate students interested in criminology, thereby increasing the likelihood that many of these future scholars will develop research agendas along government-supported lines of inquiry. Meanwhile, as public financing of universities shrinks, university administrators become increasingly insistent that new faculty bring in overhead-generating research dollars, further ensuring that most criminologists will have little choice but to dance to the tune paid for by the governmental pipers of research dollars. Finally, the most prestigious private and public universities are closely linked to governmental and business interests. Scholars who pose serious challenges to the hegemonic social system have long been seen as unattractive candidates for employment or promotion in these schools (Schrecker 1986).

Taken together, these factors have meant that social harms resulting from decisions by economic and political elites have figured less prominently within criminology.

Criminological Consciousness and Mass Media

The characteristics of modern criminology described above did not evolve in a vacuum. They are expressions of a hegemonic consciousness which, as Gramsci (1971) theorized, combines established cultural beliefs with political ideology to create dominant thought-ways that serve as filters for all information and experience. Since the beginning of the twentieth century the creation and maintenance of hegemonic consciousness have relied heavily on the communicative networks of electronic mass media, beginning with radio, then television, and now both of these plus Internet media distribution (Ewen 2001).

Economic and political elites enjoy an overwhelming (though not absolute) advantage in shaping hegemonic consciousness through their ability to influence the content of mass media. In liberal democratic states, such as the United States and the European Union, political and economic elites exert significant indirect influence over media content by setting the terms of national discourse and capitalizing on media dependence on business and government sources for information to ensure that media reportage will be dominated by pro-systemic images (O'Shaughnessy 2004). In some cases governments, such as the United States, directly manipulate mediated messages by creating apparent "news" stories that are little more than "infomercials" for government perspectives. According to a report by the U.S. inspector general issued in March 2005, for example, between 2000 and 2004 the Bush administration produced several hundred supposed news segments that were distributed to local television stations around the United States. Unlike commercials and political ads, however, these government propaganda pieces masqueraded as "objective" news by hiding from viewers any indication they had been made by the government (Barstow and Stein 2005).

Although governments play a role in shaping news, in modern capitalist democracies the primary determinant of media content derives less from government influence or manipulation than from the economic character of modern mass media itself. Increasingly, communications networks are parts of megacorporations such as Viacom and AOL Time Warner. Their primary goal is not producing a well-informed and thoughtful public; it is generating profit by keeping people watching and reading. Among other things, this goal means avoiding serious critical analyses that leave audiences concerned and discomforted rather than relaxed and satisfied. The most cost-effective way to achieve the goal of a large audience is to keep people entertained, and one of the best ways to keep people entertained is through stories that fit ideal-typical images of crime.

The hegemonic consciousness of crime as a problem involving a straightforward causal chain flowing from a premeditating evil-doer to a specifically targeted individual victim is substantially strengthened by the predominance in news media, novels, movies, and television dramas of stories featuring murder or some other type of individualized violence (Hamilton 1998; Lichter and Lichter 1983; Soulliere 2003). Whether real or fictional, tales of crime, as Aristotle informed us long ago, captivate our attention because they symbolize human moral dilemmas. They also provide a perversely entertaining sense of frisson, in much the same way that people enjoy the controlled fright of rollercoasters and other carnival rides. Finally, compared with the difficulties of uncovering and sorting through the complexities of economic and political crimes, street crime stories are inexpensive and easy to produce. Their raw material is continually being created by the justice system as it reports on crimes, captures criminals, and performs real-life dramas of judgment and punishment. The justice system is a bottomless well of storylines for news and entertainment media. As a result, media conglomerates reproduce the dominant consciousness of crime by providing a continuous array of narratives about crimes of vengeance, lust, greed, or insanity. Narratives of elite wrongdoing—unless they too happen to involve vengeance, lust, greed, or insanity—are less entertaining and more costly. They will consequently be far less attractive as grist for the corporate media system.

STATE-CORPORATE CRIME: ORIGINS AND DEVELOPMENT

It is relatively easy to critique the consciousness that dominates popular understandings of crime and, through those understandings, of criminology as well. It is similarly easy to delineate the mass-mediated channels of communication through which this consciousness is formed and rendered hegemonic. The more serious challenge is to construct an alternative approach to crime and criminological inquiry that avoids these limitations, but at the same time does not slip into the indulgence of "personal moralities" (see Braithwaite 1985:18).

The problem of defining crime beyond the boundaries of the law has troubled analysts of corporate crime and state crime since Sutherland first proposed that criminology broaden its horizons to include white-collar crime. Sutherland's work sparked both a spate of inquiries into white-collar criminality and a furious debate regarding whether regulatory violations by those in business were appropriate for criminological study. The assertion that white-collar crime is real crime by Sutherland (1945, 1949), and the negative critique of this proposition offered by lawyer-sociologist Paul Tappan (1947), raised two central issues: Can acts proscribed by regulatory rather than criminal law be considered crimes, and therefore within the purview of criminology? Can acts that are potentially punishable by law—but that have not been prosecuted—be considered fair game for criminological inquiry insofar as no court has yet ruled that a violation of law has actually occurred? Sutherland answered in the affirmative on both counts, Tappan in the negative.

As a theoretical matter, by the 1980s this debate had largely been resolved in favor of a broadened view of criminological inquiry. That is, studies of regulatory violations, for the most part, came to be accepted as legitimate subjects for criminological inquiry. At a practical level, however, as we have already noted, the proportion of criminologists who actually analyzed crimes of the powerful remained small in comparison with those engaged in the study of street crime and/or its control. Nevertheless, white-collar crime scholars have produced a growing body of literature that has increasingly intersected with research in economics and political science as well as in criminology (see Friedrichs 2004 for an overview).

Our approach builds on this literature, and extends it in three ways. First, agreeing with Kauzlarich and Kramer (1998) and Chambliss (1995), we suggest that the boundaries of criminological inquiry should reach beyond national laws and include violations of public international law.

Second, we argue that analogous social injuries should also be brought within the purview of criminological inquiry. Analogous social injuries are "legally permissible acts or sets of conditions whose consequences are similar to those of illegal acts" (Michalowski 1985:357). We suggest expanding criminology to encompass analogous social injuries not because we claim there is no difference between analogous social injuries and crimes, but precisely because there is an important difference; one represents harms that are legal and the other harms that are illegal. Comparing the nature and origins of analogous social injuries with those of prohibited harmful acts brings the processes of law formation—a subject of particular interest to criminologists—into sharp relief. It provides a useful standpoint from which to examine the political and cultural forces that result in some harms being labeled crimes, others regulatory violations, others noncriminal deviance, and still others praiseworthy acts. This type of inquiry is particularly important when examining corporate criminality in an age of neoliberal globalization, in which transnational corporations can often exert power over the creation of laws regulating their activities (Michalowski and Kramer 1987).

The concept of analogous social injury is also an important corollary to our contention that the scope of criminology should embrace the arena of international as well as national law. Under the current United Nations structure, powerful states—particularly the permanent members of the Security Council—enjoy significant advantages in determining the substantive content of international law and practical interpretations of what constitutes human rights (Ishay 2004; Lyons and Mayall 2003). In this context the concept of analogous social injury facilitates an inquiry into how some state actions will be considered violations of international law and others tolerable, even if regrettable, acts.

In sum, we combine existing understandings of economic and political crime with the concept of analogous social injury into a theoretical construct we term state-corporate crime. This construct enables us to examine a broad range of crimes, regulatory violations, and social injuries that result when economic and political powers intersect in harmful ways.

Origins

Knowing when an idea first appeared is far different from knowing how it began. Although the term *state-corporate crime* made its first public appearance in a series of papers presented in 1990 (Kramer 1990a, b; Kramer and Michalowski 1990), unraveling its origins and evolution is a longer story embracing more than two decades of collaborative effort to understand crimes of the powerful.

In the mid-1980s, as part of an early inquiry into globalization, we examined how the growing power of transnational corporations headquartered in cosmopolitan centers enabled them to shape laws of interest in the peripheral and semiperipheral nations to which they were increasingly outsourcing components of production and distribution. This work was eventually published in the journal *Social Problems* as "The Space between Laws: Corporate Crime in a Transnational Context" (Michalowski and Kramer 1987). We came away from this initial inquiry with a heightened awareness of the importance of understanding the intersection of economics and politics in the production of corporate crimes and social harms.

About the time we were completing "The Space between Laws," Ron began a project focused on unraveling the organizational origins of the space shuttle *Challenger* explosion. As he examined the relevant documents, he became increasingly sensitized to how the controversial *Challenger* launch decision involved interactions between a political organization, the National Aeronautics and Space Administration, and Morton Thiokol, Inc., a private business corporation. Acting in concert, these two organizations produced a technological failure of far-reaching consequence (Vaughan 1996). This case suggested a need for criminology to develop clearer conceptualizations of deviant interorganizational relationships between business and government.

In 1989, over dinner at the Society for the Study of Social Problems (SSSP) meeting in Berkeley, we discussed the issue, and Ray suggested labeling harms resulting from these interactions "state-corporate crime." Ron thought the term fit the problem, and began incorporating it into his work on the *Challenger* (Kramer 1990a, b), including "State-Corporate Crime: A Case Study of the Space Shuttle Challenger Explosion," which he presented at the Edwin Sutherland Conference on White Collar Crime: 50 years of Research and Beyond and which is included in this volume. We continued working together to refine the concept of state-corporate crime and to develop a more elaborated theoretical framework for it.

We presented our first efforts at the American Society of Criminology meeting in November of 1990 in a paper titled "Toward an Integrated Theory of State-Corporate Crime." In this paper we noted that, despite their ubiquity, structural relations between corporate and governmental organizations had been largely left out of the study of corporate crime. Instead, two nearly independent bodies of research had developed. Theory and research in the area of corporate crime had concentrated primarily on organizational deviance within private business corporations. Paralleling that work, but seldom intersecting with it, others had examined crimes and malfeasance initiated by governments, what Chambliss (1989) had called "state-organized crime." We suggested that rather than seeing these as separate problems, it would be useful for criminologists to examine how organizational deviance frequently emerges at the interstices of corporations and government. We used the term *state-corporate crime* to denote these types of crimes and offered the following definition: "State-corporate crimes are illegal or socially injurious actions that occur when one or more institutions of political governance pursue a goal in direct cooperation with one or more institutions of economic production and distribution" (Kramer and Michalowski 1990:3).

Less than a year later, in September 1991, a fire in the Imperial chicken-processing plant in Hamlet, North Carolina, killed twenty-five workers and injured another fifty-six. From reports about working conditions at the Imperial processing plant that Ray heard from his students at UNC-Charlotte, and from what he already knew about the North Carolina Occupational Safety and Hazards Administration, he recognized the Imperial fire as another potential candidate for state-corporate crime inquiry. Ray began working with his colleague Judy Aulette to gather and analyze data on the distant and proximate causes of an increasingly apparent case of industrial murder. As part of this work, Ray analyzed the ways in which larger conditions created by the state, such as an antiregulatory, pro-business climate and an underfunded North Carolina OSHA were important contributing precedents to the Imperial fire. This led him to revise the definition of state corporate crime as "illegal or socially injurious actions that result from a mutually reinforcing interaction between (1) policies and/or practices in pursuit of the goals of one or more institutions of political governance and (2) policies and/or practices in pursuit of the goals of one or more institutions of economic production and distribution" (Aulette and Michalowski 1993:175; see also chapter 2 below).

With a revised definition and analyses of the space shuttle explosion and the Imperial chicken fire in hand, we expanded our original state-corporate crime paper to incorporate both case studies and submitted it to *Social Problems*. After a long review and revision process and a change of editors, *Social Problems* declined the article, making it what David Friedrichs (1995) once characterized as "the most widely cited unpublished piece of writing in corporate crime research." It is this paper we present here, in print for the first time, as "The Original Formulation."[2]

In the years following our initial inquiry into state-corporate crime, other scholars began adapting the concept and its associated theoretical model to a number of other social harms. The concept of state-corporate crime has been used to analyze historical offenses, such as corporate collaborations with the Nazi regime during World War II, and to contemporary violations such as state-corporate corruption in the world of private military organizations. Some applications of the state-corporate crime model have examined offenses that begin with governments, such as nuclear weapons production or space programs. Others have explored injurious collaborations that began in the realm of business but that could not develop without governmental acts of commission or omission, such as the Firestone-Explorer rollover deaths or the *Exxon Valdez* oil spill. A number of these applications are published in the present volume.[3]

In this volume, we bring together the conceptual formulation and application of the theory of state-corporate crime with three goals in mind. The first is to establish the scope and gravity of state-corporate crime, not simply as a topic for criminological inquiry, but as a significant threat to social peace and human well-being on both a national and global scale. Our second goal is to offer those concerned with social harms at the intersection of business and government a theoretical framework for understanding how these harms are produced. The third is to provide readers, particularly student readers, a window into how ideas evolve over time, sometimes moving in directions that their initial creators may never have imagined.

WHAT COMES NEXT

The following chapters are, for the most part, arranged according to the timing of the analyses rather than the timing of the offense. Our organizing principle has been to show the evolution of the idea of state-corporate crime, rather than to present a chronological ordering of the crimes studied. We made this choice because in many instances more recent works—even though they may analyze chronologically older events—incorporate newer developments of state-corporate crime theory.

Chapters 2, 3 (on the space shuttle *Challenger* explosion), and 4 (on the Hamlet, North Carolina, fire) represent our initial developmental work on the concept of state-corporate crime. The presentation of the "Original Formulation" chapter prior to our earlier analyses of the space shuttle and the Imperial fire violates our chronological ordering insofar as it was written after these two papers, and includes the concept of state facilitation introduced by Ray in the analysis of the Imperial fire. We decided, however, that it would be important at the outset for readers to see the overall theoretical framework that shapes this book before delving into specific state-corporate crimes. The balance of the substantive chapters, chapters 5 through 14, present analyses approximately in the order they were written. The concluding chapter, contrary to the tradition of edited volumes, is written not by ourselves but by two other analysts of state-corporate crime, David Kauzlarich and Rick Matthews. As second-generation students of state-corporate crime, these scholars have done much both to expand the idea of state-corporate crime and to expose others to the concept's utility. We think that as second-generation analysts they may also be able to see further into the future than we can, and so we felt it appropriate for them to offer the concluding remarks.

NOTES

1. It is interesting to note that although criminological inquiry into elite crime is relatively absent from criminology journals, since the publication of Sutherland's *White Collar Crime*, criminologists have written or edited a number of influential books about crimes by political and/or economic elites. See, for instance, *Criminality and the Legal Order*, by Austin Turk (1969); *The Political Criminal*, by Stephen Schafer (1974); *Corporate and Governmental Deviance: Problems of Organizational Behavior in Contemporary Society*, edited by M. David Ermann and Richard J. Lundman (1978); *Elite Deviance*, by David Simon and David S. Eitzen (1982); *The Criminal Elite*, by James W. Coleman (1985); *On The Take*, by William Chambliss (1988); *Crimes by the Capitalist State*, edited by Gregg Barak (1991); *Beyond the Limits of the Law*, by John McMullan (1992); *Political Crime in Contemporary America*, Kenneth Tunnell (1993); *Trusted Criminals: White-Collar Crime in Contemporary Society*, by David Friedrichs (1996); *Crimes of the American Nuclear State*, by David Kauzlarich and Ronald Kramer (1998); *Unmasking the Crimes of the Powerful: Scrutinizing States and Corporations*, edited by Steve Tombs and Dave Whyte (eds.) (2003); and *State Crime: Governments, Violence, and Corruption*, by Penny Green and Tony Ward (2004).

2. We present this later development of our initial work because the very first paper in which we used the term state-corporate crime has been lost to the passage of time—or, more correctly, to the replacement of computers and changes of operating systems.

3. Unfortunately, among those not included are some valuable non-American applications of the concept. Their absence from this volume is by no means a comment on their quality, but rather one involving the complexities of international publication. See, for example, "Toxic Steel: State Corporate Crime and the Contamination of the Environment in Atlantic Canada" (McMullan 1996); "The Killing of the Fly: State-Corporate Victimization in Papua New Guinea" (Harper and Israel 1999).

CHAPTER 2

The Original Formulation

Ronald C. Kramer and Raymond J. Michalowski

THE CONCEPT OF STATE-CORPORATE CRIME provides a framework for studying forms of organizational deviance created or facilitated by the intersection of political and economic institutions. The proposed framework situates individual actors within specific institutional contexts, and situates these institutional contexts, in turn, within the broader network of political-economic forces that define their operating environment. The concept of state-corporate crime is further refined to distinguish between state-initiated and state-facilitated forms of organizational deviance.

INTEGRATING THE CRIMES OF THE POWERFUL

We suggest that a textured understanding of many forms of what is often termed "corporate crime" can be obtained by utilizing an integrated approach that is sensitive to the ways in which the interactions between economic and political institutions can generate deviant organizational outcomes.

On January 28, 1986, the space shuttle *Challenger* exploded shortly after take-off, killing all seven crew members. Subsequent investigations revealed that it was the relationship between a private business corporation, Morton Thiokol, Inc. (MTI), which built the solid rocket boosters used on the shuttle system, and a government agency, the National Aeronautics and Space Administration (NASA), which was responsible for assembling the shuttle system and making decisions about its launch schedule, that ultimately led to the destruction of *Challenger*. Five years later, on September 3, 1991, an explosion and fire at the Imperial Food Products chicken-processing plant in Hamlet, North Carolina, killed twenty-five workers and injured another fifty-six. These deaths occurred because fire doors that could have led the workers to safety were "routinely locked to keep employees from stealing chicken nuggets" (Drescher and Garfield 1991b:1). Subsequent inquiry found that it was not only locked fire doors but also a pattern of interwoven regulatory failures that created the conditions that led to the tragedy.

These two heavily reported tragedies, occurring five years apart, share a common characteristic. Both events were animated by the interplay between corporate and governmental units that fostered conditions for organizational deviance. The technical cause of the *Challenger* explosion was the failure of the O-ring seal in a field joint of the right-side booster rocket manufactured by MTI. This failure, however, was more than a mechanical breakdown. It was the consequence of a series of organizational decisions involving MTI and NASA. These two organizations followed a pattern of relations that resulted in decisions to use a design for the field joint that was known to be flawed, and to launch the shuttle despite information that suggested there was an unspecified probability of a catastrophic failure. Moreover, both the Rogers Commission (Presidential Commission on the Space Shuttle Challenger Accident 1986) and the Committee on Science and Technology of the U.S. House of Representatives (1986) concluded that NASA and MTI, in making these decisions, repeatedly engaged in practices that violated legal standards of safety concerning the *Challenger* shuttle.

The technical cause of the Imperial plant fire was the rupture of a hydraulic line near a deep fryer. The resulting explosion and fireball destroyed the plant, killing workers trapped by locked fire doors and injuring many others. Those who died or were injured in the Hamlet fire, however, were the victims of much more than a mechanical breakdown. They were the victims of a complex process of institutional relations that limited the protection of worker health and safety. Participants in this process include Imperial Food Products, the U.S. Occupational Safety and Health Administration (OSHA), the U.S. Food and Drug Administration (FDA), the legislature and governor of the state of North Carolina, the North Carolina Occupational Safety and Health Administration (NC-OSHA), and local building authorities. These organizational units pursued a pattern of actions and relations that made it possible and routine that workers in the Imperial chicken-processing plant would be subjected to a variety of hazards, including inadequate escape routes in case of fire.

We suggest that understanding the processes that led to the destruction of *Challenger* and the fire in Hamlet, as well as many other, less dramatic, yet nevertheless harmful forms of organizational deviance, can be advanced by linking the frameworks currently available for the study of corporate crime, on the one hand, and governmental deviance, on the other. Specifically, we suggest that combining these two foci into the concept of state-corporate crime directs attention to how the interaction between different organizational units plays a critical role in creating the conditions for socially injurious organizational actions.

This inquiry into the nature of state-corporate crime is divided into two parts. First, we ground the concept of state-corporate crime in the theoretical framework of organizational deviance. Second, we offer an integrated analytical scheme for the study of state-corporate crimes. We term our approach here an "analytic scheme" in keeping with Turner's (1991) observation that much theoretical work in sociology consists of organizing concepts into a classificatory scheme that denotes the key properties and the interrelations among these properties as they relate to concrete events in the social universe. Explanation of an empirical event "comes whenever a place in the classificatory scheme can be found for the empirical event" (Turner 1991:10).

Since its inception, the study of corporate crime has been shaped by an important insight and an important oversight. The insight is that corporate crime is actually a form of organizational deviance (Clinard and Yeager 1980:17; Hagan 1988:3). To the extent that corporations are formal organizations, the study of corporate crime can and should incorporate the theoretical and substantive insights of organizational research (Vaughan 1983).

The oversight is the limited attention given to the functional interdependency between corporations and government that has existed since the corporation emerged as the basic unit of economic activity within private-production systems in the nineteenth century. Modern corporations could not have developed, nor could they currently function, without the legal, economic, and political infrastructure provided by the government (Sklar 1988). Governments in private-production systems, in turn, depend upon private corporations and private financial institutions to facilitate state legitimacy by providing a degree of economic stability, to supply goods and services needed for government operations, and to provide the economic base upon which governments depend for their tax revenues (Offe and Ronge 1982).

Despite their ubiquity, the structural relations between corporate and governmental organizations have been relatively peripheral to the study of corporate crime. Instead, two nearly independent bodies of research have developed. Theory and research in the area of corporate crime have concentrated primarily on organizational deviance within private business corporations.

Paralleling corporate crime researchers, but seldom intersecting with them, others have examined crimes and malfeasance by governments, what Chambliss (1989) terms "state-organized crime." We suggest, however, that many forms of organizational deviance are generated precisely at the point where corporations and governments intersect. It is these forms of organizational state-corporate deviance that we term state-corporate crime. We offer the following definition: "State-corporate crimes are illegal or socially injurious actions that result from a mutually reinforcing interaction between (1) policies and/or practices in pursuit of the goals of one or more institutions of political governance and (2) policies and/or practices in pursuit of the goals of one or more institutions of economic production and distribution."

State-corporate crimes within private-production systems involve two or more organizations, at least one of which is in the civil sector and one of which is in the state sector. Thus within a capitalist economy, state-corporate crimes are the harmful consequences of deviant interorganizational relationships between businesses and governments. This definition can be applied to illegal or socially injurious practices in societies organized around private-production systems and in those based on centrally planned economies. Our focus here, however, is upon state-corporate crimes within the private-production system of U.S. capitalism.

The deviant interorganizational relationships that serve as the basis for state-corporate crime can take two forms. One is state-initiated corporate crime, and the other is state-facilitated corporate crime. State-initiated corporate crime occurs when corporations employed by a government engage in organizational deviance at the direction of, or with the tacit approval of, that government. State-facilitated corporate crime occurs when government institutions of social control are guilty of clear failure to create regulatory institutions capable of restraining deviant business activities, either because of direct collusion between business and government or because they adhere to shared goals whose attainment would be hampered by aggressive regulation.

The term "state-corporate crime" has three useful characteristics. First, it directs attention toward the way in which deviant organizational outcomes are not discrete acts, but rather the outcome of relationships between different social institutions. Second, by focusing on the relational character of the state (Wonders and Solop 1993), the concept of state-corporate crime foregrounds the ways in which horizontal relationships between economic and political institutions contain powerful potential for the production of socially injurious actions. This relational approach, we suggest, provides a more nuanced understanding of the processes leading to deviant organizational outcomes than approaches that treat either businesses or governments as closed systems.

Third, the relational character of state-corporate crime also directs us to consider the vertical relationships between different levels of organizational action: the individual, the institutional, and the political-economic. This scheme, to some extent, helps address the subject-object dilemma characteristic of much corporate crime research and theory.

STATE-CORPORATE CRIME AS ORGANIZATIONAL DEVIANCE

There are three major theoretical approaches to the study of corporate crime, and each corresponds to a different level of social action. The first is differential association theory as developed by Sutherland (1940, 1949). The second is based on organizational theory and argues that organizations can be criminogenic either due to the performance emphasis on goals (E. Gross 1978) or as a result of defective standard operating procedures (Hopkins 1978). The third perspective locates the criminogenic forces in the wider political-economic structure of society (Barnett 1981).

Differential association addresses the individual level of action; organizational theory focuses on institutional factors promoting or retarding corporate crime; and political-economic approaches focus on the way broad, preexisting societal characteristics interact with both the individual and the organizational levels of action.

Differential association theory, as proposed by Edwin Sutherland (1949), is a social psychological approach that seeks to identify the individual learning processes that lead to deviant activities. Partial support for differential association as an explanation of white-collar crime has been found by a number of researchers (Albanese 1982; Clinard 1946; Cressey 1953/1971; Geis 1967; Lane 1953). While there can be no doubt that important insights have been derived from this approach, some criminologists have criticized differential association for its failure to incorporate the institutional level of analysis (Braithwaite 1985; Ermann and Lundman 1987; E. Gross 1978; Schrager and Short 1978). As Schrager and Short (1978:410) observe, "preoccupation with individuals can lead us to underestimate the pressures within society and organizational structure, which impel those individuals to commit illegal acts."

By the late 1970s and early 1980s, in response to the overly microlevel orientation of differential association theory, a number of analysts began examining the organizational characteristics of corporate and governmental crime (Albanese 1982; Clinard and Yeager 1980; Cullen, Maakestad, and Cavender 1987; Ermann and Lundman 1982, 1987; E. Gross 1978; Hopkins 1978; Kramer 1982; Needleman and Needleman 1979; Schrager and Short 1978; Sherman 1980; Vaughan 1982, 1983). The organizational perspective holds that, for various reasons, "there is built into the very structure of organizations an inherent inducement for the organization itself to engage in crime" (E. Gross 1978:56).

By far the most popular explanation of organizational crime within this approach is the rational-choice, blocked-opportunity model (Coleman 1987). Following Merton (1957) and Cloward and Ohlin (1960), this approach argues that organizations break the law because they are blocked in some fashion from access to legitimate means to achieve organizational goals. As Gross (1978:57) puts it, organizations "live in competitive environments, even in socialist society," and given the subsequent uncertain access to the necessities for goal attainment, "one can predict that the organization will, if it must, engage in criminal behavior to attain those goals."

A related approach within the organizational perspective is one that stresses that deviant outcomes can result from a variety of problems in the internal structure of the organization. This approach focuses on the standard operating procedures (SOPs) of the organization, arguing that "corporate crime is the outcome of defective S.O.P.s" (Hopkins 1978:217). Defects in the SOPs or the internal structure of the organization may also reduce access to legitimate means for goal attainment, thus creating additional pressure to turn to illegitimate ones.

The third perspective on organizational crime is that of political economy (Barnett 1981; Box 1983; Chambliss 1988,1989; Michalowski 1985; Michalowski and Kramer 1987; Young 1981). Barnett (1981:5), for example, argues that "corporations pursue goals of profit, growth, and expanded market share subject to constraints imposed by markets and the state," and corporate crime will occur "when management chooses to pursue corporate goals through circumvention of market constraints in a manner prohibited by the state." For some, "only the dynamics of capitalism—profit maximization and private accumulation" can explain corporate crime (Young 1981:333). The limitation of this approach is that profit pressures are not unique to capitalist economies. Socialist command economies, such as that in the former Soviet Union, also generate pressures for capital accumulation (Verderey 1991). However, if a political-economic analysis is focused on the dynamics of the accumulation process under different forms of economic organization, rather than only on its manifestations under capitalism, this perspective can be a useful guide in examining how the intersection of political and economic organizations can generate deviant outcomes.

Although the criminogenic potential of pressures for profit maximization might be useful in understanding crimes by corporations, it would appear to offer a less convincing model for crimes by governments. There is, however, a common thread linking deviance by economic organizations and deviance by political ones. Most corporate crimes and most crimes by government are ultimately crimes of capital, that is, they are "socially injurious acts that arise from the ownership or management of capital or from the occupancy of positions of trust in institutions designed to facilitate the accumulation of capital" (Michalowski 1985:314).

The political state is not simply the subordinate executive of an accumulative class, so we are not suggesting that states commit crimes merely to advantage capitalists. The state is, however, the mechanism for managing class conflict (Offe and Ronge 1982). In doing so, the political state must resolve conflicts and dilemmas that stem from underlying structural contradictions in the political economy. The contradictory nature of these structural arrangements, however, can force the state to adopt deviant strategies to achieve what cannot otherwise be accomplished (Chambliss 1988, 1989).

Another source of governmental deviance is the complex institutional structure of most modern states. The goals of different organizational units within any government may contradict those of other units. To the extent that pursuit of organizational goals by one governmental unit blocks the attainment of organizational goals by another, the blocked unit may experience pressures toward deviant strategies. The conflict between the goals of Congress and those of the National Security Council, for example, constituted the basis for the Iran-Contra scandal (Hackel and Siegel 1987). Similarly, the Drug Enforcement Agency's pursuit of its goal of drug interdiction became a constraint on key aspects of the CIA's contra resupply operation, leading to a variety of illegal strategies on the part of the CIA (Sharkey 1988).

Although the differential association, organizational, and political-economic perspectives represent divergent approaches to corporate and governmental crime, they can be brought together into an integrated theoretical model (Braithwaite 1989b; Coleman 1985, 1987; Finney and Lesieur 1982; Messner, Krohn, and Liska 1989; Vaughan 1983). The structure, dynamics, and cultural meanings associated with the political-economic arrangements of any society will shape the goals and means of both economic and political institutions, as well as the constraints they face. The organizational level of analysis links the internal structure of specific economic or political units with the external political-economic environment, on the one hand, and with the way in which the work-related thoughts and actions of the individuals who occupy positions in those units are conditioned by the requirements of the positions they hold and by the procedures of the organization, on the other. Differential association, by focusing on the social relations that give meaning to individual experience, directs us to examine the symbolic reality derived from social interaction within bounded organizational niches.

Table 2.1 presents an analytic scheme for this integrated theory of organizational deviance. This framework links the three levels of analysis discussed above with three catalysts for action. These catalysts are (1) motivation or performance emphases, (2) opportunity structure, and (3) the operationality of control. This framework is designed to indicate the key factors that will contribute to or restrain organizational deviance at each intersection of a catalyst for action and a level of analysis.

The schema we offer is based on the proposition that criminal or deviant behavior at the organizational level results from a coincidence of pressure for goal attainment, availability and perceived attractiveness of illegitimate means, and an absence of effective social control. The first catalyst for action is the level of emphasis on goal attainment. Political economies, organizations, and individuals may place greater or lesser emphasis on the attainment of rationalized goals as the engine for social action. Thus a highly goal-oriented individual, working in an organization that evaluates performance strictly on goal attainment by its workers, in a society whose cultural and institutional framework emphasizes goal attainment above all else, will be more susceptible to pursuing deviant organizational strategies than if one or more of these conditions is absent.

The second catalyst for action suggests that organizational deviance is more likely in a society where legitimate means are scarce relative to goals. The likelihood of deviance increases for those organizations or organizational subunits where the allocation of means by the internal structure is inadequate relative to the organization's goals, increasing the likelihood that individuals will

TABLE 2.1.

An Integrated Theoretical Model of State-Corporate Crime

Levels of Analysis	Catalysts for Action		
	Motivation	Opportunity	Control
Institutional environment	Culture of competition Economic pressure Organizational goals Performance emphasis	Availability of legal means Obstacles and constraints Blocked goals/strain Availability of illegal means Access to resources	International reactions Political pressure Legal sanctions Media scrutiny Public opinion Social movements
Organizational	Corporate culture Operative goals Subunit goals Managerial pressure	Instrumental rationality Internal constraints Defective SOPs Creation of illegal means Role specialization Task segregation Computer, telecommunication, and networking technologies Normalization of deviance	Culture of compliance Subcultures of resistance Codes of conduct Reward structure Safety and quality control Communication processes
Interactional	Socialization Social meaning Individual goals Competitive individualism Material success emphasis	Definitions of situations Perceptions of availability and attractiveness of illegal means	Personal morality Rationalizations and techniques of neutralization Diffusion of responsibility Separation from consequences Obedience to authority Groupthink

perceive themselves to be blocked from access to legitimate means and will subsequently seek deviant alternative routes.

Finally, the operationality of social control at all three levels will serve both as an important restraint on organizational deviance and as a critical element in constructing symbolic frameworks that will operate at the societal, organizational, and personal levels as time passes. Thus societies with high operationality of social control are more likely to produce organizations with strong corporate cultures favoring compliance. Individuals who function in these organizations in such a society will be more likely to develop forms of personal morality that would mitigate against engaging in organizational deviance. By its very nature state-corporate crime directs us to examine the linkages between levels of analysis and catalysts for action. When the topic is profit-oriented violations of law by some business, it is possible—although, as our analysis of the Hamlet fire will show, not necessarily sufficient—to treat the crime as organizationally self-contained (see chapter 4). Injurious social actions that result from concerted actions by organizations operating in different social spheres (for example, production versus governance), however, require that we must expand the frame of analysis. The case study that follows in chapter 3 will examine such processes that ultimately resulted in the explosion of the space shuttle *Challenger*.

NOTE ON SOURCE

Updated, adapted and revised from Raymond Michalowski and Ronald Kramer, "State-Corporate Crime: Toward an Integrated Model," (1993). Prepared for *Social Problems* (not published).

The Space Shuttle Challenger Explosion

Ronald C. Kramer

ON JANUARY 28, 1986, the world was stunned by the explosion of the space shuttle *Challenger*. The *Challenger* exploded in midair shortly after liftoff, sending six astronauts and schoolteacher Christa McAuliffe to their deaths. As this study will document, the *Challenger* disaster was the collective product of the interaction between a government agency, the National Aeronautics and Space Administration (NASA), and a private business corporation, Morton Thiokol, Inc. (MTI). The space shuttle tragedy thus falls into the special category of organizational misconduct that Kramer and Michalowski (1990) have identified as "state-corporate crime."

THE CASE OF THE *CHALLENGER* EXPLOSION

To understand more fully why the *Challenger* explosion constitutes state-corporate crime and to assess the ability of the integrated theoretical model of organizational crime to explain this interorganizational act, we will examine four components of the story. First, the political history of the shuttle will be reviewed as part of the societal context within which the problem emerged. Second, the O-ring problem, the "fatal flaw," which places the emerging problem within its dual-organizational context, will be described. Third, we will discuss the process through which specific individuals made the concrete decisions that led to the tragic flight. Finally, the failure of various social-control mechanisms relating to the shuttle system will be evaluated.

SOCIETAL CONTEXT: THE POLITICS OF THE SPACE SHUTTLE

NASA was a product of the cold war between the Soviet Union and the United States. In the 1950s, the cold war gave rise to an arms race and a related science and technology race between the two superpowers (Nieburg 1966). The launch of the first *Sputnik* by the Soviet Union in 1957 caused a political firestorm in the United States that eventually resulted in the creation of NASA in 1958 (McDougall 1985). The new space agency was put under civilian control, but found itself constantly battling the military's attempt to influence its direction and policies (Trento 1987). The glory days of NASA came in the 1960s, with the Apollo program and the race to the moon. During this period NASA had generous budgets and unlimited political support. With these resources the agency was able to recruit top scientists and technicians and cultivate a "can-do attitude" together with a serious commitment to safety and quality control (R. S. Lewis 1988; Trento 1987).

In the 1970s, however, the political and economic environment of NASA changed dramatically. Economic conditions caused a string of budget problems at the same time that political and public support for the agency began to decline (R. S. Lewis 1988; Trento 1987). As the Apollo program wound down, NASA faced an uncertain future. This was the environment that shaped the development of the space shuttle program.

The idea of a reusable spacecraft that could provide frequent, economical access to space first surfaced in the late 1960s. In September 1969, a Space Task Force report to the president offered a choice of three long-range plans. In varying combinations these plans called for (1) a manned Mars expedition, (2) a lunar-orbiting space station, (3) an earth-orbiting station, and (4) a reusable space shuttle to link the orbiting station to Earth. For budgetary reasons, the Nixon administration scrapped the Mars project and the space platform, but ordered the development of the shuttle vehicle. As the Presidential Commission (1986:2) pointed out: "Thus, the reusable Space Shuttle, earlier considered only the transport element of a broad, multi-objective space plan, became the focus of NASA's near-term future."

The decision to proceed only with the shuttle component of the space plan forced NASA to put all of its eggs in one basket and significantly shaped NASA's goals in the post-Apollo era. But NASA's troubles were only beginning. Financial restrictions from the Office of Management and Budget (OMB) would have a major impact on the design of the shuttle, and to win political support NASA would have to allow the air force to help plan the design of the shuttle to accommodate military missions.

NASA's original design for the new shuttle craft was changed several times due to severe budget constraints. R. S. Lewis (1988:54) notes that "from a long-term point of view, the 51-L [*Challenger*] disaster was the end product of budget compromises that required NASA to abandon its original design of a fully reusable spaceship and substitute a partly reusable vehicle at about half the development cost." As one critic put it, "They had to build the shuttle down to a price, not up to a standard" (54). Because of NASA's crimped budget, the agency decided to use solid-fueled rockets, which were cheaper but more dangerous than liquid-fueled engines, and to eliminate the escape hatch (Trento 1987). As Easterbrook (1987:53–54) points out, "NASA's incremental decision to rely on solid boosters with no abort mechanisms meant that priceless human lives, several billion dollars and the whole of American space prestige would be wagered time and again on the proposition that when five used rocket engines fire simultaneously, nothing can go wrong." It was a design flaw in the solid rocket booster that eventually caused the *Challenger* explosion.

The low development expenditures imposed on NASA and the military requirements the agency agreed to in order to win political support meant that the shuttle ended up being a hybrid machine created by a series of political compromises. But NASA not only had to make critical design changes in the shuttle system due to budget considerations, military demands, and the lack of political support; it was also forced into making a purely economic justification for building the shuttle. Both OMB and Congress wanted an inexpensive and efficient reusable spacecraft. In the desperate political struggle to save the shuttle program, and in the minds of many at the agency itself, unrealistic predictions concerning the ability of the shuttle program to pay for itself were continually made by NASA officials (R. S. Lewis 1988; Trento 1987). NASA began to promise the impossible in order to build the shuttle and save the agency. To be cost effective the shuttle would have to be used frequently and for a variety of purposes. Thus the myth of the omnibus shuttle was born, which eventually led NASA to shift all payloads, including all of the scientific ones, to the shuttle, take on commercial customers, and accommodate itself to further military demands (Trento 1987).

The effort to make the shuttle a cost-effective, universal launch vehicle was an enormous burden for on NASA. Once the shuttle was finally approved and under development, pressure was placed on the agency to get the system operational and begin a heavy schedule of flights. As the Presidential Commission (1986:201) concluded, "the nation's reliance on the shuttle as its principal space launch capability created a relentless pressure on NASA to increase the flight rate."

This pressure increased dramatically in the 1980s under the Reagan administration. Ronald Reagan came into office just as the space shuttle program was preparing to launch its first test flight. In August of 1981, the president established an interagency review of U.S. space policy chaired by Dr. George Keyworth, the president's science advisor. The Keyworth group's meetings took place as NASA completed the first of four orbital test flights. The result of these deliberations was the Presidential Directive on National Space Policy. It was issued in conjunction with Reagan's first major speech on space, delivered at Edwards Air Force Base on July 4, 1982, the day the initial orbital tests concluded.

In this speech, and in the directive, Reagan announced a national policy to set the direction of the U.S. space program during the coming decade. As part of that policy, the president stated that the shuttle system was "the primary launch system for both national security and civil government missions" (Presidential Commission 1986:164). Reagan went on to declare the space shuttle fully operational and therefore ready for a wide variety of important tasks.

The president's declaration that the space shuttle was "fully operational" increased the pressure on NASA. An operational system is one that has moved out of the research and development phase into routine operation. Problems and mistakes are expected and looked for in the development phase, but are not expected or looked for in the operational phase. By the time something is operational, the bugs in the system are supposed to be worked out. Yet this was not true of the shuttle, according to a number of experts (Heaphy 1986; Pike 1988). They argue that the system was still in the research and development phase and that the president prematurely labeled it operational. This declaration was one of the major factors that led to the relentless pressure on NASA to launch shuttle missions on an accelerated schedule. As Jim Heaphy (1986:3), editor of *Space for All People,* points out, "after the president had so promptly and vigorously declared the shuttle fully operational, the atmosphere at NASA was no longer conducive to sober and rational assessment of the under funded spacecraft's shortcomings." John Pike, associate director for space policy for the American Federation of American Scientists observed, "The blame [for the launch pressure experienced by NASA] lies with the administration, for they were clearly declaring the shuttle operational before, in fact, it truly was" (1988). The reports of the Presidential Commission and of the House Committee on Science and Technology bear this out.

The Reagan administration's eagerness for the system to become operational stemmed in part from its rather ambitious plans for the shuttle. One of the administration goals, which harkened back to the budget-crisis years of the shuttle's development in the early 1970s, was to make NASA economically self-sufficient. One way NASA could do this was to become a commercial cargo hauler, primarily of communication satellites. The agency found itself under pressure to prove that the high costs of space exploration could be at least partially recouped through the commercial use of the shuttle (Presidential Commission 1986; U.S. House 1986). NASA decided to begin carrying paying customers as soon as possible (Mark 1987; Trento 1987).

The business of launching satellites for a wide variety of customers generated further pressures on NASA. For one thing, the agency had to compete with the European Space Agency's *Ariane* satellite launcher and therefore "had to make its shuttle missions look routine and dependable" (*The Nation* 1986:164).

But the launching of commercial satellites also introduced new schedule problems and a demand for an increased flight rate that only an operational system could meet. "Pressures developed because of the need to meet customer commitments, which translated into a requirement to launch a certain number of flights per year and to launch them on time. Such considerations may occasionally have obscured engineering concerns. Managers may have forgotten—partly because of past success, partly because of their own well-nurtured image of the program—that the Shuttle was still in a research and development phase" (Presidential Commission 1986:165).

In addition to these commercial concerns, NASA was increasingly being asked by the Reagan administration to use the shuttle for military purposes as well. As noted, from the very beginning the civilian space agency had been an important element in the science and technology race that took place within the context of the military objectives and interests of the Cold War superpowers. It has also been pointed out that during the political struggle over the design of the shuttle NASA had to repeatedly accept design changes suggested by the Air Force in order to win military support for the program. But the pressure to militarize the space shuttle program increased greatly under the Reagan administration.

Another reason the administration was eager to declare the space shuttle operational was its desire for the shuttle to carry out a number of "tasks related to national security." In the 1982 Presidential Directive on National Space Policy (quoted in Heaphy 1986:3), NASA was instructed to "preserve United States preeminence in critical space activities." Keeping the shuttle on an accelerated flight schedule was deemed "vital and critical" to national defense. The directive went on to say that "launch priority will be provided for national security missions."

Pressures on the shuttle program escalated even more the next year with the announcement of Reagan's "Star Wars" plan. The administration clearly understood that, whatever form the Strategic Defense Initiative would eventually take, the testing and development of the space missile defense system they desired would require an operational shuttle capable of making a large number of flights on a regular basis. The militarization of space that was planned by the Reagan administration put additional demands on an already overburdened and underfunded space agency.

NASA's organizational goals concerning the space shuttle program were shaped by this political history. Political and economic structures outside of the organization influenced the final hybrid design of the spacecraft and pressured NASA to take on a variety of commercial, military, and scientific goals that dictated an accelerated launch schedule. This pervasive pressure to fly the shuttle and fly it often has been cited by every investigation into the *Challenger* disaster as one of the chief factors leading to the tragedy. The House Committee on Science and Technology (1986:22) concluded:

> NASA's drive to achieve a launch schedule of 24 flights per year created pressure throughout the agency that directly contributed to unsafe launch operations. . . . The Committee, the Congress, and the Administration . . . played a contributing role in creating this pressure. Congressional and Administrative policy and posture indicated that a reliable flight schedule with internationally competitive flight costs was a near-term objective. Pressures within NASA to attempt to evolve from an R&D agency into a quasi competitive business operation caused a realignment of priorities in the direction of productivity at the cost of safety. NASA management and the Congress must remember the lesson learned from the *Challenger* accident and never again set unreasonable goals which stress the system beyond its safe functioning.

THE ORGANIZATIONAL CONTEXT:
CREATING THE FINAL FLAW

The tremendous performance pressure exerted on NASA by the demands of an accelerated flight rate is a necessary but not solely sufficient condition to explain the *Challenger* explosion. This performance pressure could only be judged unreasonable if the organization did not have access to the resources that it needed to meet these demands.

Presumably, given enough resources and without encountering a major barrier or obstacle to goal attainment, NASA should have been able to carry out the shuttle flight schedule without violating any of its own safety standards or any of the external standards that were applied to the agency. As we have seen, however, NASA was not provided with sufficient resources in the development phase during the early 1970s, which led to serious design compromises, and the agency also lacked have the necessary resources to carry out the extremely ambitious flight schedule in the 1980s. A lack of spare parts, for example, was forcing NASA to cannibalize each shuttle when it returned from a mission in order to get another vehicle ready for launch.

Although any number of things could go wrong with a shuttle flight and cause disaster, what did cause the explosion of the *Challenger* was a problem with the O-ring seal in the field joint of a solid rocket motor. The faulty design of the field joint manufactured by MTI was the fatal flaw that destroyed the *Challenger*. The Presidential Commission (1986:148) placed the blame for the flawed design, and the failure to act on information concerning the flaw, on both NASA and MTI: "The genesis of the *Challenger* accident—the failure of the joint of the right Solid Rocket Motor—began with decisions made in the design of the joint and in the failure by both Thiokol and NASA's Solid

Rocket Booster project office to understand and respond to facts obtained during testing. The Commission has concluded that neither Thiokol nor NASA responded adequately to internal warnings about the faulty seal design. Furthermore, Thiokol and NASA did not make a timely attempt to develop and verify a new seal after the initial design was shown to be deficient."

Information concerning the faulty seal design was a source of organizational strain within NASA and MTI. The problem with the field joint seal was a major barrier to the ability of NASA to fly its manifest and meet its flight-rate goals in a safe or legitimate manner. Since this operating problem came from a private contractor outside the space agency, it constitutes an external blockage of the ability of NASA to use legitimate means to achieve its goals concerning the shuttle. This problem also introduces the interaction between a private business and a government agency that is at the heart of the concept of state-corporate crime.

On November 20, 1973, the Thiokol Chemical Corporation (later to become Morton Thiokol, Inc.) was awarded a cost-plus contract valued at $800 million to manufacture solid rocket boosters for NASA's space shuttle project. An early test, called a hydroburst test, revealed that there was a problem with the field joint on the booster. An MTI supervisor told the Presidential Commission (1986:1,435), "We discovered that the joint was opening rather than closing as our original analysis had indicated and, in fact, it was quite a bit." McConnell (1987:118) noted that "the implications of this discovery were ominous. Without this pressure seal, the hot combustion gas could shoot through the putty and erode the O-rings. If this erosion was widespread, an actual flame path would quickly develop and the booster would burst at the joint, destroying the entire booster, and, of course, the space shuttle itself."

MTI did report this test effect to NASA, but the company said it did not believe that the joint rotation would cause problems; it did not schedule any additional tests on the joint-gap effect. A number of engineers at NASA's Marshall Space Flight Center, however, did express concern about the gap in a series of memos written in the late 1970s (Presidential Commission 1986). One of these memos, written in 1978 by John Q. Miller, Marshall's chief of the Solid Rocket Motor Branch, argued that the MTI design was so dangerous that it could produce "hot gas leaks and resulting catastrophic failure" (Presidential Commission 1986:123). The project manager at Marshall, however, did not pass these memos on to MTI, and in the end "the alarming concerns of knowledgeable Marshall engineers did not result in a redesign of the SRB field joint before flights began" (McConnell 1987:119).

In September of 1980, the Shuttle Verification and Certification Committee certified the solid rocket motor for flight, and the field joint on the motor was classified on the shuttle critical items list as 1-R, or redundant, meaning that there was a backup in case of a failure. After the second test flight in November 1981, it was discovered that hot gas had penetrated the putty and damaged the primary O-ring in the field joint of the right booster. This information, however, was not passed on from Marshall to higher levels within NASA (Presidential Commission 1986:125). This failure was indicative of a major flaw in the organizational structure of NASA: a major communication problem between Marshall and the other units within the agency. The Presidential Commission (1986:104) said that it was "troubled by what appears to be a propensity of management at Marshall to contain potentially serious problems and attempt to resolve them internally rather than communicate them forward." Marshall tended to keep "bad news" and problems to itself, and this flaw in the communication system would repeatedly be in evidence in the shuttle project in the days before the *Challenger* explosion.

Following further O-ring tests in May 1982, Marshall finally accepted the conclusion that "Thiokol's dual O-rings did not provide a fully redundant system because the secondary O-ring would not always function after joint rotation following ignition" (R. S. Lewis 1988:74). In December, the O-ring seals were reclassified as "criticality 1," which meant that they did not meet the fail-safe definition of the Space Shuttle Program Requirements document (Presidential Commission 1986). The O-rings were now considered to be a potential "single failure point due to the possibility of loss of sealing at the secondary O-ring because of joint rotation" that could result in "loss of mission, vehicle and crew due to metal erosion, burn through, and probable case burst resulting in fire and deflagration" (Presidential Commission 1986:126).

Despite the reclassification of the O-rings to criticality 1, no one at Marshall called for a halt in the program to fix the problem. The solid rocket managers believed that the secondary O-ring actually was redundant except in rare cases (R. S. Lewis 1988). In March of 1983, NASA associate administrator L. Michael Weeks settled the issue of whether the shuttle should continue to fly in its current condition when he approved a waiver on the criticality 1 field joint. As the shuttle program picked up speed, signs of O-ring erosion and damage became more marked and more frequent (R. S. Lewis 1988; Presidential Commission 1986). The managers at Marshall, however, continued to define the erosion of the O-ring to be an "acceptable risk" (McConnell 1987:120).

Nevertheless, the O-ring problem was slowly coming to the attention of higher-level officials at NASA. As an outgrowth of a flight readiness review in April 1984, NASA deputy administrator Hans Mark issued a directive to Lawrence Mulloy at Marshall requesting a formal review of the field joint sealing process. Mulloy, in turn, had a letter sent to MTI asking for a formal review to identify the cause of the erosion, determine whether it was acceptable, and define necessary change (Presidential Commission 1986). MTI replied in May with a proposal, but its final response to this directive would not be completed for another fifteen months. In the meantime, the primary O-ring of a nozzle joint failed and hot gases badly scorched the secondary ring in an April 1985 *Challenger* flight. Even though the secondary O-ring had held that time, the obvious failure of a critical component forced Marshall to impose a launch constraint on all future flights until the cause could be analyzed and dealt with. Yet this launch constraint, which meant that the shuttle could not fly unless the cause of the constraint were taken care of, was waived for the next flight and each subsequent flight through the 51-L mission of the *Challenger.*

By the summer of 1985, "the engineers at Marshall and Thiokol most intimately involved with the boosters could no longer deny that they had a potentially catastrophic situation facing them" (McConnell 1987:121). The interaction between NASA and MTI over the O-ring problem increased substantially that summer. In July two MTI inspectors were sent to Marshall to discuss O-ring problems with engineers there. Meanwhile, engineers back at Thiokol were increasingly concerned about the O-rings and urged the company to move quickly to solve the problem. In a July 31 memo, one engineer, Roger Boisjoly, pointed out that a failure of the field joint would result in "a catastrophe of the highest order and a loss of human life" (Presidential Commission 1986:249). Boisjoly recommended setting up a team to work on the O-ring problem and concluded: "It is my honest and very real fear that if we do not take immediate action to dedicate a team to solve the problem, with the field joint having the number one priority, then we stand in jeopardy of losing a flight along with all the launch pad facilities" (Presidential Commission 1986:249).

Concern at NASA was also escalating. Richard Cook, a budget analyst at the agency, wrote a memo only days before Boisjoly's July memo concerning the cost implications of fixing the O-ring problem he had been requested to investigate. Cook warned that the budget impact could be immense. He also concluded that "there is little question, however, that flight safety has been and is still being compromised by potential failure of the seals, and it is acknowledged that failure during launch would certainly be catastrophic" (Cook 1985:1). That same month, NASA officials quietly began to embark on a program to solve the problem of the leaky booster rocket seals. They ordered seventy-two new steel cases so they could install capture features, which would lock the seals tightly in place, in boosters already in use (Broad 1986). The capture feature was called the "big fix" by Marshall engineers, but while they waited for the big fix to become available, the shuttle continued to fly.

With the proposed big fix and the events of late summer and early fall 1985, McConnell (1987:121) argues that there was "irrefutable evidence that both Marshall and Thiokol realized that they were risking disaster by allowing shuttle flights to continue despite the chronic O-ring erosion." On August 19,

MTI and Marshall engineers briefed NASA headquarters on the O-ring erosion problem. The briefing was "detailed," according to the Presidential Commission (1986:140), and the conclusion presented by the engineers was that
the seal was a critical matter and that an accelerated pace was recommended
to eliminate erosion, but it was safe to fly. In view of this high-level briefing,
the statement by the Presidential Commission that "those who made that
decision [to launch] were unaware of the recent history of problems concerning the O-rings and the joint" seems contradictory.

The next day MTI, noting that a leak at any of the joints would be catastrophic, announced the formation of an O-ring task force "to investigate the
solid rocket motor case and nozzle joints, both materials and configurations, and
recommend both short-term and long-term solutions" (Presidential Commission 1986:140). The task force, however, was plagued with resource problems
and foot dragging on the part of top management during a period when the
company was renegotiating its contract with NASA. McConnell (1987:181)
observes: "It might be reasonable to assume, therefore, that Thiokol was hesitant
to have its engineering task force act too quickly on the booster redesign and by
doing so expose the inherent weakness of the original field joint design to hostile Congressional scrutiny." Whatever the reason for the delays, Boisjoly and
others on the MTI task force complained that they were being blocked in their
efforts to accomplish the task (Boisjoly 1988; R. S. Lewis 1988; Presidential
Commission 1986). Incredibly, without arriving at any solution to the problem,
MTI sent a request to NASA asking that the O-ring problem be closed out—
that is, considered resolved. On January 23, 1986, five days before the *Challenger*
explosion, an entry was made in the Marshall Problem Reports that "the problem is considered closed" (R. S. Lewis 1988:88).

Information concerning the flawed design of the field joint seal was
clearly a source of organizational strain at both NASA and MTI. Both organizations knew of the serious nature of the problem and the possible consequences of a failure of the O-ring seals. To fix the problem, however, would
require that the shuttle program be grounded, probably for a lengthy period of
time. To do so would have greatly slowed down the space shuttle's flight
schedule, cut into MTI's profits, and perhaps jeopardized the second phase of
their lucrative contract with NASA. From NASA's perspective, a long delay
was to be avoided at all costs. Heaphy (1986:3) noted: "An environment had
been created where anyone calling for a halt to the shuttle program for a safety
design was opening themselves up to a charge of advocating economic collapse, nuclear destruction and communist control of Mars."

How did NASA and MTI respond to the strain? They responded by keeping the space shuttle flying, and at an accelerated pace. The problems with the
seals were defined as "not serious" and as an "unavoidable" and "acceptable
flight risk." Unsafe or illegitimate means were used to attain the organizational

goals that had been established. These unsafe means were available simply because, as Commissioner Richard Feynman put it, "they got away with it last time." As Feynman (Presidential Commission 1986:148) observed, the decision making was "a kind of Russian roulette . . . [the shuttle flies with O-ring erosion] and nothing happens. Then it is suggested, therefore, that the risk is no longer so high for the next flight. We can lower our standards a little bit because we got away with it last time. . . . You got away with it, but it shouldn't be done over and over again like that."

Actors in Context: The Decisions to Launch Flight 51-L

We have presented data on the general performance pressure that NASA was subjected to with regard to the shuttle program and its flight-rate goals, and the organizational strain caused by the O-ring problem that NASA resolved by continuing to fly an unsafe vehicle. We focus now on the specific pressures surrounding the flight of the *Challenger* on January 28, 1986.

Mission 51-L, with the space shuttle *Challenger,* was originally scheduled for launch December 23, 1985. Bad weather, however, had forced numerous delays of the previous mission, 61-C, a *Columbia* flight. The 61-C delays made it necessary to reschedule flight 51-L to January 23, 1986. The 51-L mission itself would be postponed four times and scrubbed once for a variety of reasons. These launch delays were exerting tremendous pressure on NASA and the shuttle launch schedule. The space agency had scheduled fifteen launches for 1986, its most ambitious schedule yet, and nineteen missions in 1987. As Lewis (1988:52) observes, "there was no question that launch delays during the unusually cold winter of 1985–86 in Florida were eroding NASA's ability to meet commercial and military satellite launch commitments."

NASA also planned to launch three important scientific missions that spring. Two of these missions, the *Ulysses* and the *Galileo,* were dependent on the orbit of Jupiter. The other mission, the *Astro 1* observing mission for the appearance of Halley's comet, was also on a tight time schedule. The *Challenger* 51-L launch, therefore, was time-critical. NASA had to get the *Challenger* launched and returned within a very short time frame so that the orbiter could be reconfigured for one of these scientific missions, and preparations could be made at the launch facility for the other time-critical missions.

The 51-L mission was also special because of the presence of teacher Christa McAuliffe. She was to be the first private citizen to ride into space, where she was scheduled to deliver a school lesson to millions of American students. McAuliffe had captured the hearts of many Americans, who were therefore following this shuttle flight much more closely than they normally did. Media attention was also high, and NASA had come in for some criticism from the news media for the numerous delays in late 1985 and early 1986.

Lewis (1988:52) notes that "news media critics tended to view launch delays caused by engineering problems as evidence of inadequate quality control, and [those] caused by weather as indicative of excessive caution and lack of confidence."

For all of these reasons, NASA officials were feeling the heat as they rescheduled the 51-L flight for January 28, 1986. This date also presented NASA with an important opportunity. The president was scheduled to give the State of the Union address that night. There is evidence that NASA had suggested to the White House that the president include a reference to the shuttle program and the teacher Christa McAuliffe during the address (Cook 1986:20). According to former NASA budget analyst Richard Cook, NASA saw the speech as an opportunity to counter media criticism and rally public support around the agency once again (1988). Cook argues that the timing of the State of the Union address created additional pressure within NASA to finally launch 51-L on the morning of January 28.

But as the pressured space agency prepared to launch the *Challenger,* another major strain arose in connection with the O-rings. The weather forecast for the morning of January 28 predicted extremely low temperatures. At MTI in Utah, several Thiokol engineers became concerned when they heard about the low temperatures anticipated for launch time. They had evidence that suggested that the O-rings lost some of their resiliency in cold weather and that this problem would make it even more difficult for them to seal out the hot gases when joint rotation occurred. During the afternoon of January 27, MTI engineers presented their concerns about the effects of cold weather on the booster seal joints to level III officials in the NASA readiness review process at Marshall and recommended that the launch be delayed again.

Late in the afternoon on January 27, there was a crucial interaction between MTI and NASA, one that would lead directly to the state-corporate crime of the *Challenger* explosion. That afternoon and evening, a teleconference took place between MTI officials and Marshall officials. At this teleconference, which was also attended by senior executives and managers, MTI engineers presented their evidence on the effects of cold weather on the O-rings and the joint seal and recommended that NASA not launch the shuttle under the temperature of 53 degrees Fahrenheit. NASA's reaction to this information was swift and harsh (Boisjoly 1988). Lawrence Mulloy's response was "unusually heated" (McConnell 1987:196). He attacked MTI's data and their conclusions and accused them of trying to establish new launch commit criteria based on the 53-degree benchmark. It was at this point that Mulloy made his famous comment, "My God, Thiokol, when do you want me to launch, next April?" Another Marshall official said he was "appalled" at the MTI decision (Presidential Commission 1986:90). The mood of the teleconference quickly shifted and MTI officials found themselves on the defensive.

Congress must apply the same strong oversight to NASA that it does to any other government agency" (Benedict 1986:4). Representative Manuel Lujan, then the senior Republican on the Science and Technology Committee, confessed, "As a committee, we may have been too trusting when NASA gave us glowing reports about the space shuttle program" (Benedict 1986:4).

As with congressional oversight, NASA had generally been given favorable treatment in the media and had been held in high esteem by the public. The excitement and romance of space travel, its high entertainment value, and the genuine successes of NASA had all combined to produce public approval of the space agency and its worship by the media, especially television. McConnell (1987) reports that journalists covering NASA were taken in by the plush nature of the assignment and the skillful manipulations of the public relations staff, and did not do their job correctly. Despite their carping about launch delays (R. S. Lewis 1988), the media did not ask the tough questions, probe behind the press releases, or investigate the agency as thoroughly as they should have (Lindee and Nelkin 1986; Mann 1986; McConnell 1987). A more sober, objective, and critical stance toward NASA and the issue of safety on the part of the media, which was evident in the coverage of the agency in the aftermath of the disaster, might have been able to exert some counterbalancing pressures on NASA before the explosion.

Given the lack of external social control over the space agency, the responsibility for close surveillance was left to NASA itself. Vaughan (1988:6) points out that "the space agency, from its inception, was to guide its own regulation." This self-regulation was inadequate. As Vaughan (1988:3) notes, NASA's efforts at self-regulation concerning safety and quality control were marked by a variety of problems. Specifically, "the organizational response was characterized by poor communication, inadequate information handling, and failure to comply with regulations instituted to insure safety. Moreover, the regulatory system designed to oversee the safety of the shuttle program failed to identify and correct program management and design problems related to the O-rings. NASA insiders referred to these omissions as 'quality escapes': failures of the program to preclude an avoidable problem."

One major social control problem within the organizational structure at NASA was the absence of an effective communication system (Brody 1986). A strong communication system is essential to handle the problems of coordination and control. Without effective vertical and horizontal communication, top management may experience authority leakage and lose control over subunits within the organization. According to the Presidential Commission (1986:82), "failures in communication that resulted in a decision to launch 51-L based on incomplete and sometimes misleading information" were a contributing cause of the shuttle disaster. The tendency at Marshall toward management isolation in particular was cited by the Presidential Commission as a major factor in the breakdown of communication at NASA. This finding was ironic, since the Marshall Space Flight Center had been lauded in the 1960s as having an extremely effective communication system (Thompkins 1977, 1978).

Another internal social control problem was the reduction in the safety program at NASA since Apollo (Perrow 1986) and the lack of independence for those safety personnel who remained (Vaughan 1988). The Presidential Commission (1986) devoted an entire chapter of its report to the "silent safety program" at NASA. The commission found that the safety, reliability, and quality assurance workforce at NASA had been reduced, and that this reduction had seriously limited NASA's capability in these vital functions, which, in turn, adversely affected mission safety. The commission (1986:152) noted:

> The unrelenting pressure to meet the demands of an accelerating flight schedule might have been adequately handled by NASA if it had insisted upon the exactingly thorough procedures that were its hallmark during the Apollo program. An extensive and redundant safety program comprising interdependent safety, reliability and quality assurance functions existed during and after the lunar program to discover any potential safety problems. Between that period and 1986, however, the program became ineffective. This loss of effectiveness seriously degraded the checks and balances essential for maintaining flight safety.

Although there had been a reduction in the overall safety program at NASA, there still remained myriad safety, reliability, and quality assurance units within the overall structure. The ability of these units to act as social control mechanisms, however, was seriously eroded by their lack of independence within the structure. Both the Kennedy and the Marshall flight centers had placed safety personnel under the supervision of the very offices and activities whose efforts they were to check and control. This structural flaw was described well by the Presidential Commission (1986:153): "In most cases, these organizations report to supervisors who are responsible for processing. The clear implication of such a management structure is that it fails to provide the kind of independent role necessary for flight safety. At Marshall, the director of Reliability and Quality Assurance reports to the director of Science and Engineering who oversees the development of shuttle hardware. Again, this results in a lack of independence from the producer of hardware and is compounded by reductions in manpower, bringing about a decrease in effectiveness which has direct implications for flight safety."

Still another social control problem within the internal structure at NASA was the erosion of norms supporting the use of legitimate means to accomplish organizational goals. Braithwaite (1989b) argues that the internal culture of the organization is a critical factor in either promoting or controlling organizational crime. At NASA, an internal culture had developed in which safety

U.S. government and weapons manufacturers in the production of a nuclear arsenal, again emphasizing the central role of the government in organizing a cooperative activity involving both government and business. The case at hand, however, suggests a different kind of relationship, one in which government omissions permit private businesses to pursue illegal and potentially injurious courses of action which, in a general way, facilitate the fulfillment of certain state policies.

The relationship between overarching government policies and the specific goals of business and industry is well illustrated by North Carolina's labor history. Since the late nineteenth century the political leadership of North Carolina has pursued a policy of industrial development through, among other things, limiting unionization and blocking the power of regulatory agencies. This pursuit of industrial development is a more general and less delimited goal than the pursuit of specific projects such as a space program or nuclear weapons production. By contrast, the Imperial Food processing company, like most industries, had a specific goal of profit maximization through (among other things) worker discipline. This goal and the methods used to attain it, however, dovetailed with the state's general concern with industrial development through (among other things) creating a climate within which businesses were not burdened with either unions or extensive safety regulation.

Like the state-corporate crimes examined by Kramer and Michalowski and Kauzlarich and Kramer, the Imperial plant fire depended on the interaction between the pursuit of government goals and corporate goals. We therefore find that the general framework of state-corporate crime is appropriate for the task at hand. We would, however, modify the definition of state-corporate crime to read:

> State-corporate crimes are illegal or socially injurious actions that result from a mutually reinforcing interaction between (1) policies and/or practices in pursuit of the goals of one or more institutions of political governance and (2) policies and/or practices in pursuit of the goals of one or more institutions of economic production and distribution.

State-corporate crimes occur within a capitalist economy when two or more organizations, at least one of which is in the civil sector and one of which is in the state sector, pursue goals that intersect in a way that produces some form of social injury.

The following discussion of the Imperial plant fire as state-corporate crime is divided into three parts. First, we establish the societal context in which the Imperial fire occurred by examining the history of industrial regulation in North Carolina as it relates to the state's overall development policy. Second, we construct the institutional context for the disaster by examining the specific pattern of industrial relations characteristic of the Imperial Food processing company. And last, we examine the control context within which the fire occurred by exploring the ways in which the activities of regulatory agencies intersected with the activities of Imperial in a way that resulted in the disastrous fire of September 3, 1991.

THE SOCIETAL CONTEXT

Political-Economic History of North Carolina

The societal context within which the Hamlet fire occurred is characterized by a set of political-economic arrangements that have historically centered around broad, state-supported latitude for investors and extensive state-enforced or state-permitted controls over labor (Wood 1986). The overall climate in North Carolina, since the end of the Civil War, has been one in which state policies toward both development and labor have been tilted in favor of capital accumulation and away from advancements in wages or work conditions for labor (Myerson 1982). The result has been a history of economic growth without real economic development. As Tomaskovic-Devey (1991:2) observes, "economic growth is a process of economic change which leads to increased employment and production activity. Economic development, on the other hand, is a growth process which leads to increased standards of living for the people in a region."

Between 1970 and 1990 North Carolina's economic policies produced economic growth, but development, in the form of improved living standards for the mass of the state's industrial workers, lagged behind substantially. Between 1976 and 1986 nonagricultural employment in the South overall grew by 44 percent, as compared with only 10 percent in the Northeast (SWEC 1986:11), and North Carolina enjoyed a substantial share of this growth explosion in the so-called Sunbelt. By 1987 the state was ranked first among all the states in the number of new manufacturing plants opened, and the North Carolina Department of Commerce boasted that businesses had invested nearly $5.4 billion dollars in new and expanded industrial facilities with the subsequent creation of 76,600 jobs. Yet at the same time the state retained its long-standing position as last among the fifty states in average manufacturing wage, as well as suffering from the highest infant mortality rate of any state in the United States, and being only forty-fourth in median family income (Tomaskovic-Devey 1991:27).

Since the emergence of the "New South" at the end of the nineteenth century, North Carolina's ability to attract capital investment in industry has been linked to the state's ability to offer what state officials refer to as an "attractive business environment." In practice this has meant high rates of return due to lower production costs, preferential tax policies for industry, and, most important, extremely low rates of unionization which, in turn, both lowered the wage bill for investors and limited the ability of workers to press for improvements in working conditions.

emerged. Some authors have likened the attraction of outside investment to the state to a great buffalo hunt. One report observed: "The stampede of plants to the South is definitely over—especially for the rural areas that lack a skilled workforce, transportation, infrastructure, and cultural amenities" (MDC 1986). This slowdown of economic growth has been reflected in lessened growth in state revenue, which in turn meant that the state had to make cutbacks in its already low level of public service, and felt a need to intensify its pro-business/ antilabor stance in order to compete for the remaining few domestic industries that might relocate to North Carolina.

Blocking Worker Safety: The Case against NC-OSHA

The second factor Wood (1986) suggests might be an avenue for North Carolina workers to improve their situation is through federal regulation. In the case of workplace safety, a relatively strong federal law has been in place since 1970 in the form of the Occupational Safety and Health (OSH) Act. The act's stated goal is "to assure as far as possible every working man and woman in the Nation safe and healthful working conditions." The act requires that each employer furnish each employee "a place of employment which is free from recognized hazards that are causing or likely to cause death or serious physical harm" (Public Law 91–596, quoted in Noble 1986:3).

The law gives impressive rights to American workers. First, it obliges companies to reduce the risks in the workplace. While other labor laws limit businesses from preventing efforts by workers to make improvements in the safety of their workplace, the OSH Act not only allows workers to fight for safety and health but places the burden of responsibility on the employer, demanding that the company take action to improve the workplace in ways that benefit the worker. Second, the act provides an impressive breadth of coverage compared with other protective legislation. Nearly all workers are protected by the act; public-sector employees are the only group of workers who are not (Noble 1986).

The OSH Act was not the first attempt to protect American workers' health and safety. Massachusetts passed the first worker safety law in 1877, and all other states eventually provided some kind of legal protection for at least some workers. The OSH Act, however, was the first federal law to protect workers' health and safety, and it was the first law to require federal inspectors and a federal system of fines. The OSH Act also differs from all previous worker health and safety legislation because it gives employees the right to participate in agency inspections (Noble 1986).

But despite its positive potential for American workers, the OSH Act is not as progressive as similar legislation in other countries. For example, U.S. employers, unlike those in some other nations, are not required to establish health and safety committees, nor are they required to involve workers in decision making about health and safety issues. In addition, some property rights of the employer are protected through an appeal system that facilitates employer challenges to cited violations (Noble 1986).

The establishment of the Occupational and Safety Health Administration (OSHA), nevertheless, threatens the interests of investors because it can make inroads into profits. In order to maintain profit levels, employers need to either keep their production costs low or be able to pass on any increase in costs to consumers. Profit pressures can inhibit the development of a safe workplace, because minimizing costs usually means forgoing the establishment of safety measures that absorb workers' time or the company's money (Noble 1986). The OSH Act, which insists that safe practices be implemented, even if they have a negative impact on profits, is particularly threatening to competitive-sector industries, which are less able to pass on the cost of a safe workplace to consumers. The OSH Act potentially restructures the relations between workers and managers of capital by insisting that profits are not the only standard by which businesses will be judged. It creates new rights to health and safety for employees and empowers the federal government to enforce them.

Many employers have seen the OSH Act as an unwelcome intrusion on the rights of investors in a private production system, have fought vigorously against its implementation, and in many cases have sought to circumvent its requirements. Especially after the economic downturn of the mid-1970s, investors and capital managers worked hard to neutralize the effects of the OSH Act. Employers found an ally for these efforts in the federal executive branch. Every president since the mid-1970s has sought support from the business community by backing its demands that economic costs be weighed when any new worker safety or health standards are considered. This support includes, for example, backing the right of employers to claim economic hardship as an acceptable reason for not implementing health and safety standards.

In addition, Congress sought to appease states' rights advocates by allowing states to create their own version of OSHA that was to be controlled by the state rather than by the federal government. In a last-minute compromise during the passage of the bill, state governments successfully lobbied for this joint program. According to the hearings held by the Committee on Education and Labor of the House of Representatives to inquire into the Hamlet fire (U.S. House 1991a), North Carolina was one of the twenty three states that opted for a state-run program, establishing the North Carolina Occupational Safety and Health Administration (NC-OSHA) in 1974. Of these twenty-three states, ten were only conditionally approved because they were not in compliance with federal OSHA regulations. At the time of the fire in Hamlet North Carolina was one of these ten on probation.

If a state chooses to establish its own OSHA operation, it has the option of setting its own penalties and priorities. NC-OSHA has used this prerogative to minimize the effect of penalties for violations of safety and health standards. In 1991, for example, North Carolina increased the fines for OSHA violations for the first time since the establishment of NC-OSHA in 1974. The new maximum fine in North Carolina (and by no means the most common one) was $14,000, just a fraction of the federal maximum fine of $70,000 (Parker, Menn, and O'Brien 1991).

Workers in North Carolina, like other American workers, could be protected by federal regulation under the OSH Act. The implementation of the OSH Act, however, has been diluted at the federal level by the executive branch. In addition, the proponents of states' rights allowed the state of North Carolina to organize its own version of OSHA, one that was even less effective than the federal version. In this way, the potential for protection of North Carolina workers by federal regulation was been successfully blocked by the mutual efforts of business and government in that state.

INSTITUTIONAL CONTEXT

The history of North Carolina's political economy reveals a state in which workers have been most often blocked in their efforts to control their work environment by a business-government coalition favoring a relatively laissez-faire industrial policy. But this political-economic climate alone does not explain the complex dynamics that led to the fire at Hamlet. Word could have reached authorities about the unsafe practices in the plant and NC-OSHA did have the legal authority to unlock the doors. What kept these remedies from taking place? This question is partially answered by examining the institutional context in which the fire occurred and by delineating the specific pattern of industrial relations among Imperial management, Imperial workers, and NC-OSHA.

By the late 1980s Imperial Foods was under considerable pressure because of the general economic decline and because of fiscal problems within the corporation. Even before the fire in Hamlet, it appears that Emmett Roe, the owner of Imperial Foods, was facing financial difficulty. In 1990 he had closed a plant in Alabama without giving his employees proper notice. The courts had awarded the laid-off workers $250,000 in severance pay, although at the time of the fire no payments on this obligation to the Alabama workers had been made. Roe was facing suits for $350,000 in debts owed to his creditors and a $24,000 bill for unpaid taxes (Greif and Garfield 1991). The financial difficulty that Roe faced may have increased the likelihood of decisions that placed profitability ahead of the health or safety of workers. This interpretation would be consistent with the findings of Clinard and Yeager (1980), which suggest that the greater the financial strain faced by businesses, the greater the likelihood that they will engage in regulatory violations.

Regardless of the decisions Roe's financial pressures or management policies may have provoked, however, NC-OSHA could have intervened in a way that would have ultimately protected the workers in Hamlet. What were the factors that disrupted the ability of NC-OSHA to regulate the conditions at Hamlet? Two issues stand out. First, there is some evidence suggesting that workers who recognized hazards at the plant found it difficult to make their concerns for a safe workplace heard. Second, NC-OSHA failed to effectively regulate Imperial's safety practices because it was not adequately funded and because, according to some observers, it was not efficiently organized.

Unheeded Warnings

In order for workers to be protected from dangerous work environments, at least in any work environment where they are not empowered to alter their own work conditions, someone must recognize the problems and make them known to those who do have the power to alter the hazardous conditions. There is evidence that the workers at the Hamlet plant were aware of safety problems and that they attempted to make their voices heard.

At the hearings on the fire, Bobby Quick, an employee at the plant, was asked if any fellow employee had made a complaint about the locked doors. Quick said his immediate coworkers knew about the problem, although they had not gone to management: "The maintenance [workers] talked about it amongst ourselves. We never took it to the office. We said amongst ourselves we hope a fire doesn't break out" (U.S. House 1991a:55).

Among other departments in the plant, however, people did complain to management, although their efforts apparently did not lead to any changes in the hazardous conditions. Quick testified that "a lot of people talked about it catching on fire and killing people. I recall one day Brad [plant supervisor and the son of its owner, Emmett Roe] was there. I think it was a white lady who told him, it was the day that it smoked up. She said 'This thing is going to kill somebody.' Brad did not pay her no attention. He was always rushing the maintenance men to fix something so they would not lose money and product. All they cared about was the product, getting it out" (U.S. House 1991a:56).

At the congressional hearings, representatives asked why more people did not question the safety of the plant, or why they were not more persistent in their complaints. Quick was asked if people were fearful of making a complaint. He answered by saying, "If you try to make a statement to Brad he did not want to hear it. What you said did not matter. He was running the show. If you keep making a stink, he will fire you, you know" (U.S. House 1991a:55).

The threat of firing in response to voicing concerns about safety was also revealed in the testimony of North Carolina's governor before the hearings committee. Governor James Martin referred committee members to Alfred Anderson, whose wife had died in the fire. Martin said that prior to the fire Anderson had accompanied his wife to talk to her boss about conditions at the plant. She was reprimanded for taking her complaint outside of the plant, even to her husband (U.S. House 1991a:122).

Another witness, Fred McQueen, a local physician who examined the twenty five bodies, indicated that Mrs. Anderson's experience was not unusual. McQueen said that a system should be designed to allow workers to make anonymous complaints. He wrote that "many workers present me, a physician, with complaints but do not want to follow through with their complaints because of the fear of losing their jobs" (U.S. House 1991a:122).

The testimony in this case suggests that there were workers who recognized safety hazards in the plant and in its method of operation, and who did try to have them remedied. Their expressions of concern, however, did not result in any changes. Additionally, the evidence suggests that many other workers at Imperial felt they inhabited a chilling climate when it came to suggesting to management that safety problems existed. The perception among workers that there are costs attached to making complaints regarding job safety, perhaps costs as high as losing one's job, represents a critical institutional flaw in any work setting where the only power workers have to rectify unsafe conditions is through appeals to management. In the case of Imperial this flaw was a significant factor in the loss of twenty-five lives.

The Failure of OSHA

Had the concerned workers at Imperial chosen to contact OSHA instead of bringing their complaints directly to the plant's management, they, like many other workers in North Carolina, were unlikely to have met with success. First, they would have been informed by a poster in the plant to call an 800 number. Three-fourths of the 160,000 workplace posters publicizing the phone number for safety complaints, including the posters at Imperial, listed a number that had been disconnected, with no forwarding number. Thus the basic requirement of being able to contact the safety agency could not be met. A highly motivated worker, familiar with the process of hunting through a bureaucratic tangle of phone numbers and disconnected lines, might have reached OSHA. But the more likely response of the average worker who called the NC-OSHA number, only to be told it was disconnected, would be to conclude that the office was no longer in operation. At the very least, the incorrect posters, and the failure to replace them with correct ones, constituted a serious limitation on the accessibility of OSHA to the workers at Imperial and elsewhere in North Carolina.

The incorrect posters and other problems faced by NC-OSHA in part reflect the organization's inadequate level of funding. Nationally OSHA is seriously underfunded, and NC-OSHA is comparatively even less well funded. North Carolina governor James Martin testified before Congress that although federal OSHA guidelines required a minimum of sixty four safety inspectors to be working in the state, the legislature had authorized only thirty four. He went on to say that in January of 1991 he attempted to have nineteen more inspectors authorized, but that the legislature had denied his request. Even if Martin's request had been granted, however, North Carolina would have remained eleven short of the minimum number of required OSHA inspectors. Only nine states in the United States have fewer inspectors than is recommended by federal OSHA regulations. Of these nine, North Carolina falls the farthest below the recommended number, funding only 53 percent of the total number of inspectors required. As a consequence, although North Carolina has, for example, eighty three poultry plants, only half have ever been inspected since the inception of NC-OSHA.

In 1980 North Carolina had 1.9 million workers and forty-seven OSHA safety inspectors. Ten years later, when North Carolina's work force had grown by 37 percent, to a total of 2.6 million, the number of OSHA inspectors had declined by 12 percent, to forty-two inspectors. According to the Bureau of Labor Statistics, between 1977, when John Brooks, commissioner of the Department of Labor and head of NC-OSHA, first took office, and 1988, the number of North Carolina workplace injuries grew from 120,000 a year to 177,300 (Menn 1991). This rate of growth in workplace injuries outstripped the growth in the actual number of workers, suggesting that between 1977 and 1988 North Carolina actually lost ground in workplace safety despite the fact that the purpose of the OSH Act was to ensure just the opposite.

In addition to the inadequate numbers of inspectors, Brooks reported to the congressional committee that until late in 1991 the inspectors NC-OSHA did employ were able to work in the field only four days a week because the department lacked sufficient travel funds. Since then they had been able to work in the field only three days a week because of further cuts in NC-OSHA funding. Brooks also noted that even if he hired additional staff, there would be difficulty in training them, because the closest training center was in Chicago and was constantly filled (U.S. House 1991a:168).

At the congressional hearings on the fire it was also revealed that $453,000, which could have been used for salaries for OSHA inspectors in North Carolina, was returned to the federal government in 1991 (U.S. House 1991a: 129). Moreover, this was not a onetime budgetary aberration. According to testimony, in five of the six years preceding the Imperial fire, federal OSHA money has been returned to Washington by NC-OSHA. These funds were returned to the federal government because in order to accept them, the state would have to match them. For example, in 1991, because the state legislature was unwilling to provide the state OSHA with $243,000, it was unable to accept the matching $453,000 from the federal government (CEL 1991a:223).

Brooks also explained that the money was also not accepted because it was stipulated for salaries only. Because there was a hiring freeze on state jobs in North Carolina, according to Brooks, it would be illegal to spend the money

creation of atomic weapons. The purpose of this mission was to destroy laboratories and other facilities that were associated with nuclear energy before the planned Soviet invasion of Berlin, scheduled a few months later (Powaski 1987). The reason for the mission, code-named Alsos, was clear. As General Groves stated, "our principal concern was to keep information and atomic secrets from falling into the hands of Russia" (quoted in Powaski 1987:40). In the end, the operation succeeded, and Russia was denied access to the blueprints for the new weapon.

The end of World War II signified the beginning of a massive effort on the part of the United States to increase the sophistication of atomic weapons. At this time the U.S. military, the primary beneficiary of nuclear energy research, lost control of the rights to produce atomic weapons. Considerable debate took place between the proponents of placing atomic energy under civilian control, principally advocated by the Federation of Atomic Scientists, and those who wanted atomic energy to stay in the hands of the military. In the end, the scientists won the legislative battle. The Atomic Energy Act of 1946, sometimes referred to as the McMahon bill, established the independent, civilian-controlled Atomic Energy Commission (AEC). Under this act, the military could only gain access to the bomb by a direct presidential order. Although the AEC, in principle, was a civilian body, the military had an enormous influence over atomic energy policies and operations (Clarfield and Wiecek 1984; Powaski 1987). Powaski (1987:123) explains:

> Organizationally, military emphasis was built into the structure of the AEC from the beginning. One of its four operating divisions was military applications. A military liaison committee was appointed by the Department of Defense to participate in the AEC's weapons work. The armed services retained for themselves the intelligence function of the Manhattan Project, rather than transferring it to the AEC. The ties were so close that an incoming secretary of defense is supposed to have asked, after being shown the Department of Defense organization chart, "Where is the AEC?"

One of the first postwar responsibilities of the AEC was the transformation of military applications of nuclear energy to civilian uses. Robert Oppenheimer, the chair of the AEC, wanted to see a complete effort toward this goal, and argued vehemently for the peaceful application of atomic energy (Powaski 1987). Enrico Fermi, the scientist credited with the first successful attempt at generating a sustained nuclear reaction, and who also resided high in the AEC hierarchy, argued that primacy should be directed toward future weapons programs. In the end, according to Powaski (1987:111), "the Fermi view prevailed, and the recommendation for priority in weapons was instrumental in committing the AEC to the same view, which in turn was the basis for President

Truman's policy decision to make weapons the highest priority of the American atomic energy program."

The AEC was never required to monitor the environmental effects of the production of nuclear materials. The AEC also neglected to consider and create policy that would control the adverse environmental effects occurring during the production of nuclear weapons and nuclear materials (Steele 1989). Former AEC general manager Carroll L. Wilson stated in 1979, "Nobody got brownie points for caring about nuclear waste. The Atomic Energy Commission neglected the problem" (Steele 1989:19).

From 1945 to 1953 Truman embarked on a massive buildup of nuclear weapons. A major reason cited for this buildup was the threat of the Soviet Union. The Soviets, in 1949, successfully tested an atomic bomb, ending the U.S. monopoly and "inaugurating the era of proliferation" (Williams and Cantelon 1984:114). From this time on, relations between the United States and the Soviet Union dictated, to a large degree, the quantity and quality of the U.S. production of nuclear weapons.

Soon after the Soviets tested their first atomic bomb, a meeting was called between Truman and AEC chair David Lilienthal. Lilienthal was planning on presenting a report to Truman that argued against the development of the newly conceptualized hydrogen bomb. Truman did not read the report and, after confirming that the Soviets could build such a weapon, ordered the development of the hydrogen bomb. Recalling the meeting later, Lilienthal wrote that his effort to block the development of the hydrogen bomb was like saying "no to a steam roller" (Powaski 1987:57). The AEC, he felt, had become nothing more than a major contractor to the Department of Defense (Powaski 1987).

The decision to develop the hydrogen bomb was also conducted in extreme secrecy (Clarfield and Wiecek 1984; Powaski 1987; Williams and Cantelon 1984). Similar to the secrecy surrounding the initial development of the bomb during the Manhattan era, "there was no public, or even congressional debate, over the decision to develop the hydrogen bomb" (Powaski 1987:57). Similar circumstances thus surrounded the two major decisions to develop atomic weapons: both were conducted in secrecy, both projects operated under no formal or informal social control, and both decisions were based on the threat of an outside nation or nations. These factors put immense pressure on atomic scientists and the AEC to perform a sole function—developing bombs.

On the same day that Truman approved the production of the hydrogen bomb, he also approved the suggestions called for in a National Security Council report known as NSC-68. This study called "for an enormous increase in American defense spending in order to prevent Soviet domination of the world" (Powaski 1987:217). Nine new nuclear weapons production facilities were created to accommodate this mission.

The Atomic Energy Act of 1946 was replaced by the Atomic Energy Act of 1954. Most of the specific provisions of the new act, however, and all the licensing and related regulatory requirements applied solely to commercial reactors. Thus, the act of 1954 did little to change the prior act in relation to the government's use of nuclear energy (Clarfield and Wiecek 1984). The government's nuclear weapons production complex remained exempt from any real outside monitoring and did not have to follow the somewhat strict regulations on the emerging civilian nuclear industry. Despite Eisenhower's "Atoms for Peace" plan, the military application of nuclear energy grew substantially during these years.

The production of nuclear weapons peaked between the late 1950s and the early 1960s. During this time, twenty military nuclear weapons facilities were operating at peak capacity (Cochran 1988). As Weiner (1990:35) describes, "by 1958, nuclear weaponry was an infinitely expanding dynamo. The target list had grown to some 20,000 dots on the communist map. The target list included every city in Russia, Eastern Europe, and China." By 1960, "three thousand two hundred and sixty-seven nuclear warheads [could] annihilate the Soviet Union, China and Eastern Europe in a single blinding blow. They planned to follow this apocalyptic spasm with thousands . . . and thousands of more bombs. Ten nations would be obliterated. Five hundred million people would die."

During the Kennedy years (1961–1963), nuclear weapons production reached its zenith, with over five thousand weapons produced each year (Cochran 1988). Along with the tense climate of the Cold War and the residual effects of McCarthyism, the antagonistic relations between the Soviet Union and the United States accelerated with events such as the Berlin crisis and the Cuban missile crisis (see Powaski 1987). Between 1964 and 1976, however, nuclear weapons production decreased. President Lyndon Johnson shut down ten weapons-production facilities because of abundant stocks of plutonium (Cochran 1988). The SALT talks on arms limitation and the attitude of some high-level officials (particularly Johnson's secretary of defense, Robert S. McNamara) that weapons proliferation was futile fostered this cutback in nuclear weapons production (Powaski 1987; Williams and Cantelon 1984).

THE ORGANIZATION OF THE DEPARTMENT OF ENERGY'S PRODUCTION COMPLEX

In 1974 the Energy Reorganization Act abolished the Atomic Energy Commission and established two new organizations: the Energy Research and Development Administration (ERDA), and the Nuclear Regulatory Commission (NRC). This legislation was enacted in response to concerns that the AEC was functioning as both regulator (of civilian industries) and promoter (through the military) of nuclear programs (Powaski 1987; Radioactive Waste Campaign

1988). ERDA was established to oversee the promotional and defense productions, while the regulating and licensing operations for commercial nuclear power were assigned to the NRC (Radioactive Waste Campaign 1988).

The Department of Energy (DOE) was formed by President Jimmy Carter to "give a clear direction and focus to America's energy future by providing the framework for carrying out a comprehensive, balanced energy policy" (U.S. Department of Energy 1979:2). As a part of orchestrating this "new direction," the Department of Energy was given the responsibility of producing nuclear weapons. Although manufacturing nuclear weapons is only a small fraction of DOE's responsibilities, it has traditionally devoted one-third of its funds to warhead production (Lamperti 1984a).

The basic mission of DOE defense activities during the Cold War was to produce material for nuclear weapons and to manufacture fuel for the U.S. Navy (U.S. General Accounting Office 1986). The DOE oversaw the production of nuclear weapons and materials at seventeen major facilities around the country: six facilities produced nuclear material only, six plants produced nuclear material and assembled components into warheads, and five facilities designed and tested nuclear weapons. Almost all of these facilities had been created in the 1940s and 1950s.

The entire complex employed over one hundred thousand workers and has consistently had annual budgets of approximately eight billion dollars (Center for Defense Information 1989). The DOE, like its predecessors the AEC and ERDA, carried out most of its programs by contracting with private firms and universities. Most of the contractors who operated the majority of the DOE facilities were large multinational corporations such as Westinghouse, DuPont, General Electric, and Martin Marietta.

The U.S. government owned the equipment and materials used in the manufacturing of nuclear weapons items, and directed the contractor to produce the final product, that is, the warheads themselves or the converted nuclear materials. Thus the contractor was responsible for the actual production of the nuclear weapons, while the DOE acted as a supervisor of the contractor's activities. The organization of the entire weapons complex has much in common with the system that developed during the Manhattan Project era (Cochran 1988; Lamperti 1984b; Powaski 1987), in which private contractors maintain the important roles of researcher, developer, and manufacturer of the entire nuclear weapons program.

The DOE–Contractor Relationship

There were two kinds of financial arrangements the DOE made with its contractors. Some contractors operated on a nonprofit basis, for which they received compensation only for the costs incurred during the production of nuclear weapons. Other contractors operated on a profit basis, or "award fee" arrangement. In this type of contract, DOE agreed to pay a contractor bonus money if, during a six-month period, the contractor met certain preestablished criteria. Although each contract the DOE made with its corporate operators was different, most contracts contained essentially the same provisions (Alvarez 1990; Mobilization for Survival 1989).

The DuPont Corporation operated the Savannah River Plant in Aiken, South Carolina, from the inception of the atomic age. On a nonprofit basis, DuPont had been held responsible for the day-to-day operations of the facility. One clause in the DOE DuPont (National Academy of Sciences 1987:44) contract read, "The Contractor shall take all reasonable precautions in the performance of the work under this Contract to protect the safety of employees and of members of the public and to minimize dangers from all hazards to life and property, and shall comply with all health, safety, and fire protection regulations and requirements."

The same provision was included in DOE's 1987 contract with UNC Nuclear Industries, the operator of the Hanford facility located in Hanford, Washington. The only difference between the two contracts, in relation to the mandates of the DOE concerning the contractor's obligation to perform all activities in compliance with applicable environmental laws, was that UNC operated under a profit arrangement with the DOE, whereas DuPont operated its facility under a nonprofit arrangement (National Academy of Sciences 1987). In all other matters, the DOE placed the bulk of the responsibility on the contractor to operate the facilities in a lawful manner.

The National Academy of Sciences (1987) has argued that DOE directives to their contractors were often vague and that they provided the corporations with a great deal of latitude in the interpretation of DOE orders. For example, in the 1987 DOE–UNC contract, the DOE ordered UNC to "operate and monitor the N Reactor and support facilities in a safe, secure, and environmentally sound manner to achieve a fiscal year production goal of 705 KMWD, with less than twenty-four unscheduled outage days" (National Academy of Sciences 1987:51). Although this directive may have been legally inclusive, the DOE did not provide the contractor with the specific methods to achieve compliance with applicable environmental issues; in this sense, the DOE orders could be considered relatively vague. Additionally, the wording of the above clause suggests that the DOE wanted its contractor to know that while safe and environmentally sound procedures of waste disposal (which were unspecified) were important, it was equally important that precise production quotas be met.

The Organizational Management Structure

The nuclear weapons production complex used a three-tier approach to carry out its operations. The first tier was the contractor who actually performed the day-to-day operations. The contractor developed its own environmental protection program and periodically checked on its implementation through internal audits and self-appraisals (U.S. General Accounting Office 1986). The contractor was held responsible to meet all DOE environmental, health, and safety requirements as a condition of the contract between the DOE and the contractor (Walker 1986). The contractor thus had a high degree of responsibility in ensuring that the work was carried out in compliance with all applicable environmental laws (Alvarez 1990; National Academy of Sciences 1987; U.S. General Accounting Office 1986).

The second tier of the management structure resided in the DOE itself. The DOE field offices were directly responsible for overseeing each contractor's performance. The field offices periodically conducted appraisals and audits of the contractor's work, including incident releases and quality assurance (U.S. General Accounting Office 1986).

The final tier of the management structure was the general oversight by DOE headquarters. The office of the assistant secretary for environment, safety and health held primary responsibility for the entire complex's compliance with environmental law. There were three ways this was done: (1) appraising the field offices' environmental protection activities, (2) reviewing plans for each field office regarding how it was going to carry out its respective environmental programs, and (3) reviewing accidents and unusual occurrences at DOE facilities (U.S. General Accounting Office 1986).

THE CRIMINAL CONTAMINATION
OF THE ENVIRONMENT

Producing nuclear weapons resulted in a large amount of radioactive and nonradioactive (hazardous) waste (Lamperti 1984b; Office of Technology Assessment 1991; Reicher and Scher 1988; U.S. Department of Energy 1995c; U.S. General Accounting Office 1985, 1986, 1989). In 1986 the Savannah facility generated over 200,000 gallons of waste each day, and by the late 1980s the Hanford plant had dumped over 200 billion gallons of radioactive and hazardous wastes since its inception in 1942 (Steele 1989). Indeed, the contamination wrought by nuclear weapons production is so severe that estimates of forcing the complex into compliance with applicable environmental laws are a startling four hundred billion dollars (Congressional Budget Office 1994).

The waste disposal practices employed by most of the DOE facilities historically were grounded in the theory that "soil absorbs radioactive and hazardous elements in waste, and harmlessly extinguishes all potentially dangerous chemicals" (U.S. General Accounting Office 1986:31). Thus seepage basins and waste ponds were used as containers to filter out the harmful elements in the waste. The problem with this method of disposal, employed since the beginning of the atomic age, was that soil does not, in fact, prevent harmful elements in waste from seeping into groundwater basins (U.S. General Accounting Office 1986). A dramatic example of this is found in the waste disposal practices of the Savannah River facility. Because of its methods of waste disposal, the Tuscaloosa Aquifer, part of the Tuscaloosa Group Formation of underground water passages, is now contaminated with several harmful elements, including tritium and nitrates (U.S. General Accounting Office 1986).[1]

The Hanford facility and the Savannah River Plant have been identified by several commentators as being two of the most environmentally damaging nuclear weapons facilities (Mobilization for Survival 1989; Saleska and Makhijani 1990; Steele 1989; U.S. Department of Energy 1995c). Both facilities were involved in the production of plutonium and tritium, compounds that play an integral role in making completed warheads. The Mobilization for Survival (1989:3) has documented several adverse environmental consequences wrought by the activities of the Hanford facility. These include "100 square miles of groundwater . . . contaminated with radioactive tritium, iodine, and toxic chemicals. Over a half million gallons of high level radioactive waste [have] leaked from underground tanks and more continues to leak into the soil. Billions of gallons of liquid wastes and waste water with chemical and radioactive elements have been dumped in Hanford soil, contaminating the Columbia River and its watershed."

Steele (1989) has also documented the history of the disregard for the environment that has taken place at Hanford since the beginning of the atomic age: between 1944 and 1955, 537,000 curies of unfiltered airborne releases of iodine were let loose into the atmosphere; between 1952 and 1967, ruthenium-contaminated nitrate flakes fell on nearby farmers' fields, and ultimately resulted in the death of several hundred cattle; and over sixty "lost" burial sites of waste have not been found because of the secret methods of waste disposal used by World War II scientists. The Hanford facility, which is responsible for extremely high levels of tritium in drinking water as well as leaks from barrels containing high-level radioactive waste, has a long record of abuse and neglect concerning the environment (Office of Technology Assessment 1991; U.S. Department of Energy 1995d). Indeed, the Congressional Budget Office (1994) has determined that the cost of cleaning up this facility will be nearly one-and-a-half billion dollars.

Equally poor is the environmental record of the Savannah River Plant, which according to the Congressional Budget Office (1994) will need at least $757 million for cleanup. The groundwater near the plant is contaminated with nearly all forms of radioactive and hazardous waste, and over fifty-one million gallons of highly dangerous toxins are stored in leaking underground tanks beneath the facility (Mobilization for Survival 1989). Other problems include massive mercury leaks into the air, and high levels of tritium, strontium, and iodine in the soil (Office of Technology Assessment 1991).

The DOE regulated itself for radioactive releases into ground and surface water, radioactive waste, and radioactive leaks into water. The three principal environmental laws relevant to the DOE are the Clean Water Act of 1972, the Clean Air Act of 1970, and the Resource Conservation and Recovery Act (RCRA) of 1976. The DOE fought the applicability of these laws to its operations for several years. The department was especially tenacious in its refusal to comply with RCRA. In the eight years between the 1976 passage of RCRA and the 1984 district court ruling that the DOE was subject to this law, the DOE argued that under the Atomic Energy Act of 1954, its activities were exempt from the law because of "national security" (Radioactive Waste Campaign 1988; Reicher and Scher 1988).

RCRA gives the Environmental Protection Agency (EPA) the authority to regulate DOE's hazardous waste disposal practices. DOE's activities generate an enormous amount of hazardous waste, and it is commonly said that the department is out of compliance with this law (Alvarez 1990 personal interview; Center for Defense Information 1988; Cochran 1988; Radioactive Waste Campaign 1988; Reicher and Scher 1988; U.S. General Accounting Office 1985, 1986, 1989). Millions of gallons of hazardous waste surround some DOE facilities, and all of the production sites have been found to be operating in violation of RCRA (Radioactive Waste Campaign 1988; U.S. Department of Energy 1995d; U.S. General Accounting Office 1986). In a 1986 study conducted by the U.S. General Accounting Office (1986), all seven of the facilities reviewed were radically out of compliance with RCRA. Under RCRA (1976) an operator must identify its hazardous wastes; receive a permit in order to treat, store, or dispose of such wastes; monitor groundwater at waste sites; close and care for sites that are taken out of operation; and undertake corrective action. In 1985 a report by the Ohio EPA also found numerous violations of RCRA at the Fernald Feeds Materials Plant in Fernald, Ohio. Until the environmental laws of the 1970s, safe waste-disposal practices had been largely ignored, because there were no laws applicable to the production complex. Indeed, extreme amounts of hazardous wastes were disposed of at most DOE facilities, including the Y-12 plant in Oak Ridge, Tennessee, where four waste disposal plants were found to be leaking 4.7 million gallons of metal, acids, and solvents between the years of 1953 and 1963 (Reicher and Scher 1988).

The most publicized violations to date of environmental laws by the DOE and a DOE contractor to date were found in the June 1988 Federal Bureau of Investigation (FBI) and EPA raid on the Rocky Flats facility near Denver. Rocky Flats manufactured the plutonium parts of nuclear warhead cores and various other fission bomb components (Abas 1989). The FBI raid was prompted by Jim Stone, a six-year Rocky Flats engineer, who uncovered an internal DOE memo describing the operations at Rocky Flats as "patently illegal" and "in poor condition generally in terms of environmental compliance"

(Abas 1989:22). Stone contacted the FBI, and search warrants were issued to search the facility for possible violations of environmental law. The seventy-five-member team that raided the facility was looking for evidence to substantiate the allegations that Rocky Flats had (a) illegally treated, stored, and disposed of hazardous waste in violation of RCRA; (b) discharged pollutants without a permit in violation of RCRA and the Clean Water Act; and (c) concealed environmental contamination (Abas 1989; U.S. House 1993).

The raid on Rocky Flats marked the first time a governmental agency had gathered evidence against another federal facility for the purposes of criminal prosecution. The operation resulted in the filing of criminal charges against the Rockwell Corporation, the contractor for Rocky Flats. Rockwell responded by suing the DOE, alleging that its company was forced to violate hazardous-waste laws because the government had failed to provide a permanent storage site for liquid wastes contaminated with nonradioactive toxins (Abas 1989). In the end, however, Rockwell dropped its lawsuit against the DOE and pleaded guilty to several violations of RCRA, the Clean Water Act, and the Clean Air Act. The plea bargain reached between the Department of Justice and Rockwell cost the company over eighteen-and-a-half million dollars (Haynes 1997; U.S. House 1993).

There is no question that most, if not all, of the DOE's nuclear weapons production facilities have engaged in illegal activity. With the exception of the 1989 Rocky Flats raid and subsequent prosecution, however, official EPA and U.S. Department of Justice policy is not to take criminal action against another federal agency over environmental compliance problems (Porter 1986:9; U.S. Congress 1993). Other problems exist concerning the enforcement of environmental crimes committed by the DOE. As the Center for Defense Information (1989:2) stated, "the EPA is further handicapped by overlapping laws, a lack of statistical data on military environmental compliance, military reluctance to accept EPA oversight, and the fact that government agencies are constitutionally barred from suing each other to force compliance with the law."

Although the EPA is precluded by Article 3 of the U.S. Constitution from prosecuting another federal entity, it is not precluded from investigating alleged criminal violations by individuals at federal facilities (Thompson 1989). The contractors, however, look at the problem of enforcement in a different manner. George B. Merrick (1987:6), former vice president of the Rockwell Corporation, offers this grievance concerning DOE and EPA enforcement policy at the Rocky Flats facility: "We are in a position where the Department of Energy requires us to continue to produce weapons under threat of civil penalties even though the EPA and Justice Department threaten to prosecute our people and our company for operations essential to that production. We think that such governmental conduct is unfair, illegal, and unconstitutional."

ANALYSIS

The end of the Cold War and the revelation of massive radioactive contamination at DOE sites around the country have combined to nearly shut
down the nuclear weapons production complex. Most of the facilities are
closed and awaiting decontamination and general cleanup. The future of the
complex is not clear. What is clear is that most, if not all, of the nuclear
weapons production facilities in the United States have illegally contaminated
the environment for over fifty years.

Goal Formation

There is little question that organizations carry out most of their activities
in order to reach operative goals. Most organizational theorists stress the
importance of understanding an organization's goals if one seeks insight into
organizational behavior. Let us briefly consider the nuclear weapons production complex's goals, and the manner in which they were shaped by structural
and historical exigencies.

As we have discussed, the United States has been engaged in or preparing
for war for nearly sixty years. Given that the Cold War military strategies were
largely organized around the capabilities of nuclear weapons, and that use of
atomic weapons played a significant role in ending the hostilities of World War
II, the production of nuclear weapons became one of the most important programs of the U.S. government. This meant that the organization charged with
the responsibility of developing and producing nuclear weapons warheads had
to be, highly goal oriented and concerned with performance. Indeed, the
United States depended on these powerful weapons to deter Soviet aggression, and to gain economic and geopolitical advantages over those countries
that did not possess nuclear weapons.

Throughout the Cold War, geopolitical and economic interests caused the
United States to continually upgrade its stockpile of weapons of mass destruction, which in turn forced the nuclear weapons production complex to be
even more concerned with the achievement of production goals. The United
States had to match or beat every Soviet advance in nuclear technology. For
example, after the Soviets' first test of a nuclear weapon, Truman gave orders
to strengthen existing nuclear weapons production programs and to start production on the hydrogen bomb. Historical evidence, then, supports the contention that the weapons complex's strong commitment to producing nuclear
weapons is a result of the U.S. interest in exercising global economic and
political domination (Chomsky 1988; Ellsburg 1981).

The Selection of Means

The methods employed to produce nuclear weapons have resulted in
tremendous contamination of the environment. It is highly unlikely that the

Manhattan scientists were unaware of the adverse consequences of nuclear weapons production, given their relatively sophisticated understanding of the destructive capabilities of those weapons. Moreover, former AEC general manager Wilson admitted that the AEC neglected the problem of contamination that occurred as a result of weapons production. The production goals of the weapons complex historically have taken primacy, while the adverse environmental consequences of weapons production have never been a major concern of the contractors, the DOE, or its predecessors. A number of analysts have agreed with this conclusion (Alvarez 1990; Center for Defense Information 1989; Hodges 1991:i; Krater 1991:i; Mobilization for Survival 1989; National Academy of Sciences 1987; Reicher and Scher 1988; U.S. House 1993).

The Manhattan Project was given one objective, to produce the atomic bomb. At that time, there was little knowledge of the program outside of those who were directly involved in it. Because the operation was conducted in such secrecy and without oversight, the weapons complex was free to use any means available to meet its objectives. The scientists and the military officials in charge of the project had great autonomy and could simply select the most effective means possible for achieving their goals. Because there was complete state sponsorship of the endeavor, any method that facilitated goal attainment could be adopted as policy.

Oversight

Many students of the nuclear weapons production complex have identified the lack of interorganizational oversight within the complex as a contributor to the resulting environmental problems (Alvarez 1990; Mobilization for Survival 1989; National Academy of Sciences 1987). In the most comprehensive study, conducted by the National Academy of Sciences (1987), several specific problems were cited:

1. DOE's overreliance on the contractors to conduct their activities in compliance with environmental laws.
2. Weak ties between the DOE's Environmental, Safety and Health Department and the field offices.
3. The need for strengthening the capability of the field offices to monitor contractor activities.
4. Episodic and narrowly focused audits and appraisals into the safety of production reactors.
5. DOE's lack of offices and divisions charged with research, reactor regulation, inspections, and event analysis (as compared with the NRC).

Given the insights of the National Academy, it is possible to identify three general problems in the management structure that contribute to the lack of interorganizational oversight within the complex: a lack of communication between the various parties involved in the production of nuclear weapons and materials; DOE's apparent lack of concern for appraising the operations of the contractors; and an overreliance on the contractors to conduct their operations in compliance with applicable laws.

These three problems with the interorganizational oversight of the complex have occurred simultaneously in some instances. For example, in the years between 1981 and 1987, comprehensive DOE headquarters appraisals of contractor performance occurred only twice at the Savannah facility and only once at the Hanford plant (National Academy of Sciences 1987).

The lack of interorganizational oversight within the weapons complex seems to be the result of the lack of concern, conveyed by both the DOE and its contractors, for the adverse environmental consequences of weapons production. Many of these problems seem to reflect the general ideology of the complex, that is, the apparent disregard for the environmental consequences of warhead production and a sole emphasis on production goals.

Organizational Culture

Because the weapons production complex of the early 1990s had many similarities to that of the earlier weapons operations, it is reasonable to speculate that an organizational "culture" or "philosophy" has developed within the complex. For example, U.S. Secretary of Energy James Watkins (quoted in Olshansky and Williams 1988:29) has stated that the DOE has had "an underlying philosophy that adequate production of defense materials and a healthy, safe environment were not compatible objectives. A culture of mismanagement and ineptitude will have to be overcome in [this] department before the nation's troubled nuclear weapons manufacturing plants can be brought into compliance with environmental laws."

This statement supports the notions that environmental criminality has existed for some time and that production goals have historically taken precedence over concerns about the environmental consequences of warhead production; the priority of production goals is an integral part of the weapons complex's culture. Senator John Glenn (quoted in Steele 1989:17) makes a similar claim. He said, "The Department of Energy and its predecessors have been carrying out their mission to produce nuclear weapons with an attitude of neglect bordering on contempt for environmental protection. What they've said in effect is 'we're going to build bombs and the environment be damned.' "

Because of the peculiar history of the weapons complex as a governmental endeavor that supplied the nation's most important military weapons, the complex operated for a sustained period of time without being subject to external, independent review. This feature of the complex may have permitted the formation of an organizational culture that was autonomous and virtually immune to outside criticism.

Of the many characteristics of the organization of the weapons production complex, perhaps the most apparent is its tradition of the normalization of deviance. As a result of placing primacy on production goals through the most expedient and effective means, the complex has engaged in, and continues to engage in, the illegal disposal and storage of nuclear waste. These illegal practices can be seen as a logical result of the organization's methods of operation. Since virtually every weapons production facility is or has operated in violation of one or more environmental laws, the organization as a whole can be viewed as a "culture" of noncompliance.

NOTES

Updated, adapted, and revised from David Kauzlarich and Ronald Kramer, *Crimes of the Nuclear State: At Home and Abroad* (Boston: Northeastern University Press, 1998).

1. Tritium is a radioactive isotope that is very hazardous when assimilated into the body. Excessive nitrate levels in drinking water have been found to be harmful to all animals, especially human infants (U.S. Department of Energy 1995d).

CHAPTER 6

The Crash of ValuJet Flight 592

Rick A. Matthews and David Kauzlarich

ON MAY 11, 1996, ValuJet flight 592 crashed in the Florida Everglades, killing all 105 passengers and 5 crew members. The technical cause of the crash was a fire that erupted after one or more oxygen generators exploded in a cargo compartment. Government investigations have indicated that both ValuJet and SabreTech (an airline maintenance company) failed to comply with a host of regulations concerning the presentation, storage, and transportation of hazardous materials by air. More generally, however, the Federal Aviation Administration (FAA) has been found to be negligent in its oversight of airlines by not adequately monitoring the general safety of commercial aircraft as well as by its refusal to institute safeguards and guidelines that would have protected passengers and crews from crashes like that of flight 592. This chapter follows the tradition of state-corporate crime theorizing and research by identifying the organizational and structural forces that contributed to the ValuJet crash. This approach includes an examination of the FAA's contradictory roles as both regulator and supporter of the airline industry, as well as a discussion of both ValuJet's and SabreTech's violations of federal air safety regulations.

The present examination of the ValuJet crash can increase understanding of state-corporate crime in two ways: (1) through exposing the varied nature and form of the relationships between the polity and corporations that may lead to injurious outcomes that violate laws, and (2) through exploring the usefulness of the core theoretical concepts in the organizational crime literature by applying them to an instance of state-corporate crime.

As Michalowski and Aulette note in chapter 3, state-corporate crimes can be either state-initiated or state-facilitated. Our analysis of the crash of ValuJet 592 reveals strong evidence that this tragedy is appropriately designated a state-facilitated corporate crime. As Michalowski and Aulette similarly found in the case of the fire at the Imperial processing plant, the press and governmental officials were quick to assign culpability to ValuJet and SabreTech personnel while largely ignoring the instrumental role the Federal Aviation Administration (FAA) played in the disaster. We will demonstrate that were it not for specific omissions by a number of institutional actors in both the private and the public sector within a lax regulatory environment, ValuJet flight 592 would not have crashed.

Since state-facilitated crime usually involves acts of omission rather than commission, it is one of the least recognizable forms of state involvement in crime.[1] The utility of the concept, however, is not just in its identification of the broader structural state support of the U.S. economy and how this can be organizationally criminogenic. A variety of identifiable and specific actions or inactions by governmental agencies may lead to identifiable social harms. Our analysis of the crash of ValuJet 592 highlights not only the broader structural policies that contributed to the crash but also the specific items marginalized or overlooked by the FAA that can be directly linked to the deaths of those on ValuJet flight 592. These include ignoring two clear recommendations by the National Transportation Safety Board (NTSB) to: (1) place smoke detectors in cargo holds exactly like the area in which the fire started on flight 592, and (2) reclassify D cargo holds so that they would contain a fire and not allow it to spread to the rest of the plane.[2] Had the FAA followed these recommendations, flight 592 could have landed safely and more than a hundred lives would have been saved. Furthermore, officials in the FAA also ignored several damning reports about the low quality and maintenance of ValuJet planes, not only from other agencies, such as the U.S. Department of Defense, but also by FAA field inspectors.

In this case study we demonstrate that the crash of ValuJet flight 592 resulted from the "mutually reinforcing interaction" between private corporations (ValuJet and SabreTech) and a governmental agency (the Federal Aviation Administration). As such, the crash represents an example of state-facilitated state-corporate crime in which the pursuit of profit by corporations along with the failure of a state agency to effectively monitor them resulted in the violent deaths of 110 people. We first examine the particular events that led up to the fatal crash of ValuJet flight 592, including the specific actions of ValuJet and SabreTech employees. Although it is important to understand these specific events, the reasons why they occurred cannot be understood without placing them within the larger sociohistorical contexts of governmental regulation of the airline industry and the broader sociopolitical context of laissez-faire economics enshrined in the Airline Deregulation Act (ADA) of 1978. In order to more fully understand exactly what happened and why, we thus follow Michalowski and Aulette's approach and examine the larger "nested contexts" within which state-facilitated crime occurs.

EVENTS LEADING TO THE CRASH

The ValuJet Corporation, founded by Robert Priddy, a former baggage handler, had overcome many obstacles and quickly developed its own niche in the airline industry. ValuJet grew from two to fifty aircraft (including the acquisition of forty-eight aircraft in thirty-one months), and within four years had a profit of $6.8 million dollars (Hosenball and Underwood 1996; Levinson, Underwood, and Turque 1996). Based in Atlanta, ValuJet was approaching its fourth year of existence when flight 592 crashed. The early years of ValuJet were characterized by rapid growth and the development of a reputation for providing exceptionally low-priced airfares (as low as $39.00) and staying, in the words of Priddy, "lean and mean" (Hosenball and Underwood 1996). The lean and mean aspect of ValuJet meant, among other things, a nonunionized labor force, paying pilots about half of the industry average, having pilots pay for their own training, and outsourcing maintenance (Hosenball and Underwood 1996). Like many late-twentieth-century corporations, ValuJet viewed outsourcing as an integral component of profit making. By 1994 ValuJet was acquiring planes as fast as it could get its hands on them, and most of these aircraft were older and in need of repairs. At the time of the crash of flight 592, the average ValuJet plane was 26.4 years old (Greising 1996). Since one of the cost-cutting measures employed by ValuJet was contracting out maintenance duties, the older planes they purchased were sent to out-of-house contractors. Indeed, the only maintenance ValuJet did itself was routine inspections, and it was not equipped to do heavy maintenance. In all, ValuJet had contracts with twenty-one different certified maintenance facilities, including SabreTech (NTSB 1997).

In January of 1996 ValuJet purchased two McDonnell Douglas MD-82s from McDonnell Douglas Finance Corporation, and then in February 1996 purchased a third plane from them, an MD-83. ValuJet sent all three planes to Miami, where they were to be serviced by SabreTech.

One of the maintenance tasks requested of SabreTech by ValuJet was the inspection of oxygen generators on all three planes to determine if they had exceeded their allowable service life of twelve years. One of the planes had generators that were to expire in 1998 or later. The other two planes, however, had generators that had already expired or were going to expire shortly. Thus ValuJet contracted with SabreTech to remove the generators from these planes and replace them.

Oxygen generators are cylindrical tubes that provide oxygen in emergency situations, when cabin pressure is lost. The generators, along with the oxygen masks, are mounted behind panels above or adjacent to passenger seats in the plane. The generator cannot be activated until the spring-loaded mechanism strikes a percussion cap containing a small explosive charge at the end of the generator. When struck, this cap provides the necessary energy to create an exothermic chemical reaction, which then causes the generator to expel oxygen

CAB's safety rule-making responsibilities. The newly formed FAA thus contained within a single agency the contradictory roles of promoting the airline industry while at the same time overseeing safety regulations (Schiavo 1997).

In 1966 President Lyndon B. Johnson created the Department of Transportation (DOT), which combined all federal transportation responsibilities in order to integrate and facilitate national interests in the distribution and transportation of goods. The FAA was placed under the authority of the new department. However, CAB's accident investigation responsibilities were placed under the auspices of the newly formed National Transportation Safety Board (NTSB). The NTSB was given the responsibility of investigating accidents and making recommendations to the FAA, and the FAA, as a branch of the DOT, was given the responsibility of enforcing federal regulations within the airline industry.

Twelve years later, Congress passed the Airline Deregulation Act of 1978, which phased out CAB completely and assigned oversight of the FAA to the NTSB. Aside from phasing out CAB, the act also changed the entire airline industry. For example, the ADA of 1978 introduced fare and route competition and permitted unrestricted entry into the domestic carrier marketplace. As Dempsy and Goetz (1992:193) note, the act reflected "the economic view that increased competition in the airline industry would force prices down and eliminate excess capacity; if firms were free to set prices and enter markets without regulatory constraints, they would experiment in offering different combinations of price and service. Thus, the underlying theory of this legislation was that liberalized entry and pricing would force carriers to adhere to the competitive pressures of the marketplace to provide the range of price and service options desired by the public."

While the ADA of 1978 was grounded in laissez-faire economics, with the intention of reducing consumer costs through the pressures of supply and demand, it is also important in the history of regulatory law in its radical departure from previous approaches to fixing perceived shortcomings. Brown (1987:2) notes that "the legislation [represented] a dramatic change in the thrust of regulatory reform. Until 1978, statutory reforms served only to build upon the basic regulatory framework established by the Civil Aeronautics Act of 1938. *The 1978 legislation reflected a shift from an incremental to a decremental approach to regulatory reform in that it prescribed relaxation and eventual termination of . . . regulatory controls.* Unlike previous reform efforts, deregulation was seriously considered as a policy alternative and significantly affected the substance of airline regulatory reform" (emphasis added).[4]

Since the ADA of 1978 the airline industry has undergone several phases of growth and decline (Dempsy and Goetz 1992). Rather than an increase in the competition between airlines, however, deregulation has resulted in increased consolidation and decreased competition. For example, during the first decade of deregulation, more than 150 carriers went into bankruptcy, and by the early 1990s eight domestic air carriers accounted for nearly 95 percent of all the passenger industry (Dempsy and Goetz 1992).

Within this context, the FAA attempted to promote the growth of start-ups like ValuJet while also overseeing their compliance with FARs. While success rates for most start-ups were low, ValuJet seemed to be the exception to the rule. In many ways, ValuJet justified the laissez-faire philosophy of the ADA of 1978, and was touted as a model start-up company in the age of deregulation. Given that only 3 of the over 250 airline companies in business at the time the act was passed had survived since 1978, the success of ValuJet was important to the FAA (particularly in its capacity as promoter of the economic success of the airline industry in the wake of deregulation) and to the series of political administrations—from Carter to Clinton—that supported it.

In terms of safety, the FAA had attempted to coax ValuJet into federal compliance rather than imposing stiff penalties (Cary, Hedges, and Sieder 1996). As former inspector general Schiavo (1997) notes, the FAA inspected ValuJet planes nearly five thousand times in the three years it was in operation, and had never reported any significant problems or concerns. It has become clear that since the FAA had a vested interest in the economic success of the airline industry as a whole, and ValuJet in particular in the wake of deregulation, the agency did not adequately pursue ValuJet's violations (NTSB 1997; Schiavo 1997). Schiavo (1997:10) states that "flight is at the core of a powerful, wealthy industry of companies worth billions of dollars. These corporate giants employ tens of thousands of people and support the economies of entire cities, buy products and supplies from thousands of smaller businesses and import untold foreign money into the U.S. Their research labs keep the U.S. on the cutting edge of aviation, space and military technology. Their marketers satisfy millions of customers every day, racing to meet the increased demand for air travel."

Some FAA inspectors, however, had serious concerns about ValuJet, even though the top administration of the FAA did not. Internal reports and memos indicate that there were increasing problems that should have been addressed with regard to ValuJet's rapid growth, enormous profitability, and subsequently atrocious safety record (Schiavo 1997). According to Schiavo (1997), however, the FAA did not know what to do with ValuJet. Indeed, "the airline's safety record had deteriorated almost in direct proportion to its growth. ValuJet pilots made fifteen emergency landings in 1994, then were forced down fifty-seven times in 1995 . . . but that record would be surpassed within months with fifty-nine emergency landings from February through May of 1996 . . . an unscheduled landing almost *every other day*" (Schiavo 1997:12, original emphasis).

The Department of Defense had also conducted its own review of ValuJet during consideration of a contract to transport military personnel. The DOD report on ValuJet was comprehensive and emphatic: ValuJet was so replete with safety problems that the DOD would not give ValuJet a contract to transport government employees (Schiavo 1997). Among the problems cited in the DOD report on ValuJet was its practice of using temporary solutions to deal with major problems like breakdowns, malfunctions, and accidents.

On May 2, just nine days before the ValuJet crash, the FAA produced a nine-page report on the safety records of the various new airlines. Ordered by Anthony Broderick, who was then the FAA's associate administrator of regulation and certification, the report was prepared by Bob Matthews, an analyst with the FAA's Office of Accident Investigation (Fumento 1996). Contrary to ValuJet's claims, its safety record was far from exceeding FAA standards. While the other start-ups had one accident annually, ValuJet averaged five (Fumento 1996). To make matters worse, ValuJet's accident rate was fourteen times the major air carriers, and its serious-accident rate was thirty-two times higher (Fumento 1996). Additionally, other incidents uncovered by the FAA before the crash of flight 592 included planes skidding off runways, planes landing with nearly empty fuel tanks, oil and fuel leaks that were left unfixed for long periods of time, and inexperienced pilots making errors of judgment. In an internal FAA report on ValuJet, there were nearly one hundred safety-related problems (Stern 1996). However, the FAA did not officially recommend closing ValuJet down until after the crash of flight 592.

The rapid growth of ValuJet came at the cost of safety, particularly in the area of maintenance (Schiavo 1997). One of the most contested areas in the debate surrounding the effects of the ADA of 1978 is that of maintenance and safety (Oster, Strong, and Zorn 1992). Since deregulation, some airline companies have reduced their maintenance programs to the FAA's minimum standards—or below—in order to increase short-term profits and cash flow (Oster, Strong, and Zovrn 1992). This reduction is contrary to the initial arguments by deregulation supporters that the airline industry would be prevented from neglecting maintenance standards by the FAA, and contrary to the argument that the economic consequences of unsafe practices in terms of lost revenues would deter such practices (Brown 1987). As Oster and colleagues (1992) argue, the FAA has generally been ill equipped to ensure that maintenance programs are being adequately followed, as evidenced by the Eastern Airlines maintenance record falsification case of 1991.[5]

While ValuJet's failure to comply with safety regulations and the FAA's unwillingness or inability to enforce them are troubling enough, it is evident that the NTSB had made safety recommendations to the FAA long before the crash of flight 592 that could have prevented the accident. For example, in 1981 the NTSB had recommended that the FAA reevaluate the classification of class D cargo holds. The first recommendation (A-81-012) from the NTSB was that the FAA reevaluate the class D certification of the Lockheed L-1011, with the suggestion that it be changed to class C, which requires extinguishing equipment or changing the liner material to ensure fire containment. The second recommendation (A-81-013) was to reevaluate class D cargo holds over 500 cubic feet to ensure that any fires would die from oxygen starvation and that the rest of the plane was properly protected. This recommendation came after a plane operated by Saudi Arabian Airlines caught fire in 1980 shortly after departure. The plane landed successfully, but all 301 occupants died. The fire on the Saudi Arabian Airlines plane started in the class D cargo hold. The FAA responded by stating that the NTSB recommendations should be addressed by making sure that class D cargo liners were made of fire-resistant materials that were better than the ones that were being used at the time.

In 1988 American Airlines flight 132 experienced a fire in its class D cargo hold en route to Nashville Metropolitan Airport. As the plane was on its final approach, smoke began to enter the passenger cabin. The fire was not contained in the cargo hold, and could be felt on the floor of the passenger cabin. Fortunately the plane landed safely, and all passengers were evacuated. Contrary to FAA claims, however, the fire in the class D cargo hold on this plane did not extinguish itself, and was not confined to the cargo hold. The cause of the fire was a hydrogen peroxide solution (an oxidizer) and a sodium orthosilicate-based mixture that had been shipped in the class D cargo hold. Neither of the chemicals was properly packaged, nor were they identified as hazardous materials.

After investigating this accident, the NTSB urged the FAA to require smoke detectors in all class D cargo compartments, and to require fire extinguishment systems for them. Additionally, the NTSB asked the FAA to evaluate the possibility of prohibiting the transportation of oxidizers in cargo compartments without smoke detectors or extinguishing systems. After several exchanges of correspondence, the FAA informed the NTSB that its cost/benefit analysis revealed that the $350 million price tag attached to this recommendation was not feasible. The FAA took the position that it was not going to force the airline industry to make these improvements, because it felt they were not cost effective in terms of the amount of money required to possibly prevent a small number of accidents.

THEORETICAL INTERPRETATION

The deaths of 110 people in the crash of ValuJet flight 592 were caused by a number of factors that can be connected to three levels of analysis: individual, institutional, and structural. The proximal cause of the crash was the failure of SabreTech and ValuJet employees to follow safety procedures regarding the preparation, identification, and storage of potentially hazardous materials. Indeed, had these workers correctly capped the oxygen generators, flight 592 might have landed safely in Atlanta. One might also say that the deaths could have been avoided if the FAA had followed the NTSB's recommendation to equip class D cargo holds with smoke detectors and fire suppression equipment. To end the analysis of the crash here, however, would be a serious error, because, like most organizational crimes, a complicated nexus of relationships enveloped the actions and omissions that facilitated the crash. As Perrow (1984) has argued, understanding what he terms "normal accidents" requires attention to the interaction of multiple failures within and between systems and organizations.

Organizational crime theorists have relied on three basic concepts to explain the crimes committed by corporations and governments: (1) organizational motivation or goals, (2) opportunity, and (3) social control (Braithwaite 1992; Coleman 1987; Kauzlarich and Kramer 1998; Kramer and Michalowski 1990, 1991; Vaughan 1992). The significance of these concepts for a structural-level explanation of state-corporate crime can be encapsulated in the proposition that organizational crime results from a coincidence of pressure for goal attainment, availability and perceived attractiveness of illegitimate means, and an absence or weakness of social control mechanisms (Braithwaite 1989; Kauzlarich and Kramer 1998). Although each of these three core concepts can be examined on the micro and meso levels of analysis, our theoretical interpretation focuses more on how structural relationships affect organizational practice and policy. Following both state-corporate crime theory and the systems or "normal accident" theory (Perrow 1984; Sagan 1993), we will examine motivation, opportunity, control, and the interaction of the technical, organizational, and structural dimensions of the crash.

Motivation and Organizational Goals

Barnett (1981), Coleman (1987), Gross (1980), and Michalowski (1985) have argued that the goal of capital accumulation can be a highly criminogenic force for organizations. Often, it is posited, the motivation to secure profit can direct organizational practices and policies in a fashion injurious to consumer and employee safety.

As profit-seeking organizations, ValuJet and SabreTech employed a number of questionable techniques to maximize profit. ValuJet's radical cost-cutting procedures included using older planes in various stages of disrepair, outsourcing all of the company's maintenance, and providing very low wages and benefits to employees. SabreTech was also experiencing a high degree of pressure for capital accumulation directly preceding the crash through its agreement to complete its work on the oxygen generators quickly or incur a loss of $2,500 per day. The other organization involved in the crash, the FAA, was not a direct profit-seeking entity, but one designed to both regulate and facilitate the accumulation of capital for airline companies. The FAA's refusal, on economic grounds, to institute specific safeguards that could have prevented the catastrophe of flight 592 illustrates the injurious consequences that can result not only from pursuing capital but also from state encouragement of capital accumulation. As Barnett (1981:7) and Chambliss and Zatz (1993) have noted, a major goal of the U.S. state has been to promote capital accumulation, and the state's regulatory function "must not be so severe as to diminish substantially the contribution of large corporations to growth in output and employment." For example, while state regulatory agencies have been created to help protect workers (Occupational Safety and Health Administration), the environment (Environmental Protection Agency), and consumers (Consumer Product Safety Commission), these agencies generally do not undermine an industry's fundamental contributions to the functional requirements of the economy. In like manner, the FAA would not be expected to seriously compromise the contributions that the airline industry makes to local, community, and national economies. The difference, however, between the FAA and other regulatory agencies is its expressly stated dual mandate of both regulating the airline industry and promoting its economic success.

The three organizations involved in the ValuJet disaster, while distinct in many ways, interacted in a way that produced great social injury. Like other instances of state-facilitated state-corporate crime, the pursuit of profit was critical in the formulation of FAA, SabreTech, and ValuJet organizational policy and practice. Although organizations that refrain from crime might also have a strong interest in capital accumulation, a very distinct set of organizational relationships led to the crash of flight 592. This particular context was characterized by little social control over the actors and organizations and ample opportunity to commit crimes that together helped shape organizational definitions of acceptable risk.

Opportunity and the Failure of Controls

A basic tenet of organizational crime theory is that low levels of external social control provide opportunities for organizations to engage in crime. As Vaughan (1996:458) has noted, not only a competitive environment shapes organizational behavior, but also "the regulatory environment (autonomy and interdependence) which is affected by the relationship between regulators and the organizations they regulate." The symbiotic relationship between those who regulate and those being regulated may vary in both depth and breadth (Vaughan 1983), but the coupling of FAA and ValuJet resulted in an "interactive complexity" conducive to catastrophe (Perrow 1984).

Deregulation and the contradictory role of the FAA as regulator and promoter of the airline industry provide the larger background for ValuJet's organizational genesis and persistence. We have described the deficiencies and contradictions in the structural control of the airline industry brought about by deregulation, and have argued that this is related to the FAA's organizational disregard for the unsafe nature of many of ValuJet's planes and practices.

Instead of aggressively mandating that ValuJet place its fleet into compliance with applicable regulations, the FAA held up ValuJet as the poster child of deregulation—a victor among many losers in the market of air travel in the postderegulation era. In this sense, the FAA's failure to practice its mandate to make air travel safe for consumers through the vigorous inspection of airline companies and their planes facilitated the crash of flight 592.[6] Following this line of theoretical reasoning, had the FAA enforced federal airline safety regulations (that is, had it exerted formal control over ValuJet and SabreTech), the companies might not have been so indifferent to the quality and safety of their activities and commodities. Such oversight would have created an environment in which both SabreTech and ValuJet would have been more likely to communicate to their employees that productivity and safety are important and rewardable. In other words, the "normalization" of the deviance that produced the ValuJet "accident" would not have gone unnoticed or unchecked. The series of oversights and confusions regarding the content and condition of the boxes holding the oxygen generators is related to the ways in which SabreTech and ValuJet rewarded the behavior of employees that contributed to productivity and efficiency, but not behavior that contributed to safety. Following this line of reasoning and the available data, we suggest that the unspent and uncapped oxygen containers made it onto the airplane because employees of SabreTech and ValuJet were not adequately trained, rewarded, or encouraged to conduct careful and complete inspections of materials to be transported by air. This explanation is consistent with the findings of a number of studies that illustrate the power of organizational culture over the individual and collective actions of employees in such diverse settings as the Holocaust (Hilberg 1985; Kelman and Hamilton 1989), police violence (Skolnick and Fyfe 1993), and U.S. human radiation experiments (Kauzlarich and Kramer 1998).

Our interpretation is also consistent with Vaughan's (1996) notion of the "normalization of deviance," a condition in which deviations from technical protocols gradually and routinely become defined as normative. The normalization of rule breaking is applicable to the manner in which the oxygen canisters were processed, but it is institutionally situated as well. Risky practices, which can be an outcome of or a precursor to the normalization of deviance, became defined as acceptable for capital accumulation (ValuJet) and capital facilitation (FAA). While the crash was an undesirable outcome for all of the organizations involved, a number of matters related to the causes of the crash were defined as acceptable risks in light of organizational mandates, missions, and potential gains. Another social phenomenon, the sociology of mistakes, is also related. As Vaughan (1996) found with the *Challenger* explosion, the ValuJet crash can also be interpreted as an event that reveals how "environmental and organizational contingencies create operational forces that shape world view, normalizing signals of potential danger, resulting in mistakes with harmful human consequences" (Vaughan 1996:409).

CONCLUSION

Scholars of state crime have often bemoaned the dearth of research and theorizing on the etiology and control of such crime (Ross 1995). State crime is an emerging area of study within criminology, and it is to be expected that more rigorous research and comprehensive theory are needed. We have attempted to apply the most central theoretical concepts in the organizational crime literature to help explain the crash of ValuJet flight 592. There is little doubt that the circumstances surrounding the crash are complex, and that a comprehensive theoretical explanation would be equally complicated. A more extensive analysis is beyond the scope of this chapter. Extant organizational crime theory, however, renders the ValuJet crash intelligible. The research here supports the multidimensional theoretical proposition that the coincidence of a very strong level of motivation for the accumulation of capital by corporations and a severe lack of external control by a governmental agency results in conditions conducive to harmful organizational practices in identifiable ways.

State-facilitated state-corporate crimes like the Imperial Food Products fire and the ValuJet crash should sensitize criminologists to the manner in which acts of commission and omission are shaped by a matrix of realities constructed through the social contexts in which they occur. Modern corporations and their workers, just like state organizations and their agents, can become enmeshed in these matrices in ways that produce great harm. In some cases, this harm is an outcome of normative corporate behavior—cutting costs and maximizing profits—and normative U.S. state behavior—the support of a capitalist economy—especially when deviations from technical protocols become normalized. These behaviors are not organized for or against socially harmful outcomes per se, but levels of either or both of these behaviors represent points on a continuum of criminogenesis. When a state agency like the FAA categorically ignores the known unsafe practices and procedures of an unbridled profit-seeking enterprise like ValuJet, we can expect at some point, inter alia, a socially injurious outcome.

NOTES

Reprinted with permission from Rick Matthews and David Kauzlarich, "The Crash of ValuJet Flight 592: A Case Study in State-Corporate Crime," *Sociological Focus* 3 (2000): 281–298. Copyright *Sociological Focus*.

1. See Barak (1991) and Friedrichs (1996a) for excellent illustrations of state negligence and state crimes of omission. An interesting application of these concepts is employed by Hamm (1997) in an effort to explain the series of governmental omissions that may have provided Timothy McVeigh the opportunity to bomb the Federal Building in Oklahoma City.

largely by transnational corporations (Amin 1990, 1997; Greider 1997; Hoogvelt 1996; Mander and Goldsmith 1996). Although many argue that this trend toward a single economic system has a long history (D. Friedman 1999; Hirst 1996), most authors agree that globalization also represents significant changes in the character of capitalism (Korten 1995, 1996; Karliner 1997). We highlight two of these changes: first, the vastly increased economic and political power of transnational corporations under globalization, and second, the concomitant decline in the political power of nation-states.

With few exceptions (see, for example, Michalowski and Kramer 1987), the vast majority of literature on corporate crime has remained focused within the boundaries of individual nation-states. Today, however, such a limited focus is misleading and potentially dangerous. One of the hallmarks of globalization is the expansion of corporate control beyond the boundaries of nation-states. As others have already evidenced, the most significant and powerful corporations in the world today are transnational in character, with operations in many different countries. Korten (1996:15) summarizes contemporary corporate power this way: "The world's 200 largest industrial corporations, which employ only one-third of the world's population, control 28 percent of the world's economic output. The top 300 transnationals, excluding financial institutions, own some 25 percent of the world's productive assets. Of the world's 100 largest economies, 51 are now corporations—not including banking and financial institutions."

Corporate control is also highly gendered: "white males still hold 95 percent of the top management jobs in the country's largest corporations. The situation is remarkably similar around the world: women hold only 2 percent of the senior executive posts in most West European countries, and a discouraging .9 percent in Japan" (Seager 1993:82). Seager (1993:82) urges us to ask "what are the linkages between the power of men as leaders of capitalist enterprises and the power that derives from the broader exercise of male privilege?" In response, we posit later in this chapter that men's dominance over the global capitalist economy has tended to weaken women's economic and political position both within countries and internationally. This point is especially important in developing countries, where women's economic position has been historically strong.

Another mechanism creating heightened power for corporations is the rapid technological change accompanying the last two decades. With the rise of new computer technologies, the Internet, and virtual business transactions, corporate power might better be described as "hyper-national," operating outside the physical boundaries of geographic space or national boundaries. The implications of this shift are profound, leading some to argue that this is the dawn of a new age, what Rifkin (2000) calls "the age of access," at least as revolutionary as the industrial revolution. In this new age, important economic, political, and

cultural decisions are being made primarily by large corporations who control
not just the economic sphere but also the means of human communication
in an increasingly virtual world. "In a world in which access to human culture
is increasingly commodified and mediated by global corporations, questions
of institutional power and freedom become more salient than ever before"
(Rifkin 2000:11). It is not our purpose here to elaborate all of the changes
globalization and technological change have wrought, but we emphasize what
numerous authors have already established: the economic and political power
held by transnational corporations has increased dramatically since the 1980s.

This increased power has also led to greater corporate control over economic development, including commercial activity, and, more significantly, its
regulation. In the West, over the last fifty years a body of regulatory law had
been developed to try to curtail the most damaging aspects of corporate capitalism. In the United States, for example, national regulations attempt to protect workers' health and safety, food and product safety, the environment, and
many other areas of social and economic life. Although these regulations have
never achieved the rigor some might like, they represent a radical contrast to
the global situation. The language of "industry capture" is probably too weak to
describe many of the global organizations that discipline international economic practices today. Global commerce is dominated by a relatively small
number of global players who also serve as self-designated coaches and referees.
The most powerful corporations exert significant influence over important
international trade and development organizations such as the World Bank, the
International Monetary Fund, and, of increasing importance, the World Trade
Organization (WTO) (Millen and Holtz 2000).

The WTO was created to represent and foster transnational commercial
interests. The WTO has positioned itself as both an economic and a political
organization, with the ability to finance and support countries that agree with
its directives, and to oppose and withhold funds from countries that do not.
Health and safety regulations are largely viewed by the WTO as trade barriers,
and the presence of internal safety standards within a particular country can
lead to significant sanctions. As Wallach and Sforza (1999:18) point out, "with
the establishment of the WTO, judgments over such key areas as food safety
have been pulled from the hands of domestic legislatures and effectively ceded
to the international corporate interests that helped write the WTO rules. Following an adverse WTO ruling, Europe must now absorb $115 million annu-
ally in WTO-authorized trade sanctions to maintain a ban on beef containing
residues of artificial growth hormones."

Through the WTO and other disciplinary organizations for the global
economy, countries concerned about protecting their citizens from the potential harms caused by global capitalism are punished and regulated. The ability
of an individual country to control its own economy becomes directly linked

to its willingness to collaborate with transnational corporations. Wallach and Sforza (1999:19) argue that nations, in their effort to entice corporate investment in their countries, "are serving as corporations' servants, agreeing to challenge laws that the corporations oppose." National destinies are thus directly linked to transnational interests in the New World Order.

An obvious corollary of the increased power of corporations under globalization is the declining power of nation-states. Many scholars argue that nation-states are increasingly unable to control their own economies, let alone the global economy (M. G. Cohen 1996). For the developed world, participation in the global economy has tended to require dilution of existing regulations in order to discourage deindustrialization and corporate flight to more hospitable (less regulated) countries. For developing countries, where regulation never existed, the competition for corporate investment has all but invited and sanctioned harmful corporate practices. M. G. Cohen (1996:401) describes the dilemma this way: "As nations compete for the favours of capital, the ability to assert any type of discipline over corporate behaviour comes into direct conflict with the increased mobility of capital. Unless all nations, party to an agreement, behave in the same way with regard to corporate discipline, the corporations will not be disciplined at all. Any one nation, by acting on its own, will be disadvantaged by behaving in a stricter way. Since there is no mechanism for nations to act collectively, individual state action is critically weakened. In all nation-states, then, there is tremendous ideological and economic pressure for corporate harms to be ignored, tolerated, and even, at times, embraced "for the good of the country."

Given this changing balance of power, particularly the dependence of national economies on close economic relationships with transnational corporations, few corporate harms in the globalized world are strictly "corporate" crimes. In many cases, a better conceptualization of the harms caused by global corporations is offered by the term "state-corporate crime." A number of scholars have employed the term "state-corporate crime" to illustrate the interdependence between nation-states and corporations in generating particular harms (Aulette and Michalowski 1993; Friedrichs 1996a; Kauzlarich and Kramer 1998; Kramer and Michalowski 1990). In our work, we draw on the conceptualization offered by Aulette and Michalowski (1993:175) and in chapter three here. They define state-corporate crimes as "illegal or socially injurious actions that result from a mutually reinforcing interaction between (1) policies and/or practices in pursuit of the goals of one or more institutions of political governance and (2) policies and/or practices in pursuit of the goals of one or more institutions of economic production and distribution."

As Friedrichs (1996a:154) notes, "the premise for the concept of state-corporate crime is that modern states and corporations are profoundly interdependent." He goes on to say that "above all, the concept of state-corporate crime compels us to recognize that some major forms of organizational crime cannot be easily classified as either corporate or governmental, and that the interorganizational forms of crime that bring together corporations and government entities may be especially potent and pernicious" (156).

In employing the concept of state-corporate crime, we are not arguing that corporations and governments necessarily bear equal responsibility for the harms generated by certain capitalist practices. In the modern world, the power of transnationals frequently exceeds state power, particularly in developing countries where international commercial, financial, and regulatory organizations exert strong influence over national policy decisions. At the same time, it has been argued elsewhere (see Caulfield and Wonders 1993) that many harms against women can be viewed as political crimes, predominantly characterized as crimes of omission, since the state tacitly supports these harms by failing to protect women's basic human rights. In this chapter we extend this argument by illustrating the way that many corporate harms fostered by globalization can only occur because nation-states collaborate with or ignore the perils associated with corporate practices in their country. In making this argument we recognize that nation-states are frequently bullied, threatened, and/or punished into compliance with corporate desires.

As will be clear in the examples that follow, the International Monetary Fund (IMF) and World Bank have played a critical role in solidifying the relationship between internal national interests in developing countries and global economic interests. Over the last two decades many developing countries have had difficulty paying their debts to Western countries. The IMF and World Bank developed Structural Adjustment Programs (SAPs) as a mechanism to ensure timely payment of debts by pressuring countries to move more rapidly into a privatized commodified global capitalist economy. "Essentially such programs require countries to increase productivity and exports while decreasing government spending on social welfare" (Peterson and Runyan 1999:136). The goal of SAPs is to catapult developing countries into the world capitalist economy. Although some countries are essentially coerced into accepting SAPs, the consequences of their complicity with transnational imperatives at the expense of their citizens' health and welfare are problematic. As Aulette and Michalowski (1993:175) note, state-corporate crime is frequently characterized by a situation "in which government omissions permit private business to pursue illegal and potentially injurious courses of action which, in a general way, facilitate the fulfillment of certain state policies." Although state power may be waning, nation-states still represent one of the only strategic sites for curtailing the harmful impacts associated with globalization. Governments must be held accountable both for actions that collaborate in creating corporate harms and for their failure to protect the basic human rights of their citizens.

has costs, it is clear that these costs are disproportionately borne by women (Nikolić-Ristanović 1996). These costs include the direct harm caused to women by geographical displacement, physical violence and injury as war casualties, and the sexual assault of women during wartime; they also include the indirect costs associated with state-corporate policies to foster weapons production and militarism at the expense of other social and economic goals more beneficial to women's lives.

WOMEN'S RIGHTS, THE UNITED NATIONS, AND NGOS UNDER GLOBALIZATION

Several avenues have been identified as strategies to exert greater control over the harmful behavior of transnational corporations, including company self-enforcement, national and local government intervention, and non-governmental organizations (Millen and Holtz 2000). Because of the historic discrimination and oppression of women around the world, there is little incentive for corporations or nation-states to be concerned about the unique impact that state-corporate crimes may have on women. For this reason, women's international nongovernmental organizations have been the driving force behind the protection and advancement of women in the face of globalization. Women's NGOs both challenge and collaborate with the United Nations, which represents the single most important arena for forming and enforcing international agreements that may mediate the effects of globalization. The policies, conventions, and treaties that emerge from the United Nations, however, provide one of the only standards by which state-corporate crimes can be identified and responded to (Michalowski and Kramer 1987). For this reason, we also argue that women's NGOs will continue to have a strategic role to play in the future if women are to have collective power and representation in a globalized world.

The Historic Role of Women's NGOs

Founded in 1945 as an international governmental club, the United Nations is composed entirely of delegations of government officials. The Preamble to the United Nations Charter details its raison d'être as the promotion of peace and the end of war, "faith in fundamental human rights . . . in the equal rights of men and women," and economic and social development, in addition to a system of justice to enforce international laws. The Charter contains provisions for the involvement of nongovernmental organizations, which are formal organizations composed of private individuals or associations, neither governmental organizations nor social movements. Women's NGOs may rightly claim nearly all of the credit for the establishment in 1946 of the UN Commission on the Status of Women, and for the numerous declarations, conventions, and treaties that speak to the need to protect and empower women in the international arena in fulfillment of UN goals. It is important to note that conventions, treaties, and covenants are all international agreements among nations; thus they represent "the strongest legal tool(s) the UN has to offer" (International Women's Tribune Centre 1997:7).

International conventions and treaties emerge from United Nations conferences. UN conferences are generally a series of working sessions and meetings organized around the production of a final document. Frequently, NGOs lobby for such conferences. Because of the work of women's international NGOs, the UN authorized the International Women's Year and Conference in 1975 in Mexico City. At the close of the conference, the UN Decade for Women, Equality, Development and Peace was declared to run from 1976 to 1985. Three more World conferences followed in Copenhagen (1980), Nairobi (1985), and Beijing (1995).

Nongovernmental organizations hold forums in conjunction with world conferences. NGO forums provide opportunities to learn, educate, connect, and organize; they also send the message to the UN conference that the constituencies are watching (Prügl and Meyer 1999). Women's NGOs are responsible for the International Women's Year and Decade, the four UN conferences on women, the international women's movement, and the more formal NGO infrastructure. Without women's NGOs, few of the conventions, policies, or programs on women in and around the UN would have ever occurred (Winslow 1995).

Indeed, in combination with the UN Commission on the Status of Women, women's NGOs were responsible for ensuring that the final version of the Universal Declaration on Human Rights refers to all "human beings" rather than to all "men," as written in the early drafts. The Declaration, adopted in 1948 in part because of atrocities committed during World War II, serves as the foundation for UN women's rights documents (Tomaševski 1993:98). Article 2 states that "everyone is entitled to all the rights and freedoms set forth in this Declaration without distinction of any kind such as race, colour, sex." While the Declaration is quite broad in its recitation of rights—from political rights to the right to travel, immigrate, marry, work, and rest, among many others—it has traditionally been used to emphasize civil rights in the political arena. This focus on the right to participate in the political process and to be protected from abuses by the state, though seemingly gender-blind, ignores the realities of women's lives and their disadvantaged position in the various dimensions of social life (Young, Fort, and Danner 1994). As already noted, women's structural location makes them both more vulnerable to exploitation and less able to resist state or corporate abuses.

Because it was not a treaty or convention, the Declaration was not legally binding. It took another thirty years before the international covenants on civil and political Rights and on economic, social, and cultural Rights were adopted.

Ford's position has been that it lost its manufacturing plant in Cologne, Germany, to the Nazis and had no control over how the plant was used. Despite these claims, documents show that Ford's cooperation with the Nazis had started as early as 1940, when it began using forced labor from France and continued until at least August of 1942, well after the U.S. entered the war (Silverstein 2000). Further research has indicated that the plant was never nationalized by the Germans, and that throughout the war Dearborn maintained at least a 52 percent share of the stocks in the plant (Silverstein 2000).[4] Ford also initially resisted calls from President Franklin D. Roosevelt and British prime minister Winston Churchill to increase war production for the Allies (Silverstein 2000). Long before the war and well into it, Ford was very interested in not only profiting from its plant in Germany but also showing its alliance (symbolic or not) with Germany. This interest is best evidenced by Ford's decision to change the name of the Cologne plant to Ford Werke, in part because "there could be no doubt about the complete incorporation, as regards personnel, organization and production system, of Ford Werke into the German national economy, in particular into the German armaments industry" (Silverstein 2000:3).

Prior to Pearl Harbor Ford made huge revenues from supplying the Third Reich with war materials (Silverstein 2000). During the war, however, the value of that German subsidiary more than doubled, and after 1941 it stopped making passenger cars and focused on military trucks (Billstein et al. 2000). The United States and the Allied forces thought the plant was so strategic to the interests of Germany that they bombed it on several occasions. However, as Billstein and colleagues (2000) have noted, the plant escaped the bombing largely unscathed.[5]

One of the major problems faced by manufacturers located in Germany was a shortage of labor after the war began. Drafted into service, many German men went off to war, leaving manufacturers with serious labor shortages. The labor shortages became so acute that some plants actually saw worker protests after their working days were increased from eight to twelve hours and their pay was cut (Kugler 2000). In an act described as "revolutionary" (particularly given the forceful and brutal tactics of the SS in suppressing political dissent), some workers in one of GM's Opel plants wrote on the factory walls that "the Opel worker is hard-working but cowardly, for he does nothing as his wages are robbed" (Kugler 2000:46). The "crime" of any political dissent against the Nazis was punishable by death, and such "vandalism" represented a serious problem.

The solution created by the Reich for the labor shortages was forced labor.[6] In order for a company to use forced labor, it had to "maintain [its] own separate POW barracks, guarded by company security forces, entailing additional costs" (Kugler 2000). These costs, however, were more than offset by the fact that companies "paid" the workers minimal wages *after* deducting their lodging, food, and other expenses from their salaries (Kugler 2000). By 1943 one-half of Ford Werke's workforce was made up of captives engaged in forced labor (Silverstein 2000). They worked for twelve hours a day with a fifteen-minute break and were given meager rations of "200 grams of bread and coffee for breakfast, no lunch and a dinner of spinach and three potatoes or soup made of turnip leaves" (Silverstein 2000:4).

Internal memos indicate that Ford executives were very pleased that the Germans were allowing Ford plants in German-occupied territories to continue to operate (Silverstein 2000). Ford was very interested in "safeguarding [its] interests" in occupied territories, including Vichy, France. After the German occupation of France in 1941, the Ford plant in Vichy quickly became involved in the German war effort. It was so successful that it posted dividends under German occupation—a feat it was unable to accomplish during times of peace (Silverstein 2000).

ADAM OPEL AG AND GENERAL MOTORS

Adam Opel AG of Rüsselsheim, a division of General Motors, manufactured trucks, tanks, and aircraft engines and other aircraft parts for the Nazis (Friedman 2001). Opel's most significant contribution to Germany's war efforts probably involved its expertise in manufacturing aircraft engines (Kugler 2000). Given the vast number of aircraft engines and parts produced by Opel, as well as its proficiency in producing them, it is likely that these efforts greatly enhanced Germany's ability to conduct its air war. Historical records suggest that GM was in contact with its subsidiary during the war, and that Opel was under the same managerial staff both before and after the war started (Kugler 2000). Like Ford, Opel profited greatly from these activities, and also like Ford, Opel used forced labor. Once control of Opel was given to the Germans— with the same managers as before the war—it was determined that Opel should set aside some of its dividends to return to GM after the fighting ceased (Kugler 2000). The managers at Opel continually exceeded the output expectations placed on them by the Reich. Kugler (2000:81) writes that "Opel put its entire capacity and innovative energy at the Nazi war machine's disposal, and objectively helped pursue and extend the war."

During the war, GM headquarters in Michigan wrote off its entire investment in Opel as a loss on its 1941 tax return, a tax reduction of about $23 million (Kugler 2000). However, "this was not a divestiture, rather, General Motors retained its shares in a company now technically valued at zero" (Kugler 2000:73). After the war GM was allowed to resume control of Opel. In 1948 GM's Opel investment was "recovered at a tax value of $4.8 million requiring a tax payment of $1.8 million—about $21 million less than the company saved on its 1941 tax bill" (Kugler 2000:75).

IBM

IBM's Hollerith punch-card machines were used by Nazi Germany to advance its war efforts (the punch-cards contained standardized holes that represented particular values for individual variables). IBM's Hollerith machines performed a number of important tasks for Nazi Germany, including the scheduling of trains, counting bank transfers, and counting for the 1933 German census that provided the Nazis with important information about where Jews were living, their family history, and their professions. Once the Nazis rose to power and began their campaign against the Jews, this information would become "a means of social control, a weapon of war, and a roadmap for group destruction" (Black 2001:7).

IBM technology was also used to expedite deportation to concentration camps. There were Hollerith departments at nearly every concentration camp, including Auschwitz and Dachau (Black 2001). As Black (2001:22) notes, IBM "custom designed and leased the Hollerith card sorting system to the Third Reich for use at Bergen-Belsen and most of the other concentration camps. [IBM] also serviced its machines almost monthly [at the camps], and trained Nazi personnel to use the intricate systems. Duplicate copies of code books were kept in IBM's offices in case field books were lost. What's more, [IBM] was the exclusive source for up to 1.5 billion punch cards the Reich required each year to run its machines."

Additionally, two Hollerith experts attended the Wannsee Conference where the Final Solution of exterminating the Jews was implemented (Friedman 2001). Given this level of involvement in the day-to-day activities of the concentration camps, it appears highly implausible that IBM officials did not know the purposes for which their technology was being used.

KODAK, CHASE-MANHATTAN, AND OTHERS

There are likely hundreds of U.S. corporations that were involved in varying degrees with the Holocaust. The level of participation by most of them has not been researched to any considerable degree. For example, one corporation that is accused of profiting from the Holocaust is Kodak. Kodak profits soared in Germany during the war, when Kodak expanded to manufacture "triggers, detonators and other military hardware" (Friedman 2001:2). The French subsidiary of Kodak made so much money during the war that it was able to purchase "real estate, a coal mine and a rest home for the staff" (Friedman 2001:2). Kodak is also accused of using slave laborers in its production plants.

Chase Manhattan, which was then owned by the Rockefeller family, is another company accused of collaborating with the Nazis. Chase Manhattan is currently being sued by several Holocaust survivors on the grounds that the firm had seized their assets during the war and failed to return or account for them after the war.[7] Chase Manhattan's French branch was accused of freezing Jewish accounts at "the request of German occupation authorities" (Silverstein 2000). However, some have suggested that this historical ledger is not correct, and that in fact Chase Manhattan had seized Jewish assets before the Nazi's request (Hirsh 1998). Chase Manhattan has also been accused of giving loans to Nazi Germany to help finance the war. During World War II the Rockefellers also owned what was then known as Standard Oil (now Exxon). Rockefeller/Standard Oil was the largest shareholder in IG Farben Company—of notoriety not only for manufacturing the lethal Zyklon B gas that was used to kill tens of thousands of Jews but also for its slave labor camp located near Auschwitz that manufactured rubber for the Nazis.

THE CRIMES

A number of U.S. companies appear to have been directly involved in various criminal activities throughout the war. The most obvious were the use of forced labor by Ford and GM's Opel subsidiary and IBM's technological assistance to Nazi bureaucrats. During the war, an estimated ten to twelve million individuals worked as forced laborers, some of whom were prisoners of war. Most of these people have never been compensated, a matter that I will turn to shortly. U.S. companies benefited directly from these practices.

Further, it is questionable whether Germany could have sustained its war efforts as long as it did without the help of U.S. companies and other international banks and corporations. One can only imagine the surprise of U.S. troops landing on the shores of Normandy to find the enemy driving Ford and GM vehicles. From the trucks and cars made by Ford, to the IBM punch cards used for accounting, to the aircraft engines made by Opel, there is little doubt that the efforts of these manufacturers facilitated the criminal efforts of Germany in a significant way.

Interesting questions remain. For example, would these corporations have been guilty of violating U.S. domestic law had they continued their business with Germany after the United States entered the war (for example, under the Trading with the Enemy Act)? And, if so, why have they never been charged? In addition, have plaintiffs not had the same level of success in suing these corporations as others have had with the Swiss banks and the German corporations?

GOVERNMENTAL COMPLICITY IN THE
PROTECTION OF CORPORATIONS

Through civil litigation, Holocaust survivors have been attempting to obtain financial redress for the atrocities they or their family members suffered. A significant portion of this litigation against foreign companies, such as the Swiss banks and several German corporations, was filed in U.S. courts. The first major settlement of such a class-action lawsuit came in 1998 with the Swiss banks, who agreed to pay Holocaust survivors $1.25 billion. Later, in December of 1999, several corporations (Bayer, BMW, Volkswagen, and Daimler) agreed to create a $5.1 billion fund to pay victims of forced labor. Four important differences are evident between this settlement and the one a year earlier with the Swiss banks.

First, the settlement with the German corporations was not a settlement to a lawsuit. Second, in order to reach the agreement, the U.S. government "promised to intervene on behalf of German corporations in all future Holocaust-related litigation and to ensure that federal judges bar the court-house door to future claims" (Sebok 2000:1). Third, this settlement is the first of its kind to deal with the issue of forced labor (the Swiss lawsuit dealt only with illegally seized assets). This is important, because the number of people forced into labor during the Holocaust is far greater than the number of per-sons with assets seized by the banks, and represents not only Jews but other civilians in numerous countries and prisoners of war. However, the legal ques-tion is similar: had the corporations acted in a manner to deprive someone of what was rightly theirs (labor) without compensation? Fourth, the settlement was created by four parties: representatives from the Clinton administration, representatives from Gerhard Schroeder's administration, attorneys for the plaintiffs (including the World Jewish Congress), and attorneys for about fifty German corporations.

Sebok (2000) notes that this settlement in and of itself would not be grounds for a judge to dismiss a case against a corporation. Nevertheless, such a lawsuit against a corporation for forced labor reparations would likely fail, as the "United States and its Allies gave away the rights of their citizens to sue private companies for torts arising from the war in the treaties that were signed between 1946 and 1990" (Sebok 2000:3). The United States and other Allied countries maintained tight control over German reparations after the war and did not allow for "direct participation through private lawsuits by vic-tims" (Sebok 2000:3).

It is unclear whether this settlement or the treaties signed after the war were intentionally crafted so as to protect corporate interests. Unfortunately for the victims of forced labor, what is clear is that it seems unlikely that they will achieve monetary or other redress in civil suits because of treaties signed after the war limiting their ability to privately sue corporations, and the most recent settlement between the four parties listed earlier. This is good news for corporations like Ford and General Motors. Obviously they are protected from monetary loss in this matter. They are also protected from the powerful light of investigation that might cast doubt on their claims of unwilling par-ticipation in the war on the side of Germany.

THEORETICAL INTERPRETATION:
"ORDINARY BUSINESS"

"With the killing of the Jews I had nothing to do. I never killed a Jew, nor a non-Jew for that matter—I never killed any human being. I never gave an order to kill either a Jew or a non-Jew. I just did not do it." These were the words of Adolf Eichmann in 1961 (quoted in Markle 1995).

Making a play of words on Goldhagen's (1997) book title *Hitler's Willing Executioners,* some have suggested that Ford and GM represented Hitler's "willing mechanics." The use of the class-specific label "mechanics" detracts attention from those who were actually responsible for corporate policies. Perhaps, as Silverstein (2000) has suggested, a more appropriate term would be "Hitler's willing executives." These are, in the words of Friedrichs (1996a), the "trusted criminals" of the Holocaust; the computer experts and the corporate executives who willingly aided Hitler and his murderous regime.[8]

Various explanations have been set forth to answer the question of why so many people in Germany—and other countries—were willing to commit either directly or indirectly some of the most horrendous crimes against humanity. Some have suggested that deep-seated, mass anti-Semitism is to blame (see Goldhagen 1997). There is little doubt that many of those involved in the Holocaust hated Jews. For example, Henry Ford's pamphlet entitled *The International Jew: The World's Foremost Problem* (a polemic against Jews that accused them of controlling the world's banks, starting World War I, and ruining Christian civilization) was read by Hitler in 1923 and was published widely throughout Europe, including thirty-seven editions in Germany (Billstein et al. 2000; Silverstein 2000). Hitler explicitly praised Ford's anti-Semitism in *Mein Kampf,* citing him as a true American hero, not only for his prowess in manufacturing but also for his views on Jews. Indeed, Hitler admired Ford so much that in 1938 he gave Ford the Grand Cross of the German Eagle, which was the highest honor given to foreigners by the Nazis (Silverstein 2000).[9]

Although the case may be made that Henry Ford and others shared Hitler's racist beliefs about the Jews, it is not likely this was the sole reason for their (and their corporations') involvement in supporting the German war effort. To accept this view as the sole explanation one would have to essentially argue that Henry Ford and all of his executives and managers all suffered from the same complex of psychological disorders (Markle 1995).

Arendt's (1963) controversial work may provide a more useful explanation. During the trial of Adolf Eichmann Arendt came to the conclusion—contrary to most other observers—that there was nothing "special" about him. Rather, she argued eloquently that Eichmann's two most compelling traits were his ability to organize things and his ability to negotiate. Other than these two traits, Eichmann, according to Arendt (1963), was most accurately described as an ordinary and insubstantial person. The implications of Arendt's "banality of evil" thesis caused quite a stir for its chilling implications: that Eichmann was fundamentally no different from the rest of us.[10]

Milgram's (1963) empirical work in this area was not particularly comforting either. In a series of controversial experiments Milgram concluded that "with numbing regularity, good people were seen to knuckle under to the demands of authority and perform actions that were callous and severe. Men who are in everyday life responsible and decent were seduced by the trappings of authority, by the control of their perceptions, and by the uncritical definition of the situation in performing harsh acts" (cited in Markle 1995:52)

As disturbing as the findings of Arendt (1963) and Milgram (1963) are, others have been drawn to similar conclusions. For example, Christopher Browning, in his classic work *Ordinary Men: Reserve Police Battalion 101 and the Final Solution in Poland,* found that the reservists who carried out the mass murder of Jews were motivated to do so not out of any specific malice for their victims but rather out of a crushing sense of conformity and careerism. Ordinary Poles, Lithuanians, and Ukrainians also murdered their neighbors with little prompting from German occupying forces (see J. Gross 2002; Rhodes 2002).

How different are these corporations (and their leaders) from the "ordinary men" that Browning studied? Were the corporations "forced" or "coerced" into action, or was their contribution voluntary? In many respects, throughout the war it was largely "business as usual" for these corporations. As was mentioned earlier, those who controlled Opel were the same group of managers before and after the war started. Ford, evidently "lost control" of its plant in Cologne, but corporate headquarters still maintained contact with, and profited from, the plant.

Despite knowledge of key information that could have hampered the Nazi war machine, these corporations did nothing to stop it. In fact, most firms simultaneously facilitated the crimes of Nazi Germany and made significant profits. U.S. officials suggested to some corporate leaders that what they were doing was, at best, contrary to the interests of the United States and the Allied forces. Howard Elting, Jr., U.S. vice consul in Switzerland, in November of 1943 told Kodak, whose Swiss subsidiary was still purchasing photographic supplies from Germany, "our sole interest is to shut off every possible source of benefit to our enemies, regardless of what American commercial interests might suffer" (Friedman 2001:1). This warning was not issued, however, until long after the United States entered the war.

Both before and during much of World War II, U.S. businesses embraced an aggressively amoral position regarding the crimes of governments with which they might collaborate. Alfred Sloan, then General Motors president, said in 1938 that "an international business, operating throughout the world, should conduct its operations in strictly business terms, without regard to the political beliefs of its management, or the political beliefs of the country in which it is operating" (Levis 2000:245). There is no doubt that Germany represented a large market for U.S. corporations, and it had been a "good customer" in the sense of profitability. The buildup of Hitler's war machine prior to the outbreak of war had been very profitable for some of these corporations, Opel and Ford in particular. Like the ordinary men in Browning's study, or Eichmann on trial, these corporations did not view themselves as "evil." To the contrary, they did what corporations are supposed to do—make profits for shareholders.

MODERNITY, TAYLORISM, AND NAZISM

Traverso (2003) has warned that it would be a mistake to reduce the genocidal outcome of Nazism to an isolated moment in German history. He, like Baumann (2000), maintains that the Holocaust was the product not only of the confluence of German culture, history, and anti-Semitism but of Western culture itself: "the roots of Nazism and its violence lie in the history of the West, in the Europe of industrial capitalism, colonialism, imperialism, and the rise of modern science and technology, the Europe of eugenics and social Darwinism—in short, the Europe of the 'long' nineteenth century that ends in the battlefields of World War I" (Traverso 2003:16).

On the surface, it may seem an unfortunate coincidence that corporations like Ford, GM, and IBM were involved in the Holocaust. However, telling similarities between the features of such corporations and the Holocaust cannot be ignored if one is to understand how and why a corporation like Ford would aid—directly or not—in the murder of six million European Jews. In other words, rather than viewing the actions of the corporations and the Nazis as arising from different processes, it may be more instructive to examine the ways in which they are both products of a common historical process.

The first mass killings of Jews were carried out by the SS Einsatzgruppen. The task of Einsatzgruppen was to follow behind the invading German army and to make newly conquered areas "free of Jews." This was accomplished by rounding up the Jews in the area, directing them to an isolated area outside of town, digging a mass grave, and then shooting them. These acts were carried out by soldiers who were told to shoot Jews, including women and children, sometimes for hours on end. The psychological toll on the soldiers of shooting unarmed civilians, including women and small children, was enormous (Rhodes 2002). German officers tried to offset the psychological problems encountered by their soldiers by giving them large amounts of chocolate and alcohol (Rhodes 2002). After all, shooting unarmed women and children cannot be rationalized as an act of war, even by the most dedicated soldier.[11] Over time, high-ranking military officers and members of the SS began to view the mass shootings of Jews as too inefficient and too costly. The model of the death camp was born from these concerns.

clearly see the Ford plant, which, compared with the rest of the city, is in pristine condition, a fact not lost on many reporters who visited Cologne immediately after the war. While I am not suggesting that Ford Motor Company had enough political clout to save its Cologne plant from bombing, it is clear that through either incompetence or intention it was not destroyed.

6. Forced labor is not used in the same sense here as it was in the death camps, where the practice of "extermination through labor" was used. The forced labor refer to was known as *Reischseinsatz,* and included prisoners of war, foreign civilians, and concentration camp prisoners. These laborers came from several countries, including France, Poland, and the former Soviet Union (Billstein et al. 2000). About fifty corporations used forced or slave labor, including Bayer, BMW, IBM, General Motors, Ford, Kodak, Volkswagen, and Daimler-Chrysler. In December of 1999 several corporations (Bayer, BMW, Volkswagen, and Daimler-Chrysler) agreed to create a $5.1 billion fund to pay reparations to victims of forced labor.

7. The U.S. bank J. P. Morgan was also named in the same lawsuit; they too are accused of illegally seizing and failing to return Jewish assets during the war. The suit claims that J. P. Morgan managers openly boasted of "the anti-Jewish record and policies of J. P. Morgan."

8. In this sense it would also be instructive to look at other elites who contributed either directly or indirectly to the Holocaust, such as the physicians who experimented on the Jews and the lawyers who helped craft Germany's legal codes concerning who was and was not a Jew. In addition, far too little attention has been given to the subject of those German elites who were shuttled out of Germany after the war—many of whom were accused of committing crimes during the Holocaust—because of their strategic value to the United States and its Allies in the newly forming Cold War with the Soviets.

9. Henry Ford was not the only American businessman to receive such an "honor." Thomas Watson (from IBM) and James Mooney (vice president of GM) also received the Grand Cross of the German Eagle.

10. One must be careful, however, in drawing the conclusion that "we are all Nazis" from Arendt's statements on Eichmann. This is not what she was suggesting. What she was arguing was that the potential to become an Eichmann resides in each of us.

11. The way in which such barbaric acts were rationalized by the soldiers and those in command was that the "war against the Jews" had to be "total," so that not a single Jewish child could live and potentially come back some day to seek revenge for his or her parent's death (Rhodes 2002).

CHAPTER 9

Bridgestone-Firestone, Ford, and the NHTSA

Christopher W. Mullins

THIS CHAPTER ADDS TO THE growing body of criminological cal literature on state-corporate crime through an examination of the Bridgestone-Firestone tire tread separation case that emerged in the late 1990s. Specifically, I will demonstrate how a pattern of corporate wrongdoing on the part of the corporations involved, along with gross regulatory failure on the part of the U.S. government, contributed to a rash of avoidable deaths and injuries due to rollover accidents involving Ford Explorers.

Widely covered in the media, and the source of scores of still unresolved court cases in the United States and abroad, the tread separation case stands as one of the largest failures of the automobile industry to protect consumer safety and well-being to date. The case produced the largest automotive parts recall in history, with hundreds of thousands of tires being replaced worldwide. Two major multinational corporations, Ford Motor Company and Bridgestone-Firestone, Inc., were forced to engage in major public relations damage control and to appear before both houses of the U.S. Congress. Further, both have been named as defendants in numerous lawsuits.

The evidence for these claims is strong:

- As of November 8, 2001, the National Highway Traffic Safety Administration credited Bridgestone tire tread separations as the cause of 271 deaths and over 800 injuries.
- Out of dozens of lawsuits filed, one has been settled by Bridgestone-Firestone. The company will pay $41.5 million, with each state, as well as Puerto Rico and the District of Columbia, receiving $500,000; $10 million will go to pay state legal fees and $5 million to fund tire safety education programs.

- The U.S. government failed to take action to address the problem until May of 2000, even though it was in possession of evidence of the tire problems as early as 1997.
- The first lawsuit concerning tread separation and rollover was filed on February 12, 1991 *(Woodburn v. Firestone Tire and Rubber Co., et al.).*
- To this date, neither Bridgestone-Firestone nor Ford Motor Company has admitted culpability for the accidents or defects.

This case is unique in that it involves the intersection of two corporations with different products—Bridgestone-Firestone and Ford Motor Company—and it also highlights how, in a globalized economy, state-corporate crimes can flourish due to variations in regulation and controls placed on consumer items by different nation-states. At its core, this case involves two intertwined issues.

The first issue is tread separation on Bridgestone-Firestone tires. Primarily, it was Bridgestone-Firestone's ATX and Wilderness AT tires that showed the greatest tendency to separate. Further, most of the tires that experienced separation in the United States were traced to the Bridgestone-Firestone plant in Decatur, Illinois. The majority of these separations occurred on vehicles operating at high speeds in warm climates.

The second issue is vehicle rollovers due to tire tread separations. Ford Explorers appeared most susceptible to rollover while operating with Bridgestone-Firestone tires. Although other vehicles experienced some rollover problems, none did so with the frequency of Ford Explorers. Because of design characteristics of Ford's sports utility vehicles (SUVs) well before the Explorer line was developed, drivers frequently had difficulty in maintaining control of vehicles when they experienced various forms of tire failure. The resulting crashes were responsible for numerous injuries and deaths.

The Bridgestone-Firestone case is the product of the largest contract between an auto manufacturer (Ford) and a parts provider (Firestone) in the history of the U.S. automobile industry, a contract that represents a century-long relationship between the two corporations. The Explorer quickly became one of the most popular vehicles ever manufactured by Ford or any other company. As the sole provider of tires for the Explorer, Bridgestone-Firestone stood to make an enormous profit. Unlike many cases of state-corporate criminality presented in this volume, the Bridgestone-Firestone case involves two huge transnational, multi-unit corporations as well as the U.S. government. As we will see, it is often impossible to disentangle the facts of the case from the obfuscations of the various organizations involved.

The basics of the case have been widely reported by news media in the United States. Public Citizen (see www.citizen.org), a consumer watchdog group, constructed a detailed case history and critique of the Transportation Recall Enhancement Accountability and Documentation (TREAD) Act.

However, much information surrounding this case has been difficult to obtain—indeed, the passing of the TREAD Act has made it even more difficult.[1] It should be noted that some details in this case are still unfolding, and thus a final analysis is not possible at this time. What is provided here, however, is as thorough and accurate an examination of the case as is possible under present circumstances.

THE TIRE PROBLEM: BRIDGESTONE-FIRESTONE

According to its own records, Bridgestone-Firestone was aware of design flaws in the ATX and Wilderness AT tire designs submitted to them by Ford. Despite early protests by their engineers regarding these inherent problems, they went forward with tire manufacture. The National Highway Traffic Safety Administration (NHTSA) (2001) claims the critical design flaw in these tires rests with the belt wedge, a strip of rubber that sits between the two steel belts of the tire near the edge. With the Wilderness AT and ATX tires, the belt is thinner and narrower than on other models. As this belt naturally cracks with age and usage, its design can lead to its separation from the rest of the tire composition, thus allowing the steel belts to separate from the tire itself and producing total tire failure. This situation is exacerbated when tires of higher inflation pressure are used on heavier vehicles. Such conditions hasten the wear on the defective belt wedge. Further, the potential for tread separation increases with usage, higher temperatures, and faster driving speeds.

The majority of the defective tires have been traced to the Bridgestone-Firestone manufacturing plant in Decatur, Illinois. While other models and other Bridgestone-Firestone plants tires, as well as other manufacturers' tires, experience tread separation, Decatur tires show substantially higher failure rates. Decatur ATX tires at three years of age experience a failure rate of 200 per million; Wilson ATX tires experience a failure rate of fewer than 100 at the same age.[2] Goodyear Wrangler RT/S tires, a leading comparable competitor,[3] do not experience a measurable failure rate at this age. At four years of age, Decatur ATX tires have a failure rate of approximately 500 per million, Wilson ATX have a rate of just over 200 per million, and GY Wrangler RT/S still have an essentially minuscule failure rate. At seven years of age, Decatur ATX tires have a failure rate of over 800 per million, Wilson ATX of just under 200 per million, and GY Wrangler RT/S's failures are still minuscule (NHTSA 2001).[4] Clearly, some aspect of the problem originated within the Decatur plant.[5]

There was some debate within Bridgestone-Firestone regarding whether or not the Decatur plant operated in an appreciably different fashion than other plants making ATX tires. In 2000, NHTSA investigators claimed that more lubricant was added to the rubber mixture for ATX tires at Decatur, thereby changing the nature of the compound (*Strategic Safety* 2001). At the time, however, Decatur was making over fifty different tires, with none of the others showing failure rates as high as the ATX model. Bridgestone-Firestone also produced documents for the NHTSA suggesting that there were no differences in processes at the Decatur plant (NHTSA 2001; *Strategic Safety* 2001). What is known is that in July of 1994 Firestone workers went on strike and stayed on strike until December of 1996. In January of 1995, 943 replacement workers were hired by Firestone to operate the Decatur plant. However, it is unclear how this affected the tires produced by the plant and how many of the tires that separated were produced by replacement workers.

Internal Ford documents also indicate that the Decatur plant was the source of the majority of the tires used by Ford Motor Company in Venezuela to manufacture the Ford Explorer for the South American market. This production began in February 1996, and Ford imported 3,010 tires from the Decatur plant until Ford Venezuela was able to begin its own tire production (U.S. House 2000a). As I will discuss below, the failure of these specific tires led to the only criminal charges filed to date in this case.

All along, Bridgestone-Firestone has been vehement in insisting that it is the vehicle design flaws, not the tires, that led to the numerous fatal accidents involving tread separation. When responding to the NHTSA's investigation of the tread separations, Bridgestone-Firestone claimed that "a tread separation is not a defect" (NHTSA 2001:25); rather, it is an expected failure of any steel-belted tire. In terms of media coverage and public relations, Bridgestone-Firestone seems to have been moderately successful in shifting the blame to Ford. In court cases, Bridgestone-Firestone has settled the only cases as yet resolved.

THE VEHICLE PROBLEM: FORD MOTOR COMPANY

Ford has a well-known history of anticonsumer corporate behavior, which has been defined as criminal by some writers. From the infamous Pinto case, to falsifying emissions records (Ditlow 2000; *United States v. Ford Motor Company* 1973) to its collaboration with Nazi Germany during World War II (see chapter 8 above), Ford is often a "usual suspect" in cases of corporate negligence. Ditlow (2000:3) claims that "cover up is a culture at Ford Motor Company."

The tread separation cases came on the heels of Ford's problem with stalling vehicles—a failure in the Thick Film Ignition mounted on distributors used on over twenty two million vehicles sold from 1983 to 1995 model years (Ditlow 2000). During NHTSA's investigation of this case, Ford withheld information and presented false information. Their delays allowed the eight-year statute of limitations on NHTSA's authority to investigate to expire. In the ruling for *Howard v. Ford Motor Company* (2000:8), Ford was found guilty of "fraudulent concealment" and violating Civil Code sections 1770(a)(5) and (7). In the early stages of the tire case, with dust still settling from the Howard ruling and Ford still illegally withholding information from NHTSA about faulty starters, the corporation had every reason to want to deflect another faulty product scandal.

Internal Ford documents show that as far back as 1984, Ford knew that its sport utility vehicles experienced high numbers of rollover accidents (Public Citizen 2001). The Bronco was the first model to exhibit this tendency. The primary cause is a relatively narrow wheel base in proportion to the height and weight of the vehicle. While this was a well-known SUV problem, it went essentially unaddressed through the years while Ford created other lines of SUVs. The exact reasoning behind this is unclear, though speculation highlights two issues. Correction would require reengineering of the entire chassis system of the vehicle line—a high-cost proposition. Such modifications would also produce a vehicle closer in size and weight to the Chevy Suburban, which had proved to be less popular with buyers than the Explorer. Ford executives may have judged that such a redesigned, safer vehicle would be less "sporty" looking and less attractive to the customer base for SUVs.

As early as May of 1987, internal Ford memos indicated problems with prototypes of the Explorer (at this time called UN46). Research and development reports stated that the Explorer was less stable than the Bronco II, and it was recommended that a wider wheel base, a lower-sitting chassis, and smaller tires be utilized (Public Citizen 2001). Later evaluations raised concerns about the front suspension system on the Explorer. Problems here could contribute to poor handling of a vehicle with a tire blowout or a potential rollover.

Throughout 1989, Ford engineers tried to correct the emerging tread separation and rollover problems with the Explorer. Although top management recommended adopting suggested changes, it was also made clear that changes would not be allowed to compromise the release of the vehicle, slated for March of 1990. The vehicle was ready on schedule, with many of the problematic aspects of its engineering unaddressed. In management's own words, getting the vehicle out on time was "job one" (Public Citizen 2001).

There is evidence to suggest that Ford bears culpability not only for the rollover issue, but for the tire issue as well. According to Bridgestone-Firestone, Ford submitted the faulty tire designs to Bridgestone-Firestone. An internal 1987 Ford memo indicates that Ford approved the ATX tire design prior to manufacturing (Public Citizen 2001). The exact history of the tire and its design are unclear, but both companies were clearly aware of the tire issues, especially the issues of tread separation and the related potential for rollover accidents. However, neither company attempted to halt or delay the vehicles' release.

Vehicle failures related to these engineering problems emerged early. In 1988, Thomas J. Baughman, chassis engineering manager in the Heavy Truck Division for Truck Operations of Ford Motor, was informed of tire failures on Ford vehicles in Saudi Arabia (Baughman 2000). By 1989 there were other reports about tread failures and rollover potential. Ford responded to these concerns by altering recommended pound-per-square-inch (PSI) inflation standards. Ford sent several memos to its dealers and repair shops worldwide with various suggestions on tire inflation modifications. Ford's ultimate goal was to get the vehicles on the road with the tires in question. In 1990, the vehicles were released.

By 1991 lawsuits were filed concerning tread separation and rollover accidents. Between 1991 and May 2000 (the opening of NHTSA's investigation into ATX, ATX II, and Wilderness tires) at least fifty nine lawsuits related to this product failure were filed against the two companies involved (Public Citizen 2001). Between 1990 and 1996 Ford issued memo after memo to dealers related to tire inflation pressures on the Ford Explorer. Essentially, these documents did little other than suggest that minor manipulations of inflation pressures be made on vehicles on the lots or that came in for maintenance. There was never a concerted effort to make consumers who already owned Ford SUVs aware of these recommendations. Individual citizens were not the only victims. Many governmental agencies had contracts with Ford to provide vehicles and tires. In June of 1996, the Arizona Game and Fish Department manager sent an email to his supervisors warning of tread separations and blowouts on department vehicles using Firestone tires. In July 1996 the deputy attorney for Yuma County, Arizona, John K. White, reported the same problem on vehicles in the sheriff's department there.

In August 1997, Ford and Firestone were notified of the problem on vehicles shipped to and operated in Saudi Arabia. Similar problems arose in Malaysia, Thailand, Venezuela, and Colombia, as well as other Middle Eastern and South American nations. For example, in 1997 Ford generated an internal report based on thirteen separation cases (six in Malaysia and seven in Thailand) linking the root causes to fatigue failure accelerated by high temperatures, high speed usage, underinflation, and synergy among these factors. The field investigators suggested switching to the Goodyear Wrangler RT/S tire, which, once tested, did not experience failure under these conditions (Ford 1997). No long-term actions were taken, however, even though the Field Review Committee secretaries for Europe and North America were the principal addressees on the report, indicating that high-level Ford management worldwide had been informed of the exact nature and conditions of the problems at this time.

In 1999 another foreign market problem emerged: Explorers sold and operated in Venezuela began to experience high levels of separation and rollover. In an email dated August 11, 1999, Carlos Maron, a Ford of Venezuela (FOV) local development manager, complained to Ford U.S.A. tire development managers about the lack of action by Ford Motor Company on the tire failures brought to their attention "weeks ago." A Firestone group had been to Venezuela and claimed they found no evidence of manufacturing defects in the tires. Maron claimed that the problems were happening only on Ford Explorers and told his North American contact—a tire and wheel engineer—"We are not to stand this situation any more. We want to do a campaign of change of tires to 100% Explorers in service [*sic*]. The problem is that we don't know which tire to install because we don't know the cause of failure" (Camaron Venezuel 1999). An email dated August 19, 1999, sent by the Ford tire development unit, requested information about what tires were actually sent to FOV, saying, "This whole Venezuela thing is blowing up." Within two days the tire development unit in the U.S.A. sent emails recommending the use of Goodyear RT/S tires in the Venezuela market.

Overall, Bridgestone-Firestone and Ford largely ignored the international cases, except for blaming faulty consumer usage for tire separation and rollover accidents. This is the explanation that both companies continue to hold to in 2005, nearly fifteen years after the problem first emerged. Bridgestone-Firestone reiterated its claim of innocence during the 2000 Senate hearings (Bridgestone-Firestone 2000). Unsurprisingly, Ford insisted from the onset of the problem that the Explorer rollover problem was a tire issue, not a vehicle issue. Ford has sought to place the entire blame on Bridgestone-Firestone despite that fact that the tires in question had been built to Ford's designs. In his testimony to the U.S. Senate, Ford president, Jac Nasser (2000:4) went so far as to claim that "Ford did not know there was a defect with the tires until we received the confidential claims from Firestone in July of this year."

Such discourse was not merely a public front. In conflicts over the Venezuela separations, FOV and Bridgestone-Firestone Venezuela (BFVZ) had heated arguments regarding the nature of the problem and which corporation was ultimately liable. On May 5, 2000, BFVZ presented a letter to the president of FOV with its proposal for solving the tire issue. According to an internal BFVZ memo, Ford's response was "aggressive" in wanting "to blame Bridgestone-Firestone for their problems" and demanded a "silent recall" of all the tires. BFVZ suggested suspension modifications that FOV refused (Gonzalez 2000). On May 8, another meeting occurred. Again Ford reiterated that it would not accept a statement that the suspension of the Explorer was to blame and said that all problems were to be attributed to the tires. The corporations failed to reach an agreement (Colmenarez 2000).

From the start, neither corporation wanted to assume liability for the problem. Each had a ready-made scapegoat, and each began to construct its case against the other in private meetings long before the case became public. As seen in Ford USA's responses to FOV in the case of the earlier separations, they had a solution: switch to another brand and model of tire. When FOV complained about separations, they were given the same advice that was given in the Malaysia and Thailand cases. The problem was known, as was the solution. Yet the solution was only applied when individual branches of Ford demanded an alternative to Bridgestone-Firestone tires. Not only were the companies keeping crucial safety information from the public, but they were also keeping it from their subbranches.

brought cases against them with counter-data blaming the other company, settlements can be forced that are more favorable to the corporation than would potentially be given in court.

Controls and Their Failure

The government responded to pressures of the auto and auto-tire industries in its approach to the problem. Ignoring the needs of the public, the TREAD law does little to help and quite a bit to potentially hurt consumers and discourage public knowledge about future problems of this type. The tight intersection between the Department of Transportation and the private transportation industry blurs the line between the regulated and the regulators—an intersection made even more problematic in light of the secrecy provisions contained within the law.

It is reasonable to ask: why would the government do so little, while claiming to do so much? On the one hand, as Barnett (1981), Chambliss and Zatz (1993), and Matthews and Kauzlarich (2000) have shown, it is often the state's obligation, at least under a capitalist economy, to protect, encourage, and assist corporations in capital accumulation. Gold, Lo, and Wright (1975) argue that the primary purpose of the state in a capitalist system is to allow the corporate capitalist economy to flourish. Government becomes constrained by the needs and desires of major corporations. Even a Parsonian functionalism would predict a tight intersection between the economy and the state, with the state being in many ways subordinate to the economy. All of these perspectives would predict little to no action on behalf of the state in guarding citizen safety. On the other hand, as O'Connor (1973) noted, the state must protect the perceived legitimacy of both the capitalist system and itself. Thus in the face of widespread public concerns or panic, it must take, or appear to take, effective action to minimize the source of concern. In the Bridgestone-Firestone case, this action was the passage of TREAD, which may serve more as "symbolic legislation" (Edelman 1985) than as any real inroad into the prerogatives of the automobile industry.

Neither of the dominant American political parties has shown much interest in regulating U.S. corporations (Nader 2000). Particularly since the conservative revolution that began with the election of Ronald Reagan in 1980, both parties have presented themselves in their rhetoric and their behavior as intensely corporation-friendly. The continued high levels of U.S. government spending on corporate welfare are an excellent example of this (Nader 2000; Shields 1995). The TREAD Act can be seen as direct avoidance by the U.S. government of its obligation to establish regulations necessary to ensure consumer safety, in order to avoid imposing costly prohibitions on the auto and auto parts industries, while seeming to be sensitive to consumer needs. Such corporate protections go beyond simple attention to preserving national economic health.

Recent work on the victimology of state crimes (Kauzlarich, Matthews, and Miller 2002) highlights patterns of structural inequality, which lead disempowered groups to be more frequently victimized by such activities. Generally, this pattern holds for state-corporate crimes as well, though there is an interesting twist when looking at this case and others in which the victims are U.S. consumers. When victims come from groups that wield an amount of consumer or social power, regulatory agencies are compelled to take some form of at least symbolic action. In the case under examination here, as well as in the crash of ValuJet flight 592 (see chapter 6) and the *Challenger* disaster (chapter 3; Vaughan 1996), the victims come from more privileged social strata, which catalyzes minimally symbolic responses by regulatory agencies. SUVs are marketed to households with median incomes and above, households that are more likely to be politically engaged and generally have more political, economic, social, and cultural capital. This is not a population that can be readily ignored by either the U.S. government or major U.S. corporations. Thus while TREAD actually does little to alter the system of design and production that produced the tire failures and related accidents, it does satisfy middle-class demands for action on an issue directly related to their interests. Such interactions also point to the earlier silence on the issue when it was localized overseas—such populations did not possess the necessary capital to garner U.S. media attention, much less governmental attention. Through the exploitation of the great social distance between the earliest victims and the U.S. residence of the corporations involved, the accidents and separations could be virtually ignored, as there was no economic or political impetus to correct the issue.

Cultural Elements

The notion that American society and culture are organized for street crime has been thoroughly explored within sociology and criminology (Messner and Rosenfeld 2001). Institutional anomie theory explains high levels of street crime in the United States, especially when compared with similarly structured European nations, as a function of economic dominance and an emphasis on economic success over the processes that generate that success. While to date this theory has found its greatest applications with street offenses (homicide, specifically), it is not illogical to assume that these same cultural forces are operating within corporate and state-corporate offending as well.

Broad cultural pressures for success apply to corporate performance as well as to individuals within corporations. As United States–based transnationals expand their economic influence over the globe, they bring the same cultural structures. These corporations, while located in other nations to utilize labor and exploit markets, export the same values that make the United States a "society organized for crime." Thus as we continue to see the development of

TRAFFIC VALDEZ: Roger that.

HAZELWOOD: Okay. We'll give you the status report as to the changing situation. Over.

TRAFFIC VALDEZ: Standing by. (Davidson 1990:19)

VTC then notified the Coast Guard port captain, Commander Steve McCall, who was in charge of emergency response within Prince William Sound. "This is the big one. We have the *Exxon Valdez* aground at Bligh Reef" (Davidson 1990:19). Commander McCall got out of bed, left for the Alyeska Marine Terminal, and radioed Hazelwood on the *Exxon Valdez:*

MCCALL: *Exxon Valdez*, this is the captain of the port, Commander McCall. Do you have any more of an estimate as to your situation at this time? Over?

HAZELWOOD: Oh, not at the present, Steve . . . but we are working our way off the reef . . . the vessel has been holed. Right now we're trying to steer off the reef. And we'll get back to you as soon as we can.

MCCALL: Roger on that. You know, we've got all our planned mechanisms in place to give you what assistance we can . . . Take it, take it slow and easy and, you know, I'm telling you the obvious, but . . . take it slow and easy and we are getting help out as fast as we can.

HAZELWOOD: Okay. We're in pretty good shape right now stabilitywise. We're just trying to extract her off the shoal here and you can probably see me on your radar. And once I get underway I'll let you know.

MCCALL: Roger. Yeah. Another thing, now again, before you make any drastic attempt to get underway you make sure you don't . . . start doing any ripping. You got a rising tide. You got another about an hour and a half worth of tide in your favor. Once you hit the max I wouldn't recommend doing much wiggling. Over.

HAZELWOOD: Okay. Yeah, I think . . . the major damage has kind of been done. We've kind of . . . rolled over it and we're just kind of hung up in the stern here. We'll just drift over it and I'll get back to you. We'll be standing by. *Exxon Valdez*, clear. (NTSB 1990:13–14)

Hazelwood did not stop his efforts to free the *Exxon Valdez* from Bligh Reef for another two hours.

At 12:35 A.M., when the Alyeska Marine Terminal superintendent, Chuck O'Donnell, was awakened and notified of the incident, he called one of his subordinates, Larry Shier, and sent him to find out what was happening. The Exxon Pipeline Company president, Darryl Warner, was notified in Houston of the incident at 1:23 A.M., and he notified Exxon Shipping president Frank Iarossi immediately.

A DELAYED RESPONSE

At 5:00 A.M. Alyeska response workers reached the terminal to respond to the spill. They found the response barge in dry dock, covered with snow, and not at all ready to respond to a spill. The response was slowed even further because only one Alyeska worker was qualified to operate the forklift and crane that were needed to move equipment and materials to the barge and lift them onto its deck. This forced him to shuffle back and forth between the two pieces of equipment (Alaska Oil Spill Commission 1990). Nearly six hours after the workers had arrived, the barge set out for Bligh Reef. It arrived there some fourteen hours after the *Exxon Valdez* had been grounded.

The magnitude of the spill was not realized until first light Friday, March 24, when Alyeska officials flew over the sound and "saw a slick three miles long and two miles wide drifting south from the tanker" (Davidson 1990:24). By that evening, an estimated 240,000 barrels of oil, or nearly 11 million gallons, had escaped the *Exxon Valdez* into Prince William Sound, and the spill had spread to a size of more than eighteen square miles.

The cleanup response was slow, and it was clear from the beginning that nobody involved was adequately prepared to handle a disaster of that magnitude. For example, Exxon president Frank Iarossi made calls to mobilize booms and other cleanup equipment from as far away as San Francisco and Southhampton, England. Some thought was given to burning the spilled oil, but there were not enough of the necessary fire-resistant booms located in Alaska. Further problems would be created by smoke pollution from burning the oil, for which Exxon did not have the necessary permits. Finally, the controversial issue of using dispersants was considered.[1]

Despite all the delays, Iarossi was still optimistic. On Sunday night, March 26, he said, "starting tomorrow we are going to have all three tools—skimmers, burning, and dispersants—at our disposal [and by] tomorrow morning we're going to be going all out" (Davidson 1990:54). His optimism was short lived, because a storm hit Valdez that night, bringing with it high winds that carried the oil quickly through the sound and brought it to the shorelines, making an already bad situation even worse. "Oil from the *Exxon Valdez*—now beyond containment—would range through Prince William Sound and the coast of Southcentral Alaska, eventually striking beaches nearly 600 miles from Bligh Reef" (Alaska Oil Spill Commission 1990:61).

THE ACTORS INVOLVED

The *Exxon Valdez* oil spill was a result of the actions not only of Exxon and Captain Joseph Hazelwood but also of the Alyeska Pipeline Service Company, the United States Coast Guard (USCG), the Alaska Department of Environmental Control (ADEC), the state of Alaska, and the U.S. government. All

Exxon

Although Exxon had indicated that it would respond to large spills, it did not provide the ADEC with a plan for response. Therefore the corporation had no official plan in effect for Prince William Sound, which hindered response time. Exxon had to collect equipment from all over the world in order to respond to the spill.

Aside from Exxon's specific response to the *Valdez* oil spill, other problems within the corporation had contributed to the disaster. For example, a spill occurred a few months before the *Valdez* in New York and New Jersey due to "shoddy equipment and poor maintenance procedures." According to one writer, the *Exxon Valdez* spill, along with the New York and New Jersey spill and a fire in an L.A. refinery, "suggests that the company stubbornly refuses to embrace a policy of safety and prevention" (Randolph 1990:51). There were also questions regarding falsified overtime records. The Coast Guard had developed regulations for caps on overtime hours in order to reduce crew fatigue. On the night of the spill, it was clear that overtired crewmembers had made key decisions that contributed to the disaster. In the past, Exxon had been accused a number of times of falsifying the overtime records of employees in order to pass inspections (NTSB 1990).

In addition, problems existed with Captain Hazelwood. Hazelwood graduated from maritime college in 1968 and moved quickly through the ranks, earning "his master's license at age thirty-two, ten years earlier than most Exxon captains" (Alaska Oil Spill Commission 1990:9). His performance evaluations, however, continually noted that he only did the minimum required for his job (NTSB 1990). In 1982, 1983, and 1984, even after Hazelwood had moved up to the rank of master, his evaluations suggested shore assignment because he did "not try to achieve potential" (NTSB 1990:183). These reviews were for some reason never signed or forwarded to Exxon headquarters for final review. Hazelwood remained a shipmaster, and was eventually moved to the *Exxon Valdez* in April of 1987 (Davidson 1990). At the time of the tanker's grounding, Hazelwood's blood alcohol content may have been .20, which was five times the limit for vessel operators (Davidson 1990). This was not Hazelwood's first incident with alcohol. His problems with alcohol had led to three suspensions of his driver's license, and he had voluntarily checked into a treatment program in 1985. Bruce Amero, an Exxon employee, said that "there's a bad joke in the fleet that it's Captain Hazelwood and his chief mate, Jack Daniels, that run the ship" (Davidson 1990:66). Exxon knew of this drinking problem but failed to check Hazelwood's driving record when turning over to him the largest ship in its fleet, according to Davidson (1990).

The U.S. Government

One could make the argument that the U.S. government was solely responsible for the *Exxon Valdez* oil spill, because of its authorization of the Trans-Alaska

Pipeline System. Not only did it authorize the TAPS, but it stressed the importance of early completion because the pipeline would supply 10 to 12 percent of
the nation's oil with its two million barrels per day, which would reduce reliance
on foreign oil (U.S. House 1976). In doing so they turned the other way when
welding problems were discovered in the pipeline that could have led to leaks or
greater problems down the road (U.S. House of Representatives 1976).

But there are also more subtle ways in which the U.S. government was a
responsible party in the grounding of the *Exxon Valdez*. The responsibilities of
U.S. Coast Guard had been steadily increased over the years with the enact-
ment of several laws, including the Vessel Bridge-to-Bridge Radiotelephone
Act of 1971, the Federal Water Pollution Control Act of 1972, and the Trans-
Alaska Pipeline Authorization Act of 1974 (U.S. House 1987). The increased
responsibilities, however, were not accompanied by sufficiently increased funding.[3] Manpower actually decreased over this period (U.S. House 1987).

In 1986 the U.S. government set up the Hazardous Substance Superfund
in order to aid cleanup of hazardous substances in case the responsible party
could not afford the costs. A trust fund of $8.5 billion over five years was estab-
lished (U.S. Code, Title 42, Section 9611). At the time of the spill, the fund was
down to only three or four million dollars. Because of the lack of funds, the
U.S. Coast Guard on-scene coordinator, Admiral Paul Yost, who could have
federalized the spill and taken over responsibilities when Alyeska and Exxon
did not respond effectively and efficiently, decided not to federalize. In making
his decision, Admiral Yost noted that "we are looking at a $100 million–$200
million [a day] spill. We are looking at a corporate giant who has been a good
corporate citizen in their response so far, willing to open their checkbook, put
no limits on it. I would be very reluctant to federalize this spill with four million dollars in my pockets when I know that we are spending over $100 mil-
lion a day—by 'we,' Exxon is" (U.S. House 1989: 23).

THE VALDEZ SPILL IN CRIMINOLOGICAL CONTEXT

A lax regulatory environment existed within the organizational boundaries of most of the actors involved in the *Valdez* oil spill. According to
Matthews and Kauzlarich (2000), organizational goals, opportunity, and lack
of social control (a lax regulatory environment) are all contributing factors in
state-corporate crimes. The U.S. government failed to regulate Alyeska when
welding problems were found in the pipeline construction (U.S. House 1976),
the ADEC failed to regulate Alyeska and its upkeep of spill response equipment (Alaska Oil Spill Commission 1990), and Exxon failed to regulate its
employees and their on-duty behavior (Davidson 1990). This series of oversights and failures to reprimand wrongdoing created an environment that, when
coupled with a strong corporate profit motive, was conducive to an accident
such as the grounding of the *Valdez*.

We believe that the *Exxon Valdez* oil spill is best viewed as a form of state-corporate crime, as opposed to an "accident." From this criminological perspective, we will examine the "nested contexts" that brought about the construction of the Trans-Alaska Pipeline System. The nested contexts we will examine include the societal, political, and regulatory. In the same way that Aulette and Michalowski (1993; see chapter 4 above) suggest that the societal, organizational, and control contexts came together in a way that made the fire in the Imperial Foods chicken-processing plant inevitable, the societal, political, and regulatory contexts come together here to make the grounding of the *Exxon Valdez* and subsequent oil spill inevitable.

Societal Context

In the societal context, various events facilitated the construction of TAPS. One of the most important was the 1973 Organization of Petroleum Exporting Countries (OPEC) oil embargo that was placed on the United States. This embargo came about because many OPEC nations were angered by the U.S. support of Israel in the Yom Kippur War (Mathew 2001). OPEC cut off sales to the United States, and the resultant oil shortage caused the price of oil products to skyrocket, particularly in the Midwest. The experience of the embargo, along with increased consumption and restricted oil drilling on the Outer Continental Shelf (due to an oil spill in Santa Barbara) contributed to a growing sense that the United States faced an energy crisis (Gramling and Freudenburg 1996).

At the time of the OPEC oil embargo, the United States made up 6 percent of the world population but consumed 35 percent of the world's energy (U.S. House 1973a). During this period there were also increased regulations in the coal and natural gas industries that increased the demand for oil (Bohi and Darmstadter 1996). These factors, combined with the discovery of oil in Prudhoe Bay in 1968, led to a desire to move Alaskan oil to the market to alleviate the sense of crisis. However, this desire was not easy to fulfill. In order to move the oil to the market, a pipeline would have to be constructed to transport the oil. The question then was whether the pipeline would cross Alaska to the southern port of Valdez, where the oil would then be transported to market via tanker ships, or whether the pipeline would cross Canada to a midwestern U.S. terminus.

Many issues had to be considered before the location of the pipeline could be decided. According to Don Young, "Alaska's only representative in the House of Representatives," the Alaskan route was preferable to the Canadian route, because "the Canadian route is mired down with uncertainties, delay and extenuating circumstances which leads us to question the validity of the proposal. We know the line would take three to five years longer than the Alaskan route for construction alone. . . . Moreover, the Native people, the

environment issue, the financing, the N.E.B. [National Energy Board] requirements, the proposed ownership terms, and finally the absence of an application, are all matters which would have to be looked into before construction
of a Canadian line could begin" (U.S. House 1973a:123).

This statement can be better understood when monetary costs and benefits are taken into account. If the pipeline were to cross Alaska, construction
costs would be about three-and-a-half billion dollars, whereas if the line were
to cross Canada, it would cost about six-and-a-half billion dollars (U.S. House
1973a). The pipeline would also produce revenue and tax money: when running at full capacity, the line could produce as much as two billion dollars
per year in royalties for Alaska (Lindbergh and Provorse 1977). Because of the
shorter construction time required for the Alaskan line, "3.4 billion barrels of
oil would reach the market prior to the time deliveries from a Trans-Canadian
line would begin" (U.S. House 1973a:253). Oil companies would draw a profit
sooner and the sense of an energy crisis would dissolve more quickly.

Nevertheless, many problems were evident in the proposed Alaskan route,
both from an environmental and from a national security standpoint. According to the final environmental impact statement, because the Alaskan line
would use huge oil tankers to transport the oil from the proposed port of
Valdez to the market, major environmental harms could result if there were a
tanker accident in the difficult-to-navigate waters of Prince William Sound
(Gramling and Freudenburg 1997). The final environmental impact statement
also acknowledged that there were other environmental concerns as well,
because the pipeline would need to cut through a great deal of permafrost, possibly causing melting; cross caribou migration paths; traverse the rugged Brooks
Range; and go over the Alaskan Range, which would present earthquake hazards (U.S. House 1973b). Despite these concerns, the final environmental
impact statement stated that it was in the nation's interest to reduce dependency on foreign oil; therefore the Alaskan pipeline should be constructed. The
pipeline construction would also "improve U.S. international balance of payments, create badly needed jobs for Alaskans, and produce essential income for
the State of Alaska" (Gramling and Freudenburg 1997:79).

Political Context

The political context surrounding the *Valdez* spill involves events and decisions made by government officials that influenced the construction of TAPS
and the subsequent grounding. Important issues involved here include the government's decision to construct TAPS, concerns regarding national defense, the
Native Claims debates, and the War on Drugs.

Alaska has long been a strategic outpost for national defense. Prior to World
War II there were many military installations in Alaska both for petroleum and
for protection. Alaska became a "jumping off point for Asia" during World War

II (Berry 1975:23). Despite the military presence in Alaska, the Alaska pipeline would not be as safe as the Canadian line in terms of military defense, because shipping oil via tankers from the proposed Valdez port during a war would mean that "tankers with vital crude would be exposed to our enemy and could be dried up with a minimum effort" (U.S. House 1973b:810). Yet the U.S. military did have an interest in the construction of the Alaska pipeline, because oil plays a vital role in military affairs for such things as fuel for use in planes and tanks. The government also had set aside twenty-three million acres of the North Slope land "that [was] likely to contain oil, to be exploited by the military in the case of emergency" (Berry 1975:77). If the pipeline were to be constructed across Canada, then U.S. oil would be moving through another country, which could put the United States at the risk of another energy crisis by possibly allowing Canada rights to the pipeline and in turn rights to the U.S. government reserves of oil.

Another issue, involving the native peoples in the Alaskan frontier, came to light once TAPS was decided on. Since the time of the purchase of the Alaska Territory in 1867, many Native peoples had been moved from their traditional hunting grounds. When Alaska was granted statehood in 1959, approximately one-fourth of the land was set aside as federal land (Berry 1975). The Alaskan Natives protested this decision, because many of their native hunting grounds were included in the federal lands. At the time that TAPS was under consideration, Alaskan Natives feared that even more land was going to be taken.

> The Alaskan Natives said the land in question belonged to their ancestors and, since it had never been sold or taken from them in battle, still belonged to them. . . . In 1969, most Natives were willing to settle for 40 million acres plus money for the rest of the land they claimed. They wanted those 40 million acres to include their traditional hunting and fishing grounds and the land around their meager villages, but their leaders also wanted land that would provide an economic base for their people in the future when the simple village life might no longer be possible. They wanted protection against the change which they also knew had come to Alaska. (Berry 1975:7)

It was not until 1971 that these land claims were finally settled with the establishment of the Alaska Native Claims Settlement Act. With this act the Alaskan Natives received 40 million acres, nearly $500 million, and an economic stake in the state's future mineral sales (Berry 1975; Gramling and Freudenburg 1997).

Another issue connected to the political context that subsequently led to the grounding to the *Exxon Valdez* was the U.S. government's War on Drugs. When the Reagan administration declared a "war on drugs" and planned to spend millions of dollars to fight this war, the money to support this program had to come from somewhere. Budgetary cuts were made within the system;

specifically of importance here were the cuts in the Coast Guard budget. The cost of the War on Drugs involved billions of dollars:

> The federal government spent an estimated $3 billion to fight the war on drugs in 1988. . . . The [first] Bush administration has asked Congress for $150 million in anti-drug grants to state and local agencies alone. Law-makers are seeking $275 million for fiscal year 1990. Under the Bush pro-posals, the Drug Enforcement Agency (DEA) would receive even more money ($551 million) than it received under the Reagan administration ($546 million), and an additional $68 million would go to DEA through a separate appropriation. (Johns and Borrero 1991:68)

According to USCG commander James Woodle, the Valdez terminal was not technologically up to par. When he recommended an additional radar site on Glacier Island or Bligh Island, the USCG response was that the "$100,000 a year" would be "cost prohibitive" because of budgetary cuts. Ultimately "budget cuts and the transfer of personnel to President Reagan's war on drugs had continually drained money from the Valdez Coast Guard budget and had whittled its staff from thirty-seven to twenty-four since the pipeline's comple-tion in 1977" (Davidson 1990:12).

Regulatory Context

The regulatory context consists of acts by individuals or other involved parties that do not follow established rules or regulations. In the case of the *Exxon Valdez* oil spill, these acts typically involved careless disregard for the rules or lack of enforcement of the rules because of greater importance placed on other goals, such as profit.

Acts of disregard for the rules occurred mostly with Alyeska and Exxon. As part of the regulations set up for the establishment of TAPS, Alyeska was to have its contingency plan in place one year prior to oil flow. Its plan, however, was not in place until a month prior to oil flow. As a part of its contingency plan, Alyeska was to have a specific quantity and quality of equipment on hand for use in the event of an oil spill. At the time of the grounding of the *Exxon Valdez*, much of the equipment was covered with snow on a broken-down barge, and the emergency response team that Alyeska had promised had been disbanded (Alaska Oil Spill Commission 1990). This disregard for regulatory requirements also extended to the Exxon Corporation. For example, all crewmembers were aware of the company's alcohol use policy, yet they did not report Hazelwood when they had repeatedly noticed him drinking while on duty (Davidson 1990). The Exxon Corporation was also aware of the workload requirements put in place by the USCG, but was accused a number of times of falsifying overtime records (NTSB 1990).

Lack of enforcement of regulations is most apparent in the nonaction on the part of the U.S. government and the ADEC. The U.S. government was aware of problems in the welding of the pipeline, mentioned earlier, and took no action to have the problems fixed (U.S. House 1976). The ADEC did not check all of the response equipment when it conducted evaluations of the Valdez terminal and did not hold spill simulations to high standards, giving simulations that were merely adequate passing marks. The ADEC administrators were also aware of the compliance problems but did nothing to make Alyeska comply with regulations (Alaska Oil Spill Commission 1990).

When situated within the nested contexts described above, the events leading up to the grounding of the *Exxon Valdez* and the resulting oil spill are revealed as multidimensional and complex. The OPEC oil embargo and subsequent "energy crisis" combined with the discovery of oil in Prudhoe Bay opened the door for a pipeline project to alleviate the crisis. When discussions began regarding pipeline construction and location, Alaska, a fairly new state requiring revenue, jumped on board and argued that the TAPS project was the best option for the United States. Once TAPS was agreed upon and constructed, the Coast Guard presence increased to handle tanker traffic, but when the War on Drugs cut significant portions of the Coast Guard budget, the result limited resources within the VTC. When all of this is placed within an environment of lax regulatory enforcement, such as the ADEC's poor enforcement of rules during spill simulations and disregard for Alyeska's and violation of regulations and its poor upkeep of equipment, it becomes apparent that something like the *Valdez* spill was inevitable. Unfortunately, the inevitable turned out to be the worst oil spill experienced in North America.

ENVIRONMENTAL, HUMAN, AND LEGAL CONSEQUENCES

The *Exxon Valdez* "accident" resulted in 10.8 million gallons of crude oil being spilled into Prince William Sound (*Exxon Valdez* Oil Spill Trustee Council 1999). The slow recovery time caused the oil to pound beaches 1,300 miles away from the actual spill, killing much of the wildlife in its path. Moreover, the impacts of the spill were not only ecological: many economic hardships, social problems, and psychological difficulties surfaced in Alaskan fishing villages and towns in the aftermath of the spill. Many believe that the damages far outweigh the monetary loss that Exxon and the Exxon Shipping Company suffered as a result of the cases brought against them.

According to Lord, the *Exxon Valdez* oil spill occurred at a critical time, because various planktons were just beginning their annual bloom. In addition, "the reproductive periods for most species of marine life took place while the oil was in its most concentrated and damaging forms" (Lord 1997:103). As a result many animals were killed and many animal populations were harmed.

Alaska's commercial fishing industry, which many Alaskans heavily relied upon for their income, was especially hit hard by the spill. In the salmon fishing industry alone, sixty-five million dollars were lost in 1989 because salmon fishing was closed in oiled areas (M. J. Cohen 1997; Lord 1997).

Confronted by large economic losses, many people experienced emotional problems, which in turn resulted in increased social problems. As Cohen (1997:161) noted, "rates of mental health and alcohol counseling during the post-accident period in two local clinics were significantly higher than those recorded for the pre-oil spill years."

After the spill, attention centered on the legal struggle that ensued between the state of Alaska, the U.S. government, Exxon, the Exxon Shipping Company, the Alyeska Pipeline Service Company, and Captain Joseph Hazelwood. The state of Alaska tried Captain Hazelwood for criminal negligence as well as other charges, but an Anchorage jury acquitted him of all but one minor misdemeanor, which was later reaffirmed on appeal (Piper 1997). The state of Alaska filed suit against both Exxon and the Alyeska Pipeline Service Company for negligent operations and the botched response. Exxon filed a countersuit, claiming "the state interfered with Exxon's ability to do what needed to be done" (Piper 1997:255).

In addition to the cases brought by the state of Alaska and federal government, a large number of claims by commercial fisherman, cannery workers, and some smaller local governments were settled out of court. As a result of these out-of-court settlements, Exxon paid about $130 million (Piper 1997). The final settlement that resulted from the state and federal charges consisted of three parts: the criminal plea agreement, criminal restitution, and the civil settlement.

The criminal plea agreement levied the largest fine ever for an environmental crime, $150 million, on Exxon (*Exxon Valdez* Oil Spill Trustee Council 1999). Of the $150 million, however, $125 million was remitted (that is, forgiven) by the court because of Exxon's "cooperation with the governments during the cleanup, timely payment of many private claims, and environmental precautions taken since the spill" (Piper 1997:259). Of the remaining $25 million, $13 million went to the Victims of Crime Fund and $12 million went to the North American Wetlands Conservation Fund (Piper 1997; *Exxon Valdez* Oil Spill Trustee Council 1999). Under the criminal restitution agreement, Exxon paid $100 million in criminal fines to the federal government, which then passed on $50 million of that sum to the state of Alaska as restitution for damages (Piper 1997).

The civil settlement was much greater, with Exxon agreeing to pay $900 million over ten years. Of this $900 million, up to $72 million could be used to reimburse the state of Alaska for costs incurred during cleanup and up to $62 million could be used to reimburse the federal government (U.S. House

1991b). The $900 million was to be paid to a court-administered trust fund overseen by the *Exxon Valdez* Oil Spill Trustee Council, a panel of six members, and used for restoration projects (Piper 1997).

Many objected to the terms of the settlement. One skeptic was Dennis M. Hertel, a U.S. representative from Michigan. He remarked, "If Exxon hadn't cut this deal, they would have been going to trial next month on felony charges. Instead, they pled guilty to lesser charges while admitting that they were criminally responsible for the largest and most destructive ecological disaster in our Nation's history ... Since payment of damages are scheduled to extend through 2001, and since the settlement failed to account for inflation, Exxon will pay fewer 'real dollars' in future damage payments. In effect, the penalty will lighten with time" (U.S. House 1991b:3).

In 1994 a class-action suit was also brought against Exxon, which, when settled, was to provide more than thirty thousand people with five billion dollars to be split among them. However, because Exxon appealed the suit all the way to the U.S. Supreme Court, the money remained unpaid until 2004, over ten years after the spill. The U.S. Supreme Court ruled against the Exxon Mobil Corporation (Exxon and Mobil Corporations had merged in 1999) and allowed the five-billion-dollar settlement to stand (*New York Law Journal* 2000; Phillips 1996; http://www.exxon.mobil.com/emhistory/index.html).

New legislation also resulted from the *Exxon Valdez* oil spill, the most important of which was the Oil Pollution Act (OPA) of 1990. This act was enacted "to establish limitations on liability for damages resulting from oil pollution, to establish a fund for the payment of compensation for such damages, and for other purposes" (U.S. Coast Guard 2000). Main issues addressed by the OPA of 1990 included an "integrated contingency planning and incorporated industry response plans to enable a systematic approach to response," increased response plan exercises, a "30-fold increase in the trust fund for oil spill response," and a system of strike teams situated nationwide that are prepared with equipment to respond to spills.

In spite of this new legislation, environmental harm, and the large fines levied against Exxon as a result of the *Exxon Valdez* oil spill, problems within the oil industry in general have continued, ranging from oil spills to refusal to obey rules and lax regulation. For example, in November 2000, the *Westchester*, a tanker operated by Ermis Maritime Corporation of Greece, ran aground in the Mississippi River, spilling 567,000 gallons of oil. In January of 2001 the tanker *Jessica*, an Ecuadorian ship, ran aground off the coast of Ecuador's Galápagos Islands, spilling approximately 144,000 gallons of oil into the sea and threatening the sensitive, mostly untouched Galápagos Islands. In March of 2001 a freighter leaked about 300,000 gallons of oil and caused part of Miami Beach to be closed, and in April of 2001 a freighter and tanker collided in the Baltic Sea, causing 764,000 gallons of oil to spill (Olsen 2001).

As noted, under Title II of the Ports and Waterways Safety Act of 1972, Public Law 92-340, the Coast Guard required all tankers constructed after January 1, 1974, "to have a segregated ballast capacity and a double bottom" (U.S. House 1973a:191). Under the OPA of 1990, tankers traveling in U.S. waters are required to meet or exceed double-hull requirements by the year 2015 (U.S. Coast Guard 2000). Despite this legislation, as of July 2005 the Exxon Mobil Corporation continued to use single-hull tankers to transport oil, and over 70 percent of their world fleet remains single-hulled (Harrison 2000).

Of all those involved in the *Exxon Valdez* oil spill, Alyeska was at the top of the list when it came to oversight that led to problems with the cleanup efforts. Alyeska was responsible for faulty welding during pipeline construction (U.S. House 1976), polluting the environment when the company failed to properly construct the required incinerators, and failing to have equipment ready when the spill occurred (Sethi and Steidlmeier 1997). Despite these faults and the subsequent problems associated with the *Exxon Valdez* spill, Alyeska continues to have a lax regulatory environment. In December of 2000, two government reports charged Alyeska "with faulty management oversight in its marine-loading operations" when workers tied cables to anti-sparking equipment on the docks (Carlton 2000). Because problems still exist in the enforcement of regulations, the new legislation was not an effective means to evoke change within the oil shipping industry.

CONCLUSION: BACK TO THE FUTURE?

Oil industry leaders are not the only ones who have failed to implement the lessons that should have been learned from the *Exxon Valdez* spill. In the early years of the twenty-first century, OPEC production cuts, U.S. wars in the Middle East, and rising energy prices in the United States have sparked memories—or perhaps nightmares—of the 1970s energy crisis. U.S. president George W. Bush and other conservatives saw this climate as an ideal political moment to propose opening up more of the Alaskan frontier to oil exploration, promising that this step would reduce foreign reliance on oil. This proposal was not paired with any meaningful efforts to reduce petroleum consumption, which would reduce oil industry profits. U.S. energy secretary Spencer Abraham suggested that the administration would not go "begging the OPEC countries or anybody else" to increase oil production as long as the United States had untapped reserves that could help relieve an energy shortage (Greenberg 2001). In a triumph of this ideology, in March 2005, by a narrow margin, the U.S. Senate passed a rider to a federal budget bill to approve drilling in the Arctic National Wildlife Refuge in Alaska (ANWAR). For over twenty years the oil industry and conservative politicians have fought to open ANWAR to oil exploration, but had always failed in the face of environmental coalition opposition. This time they succeeded in their dream of expanding the exploitation of the Alaskan wilderness for its oil. Given the massive failures that resulted in the *Exxon Valdez* spill, we can only surmise that pumping an additional million barrels of oil per day to the Valdez port without widespread implementation of far more rigorous regulatory controls than presently exist portends future ecological disasters for the region.

In the tradition that has been established for the study of state-corporate crime, as in previous research by Matthews and Kauzlarich (2000:295), our analysis of the *Exxon Valdez* oil spill lends support to the proposition that the intersection of profit motives with a lax regulatory environment is conducive to producing "harmful organizational practices in identifiable ways." When events like the *Exxon Valdez* oil spill are viewed as unpreventable accidents, or what Charles Perrow would call "normal accidents" (Perrow 1999), the practices that contributed to these accidents are likely to be seen as relatively unavoidable, remain largely unquestioned, and most likely continue. Further, in a capitalist society, given the unquestioned privilege assigned to the pursuit of profit, it is easy for corporations and their government regulators to lose sight of the greater good beyond immediate bottom lines, often with devastating results. In contrast, viewing harmful outcomes like the *Valdez* oil spill as the product of wrongful intersections of business and government, that is, as state-corporate crimes, suggests a mandate for changing these practices and behaviors in order to reduce the likelihood of such events being reproduced in the future.

NOTES

1. The use of dispersants became a critical question throughout the response. Dispersants are controversial, because it is not fully understood what their effect can be on the water table; they "do not remove oil from the water; rather, they act like dishwashing detergent, breaking the oil into tiny droplets that descend from the surface down deeper into the water column" (Davidson 1990:40). Because of the controversy surrounding the use of dispersants, Alaska spent several years developing guidelines for their use in the case of an emergency. Dispersants were to be used only when skimming proved to no longer be effective, and there were three zones established for usage. Zone 1 regions were "regions that were far from sensitive shorelines," and in these areas there was standing preapproval for the use of dispersants. Zone 2 regions are regions that are more ecologically sensitive, and the use of dispersants in these regions is decided in a case-by-case basis and requires approval from the state of Alaska and Environmental Protection Agency (EPA). Zone 3 regions are regions "which are in and around resources requiring protection, such as intertidal areas, small coves, and fjords[;] the use of dispersants is not recommended at all" in these areas but is subject to approval by the state and the EPA (Davidson 1990:42).
2. The Alyeska member companies are Amerada Hess Corporation, ARCO Pipeline Company, BP Pipeline Corporation, Mobil Pipeline Company, Phillips Petroleum Company, Humble Pipeline Company, and Union Oil Company of California (U.S. House 1973b).
3. The U.S. Coast Guard Authorization Act of 1978 authorized $1,252,321,000 for the years 1978 and 1979 (U.S. Senate 1977:1). The U.S. Coast Guard Authorization Act of 1983 and 1984 allocated $1,700,000,000 for fiscal year 1983 and $2,000,000,000 for fiscal year 1984 (U.S. Senate 1982:1), as compared with 1988 allocations of $2,006,000,000 (U.S. House 1987:1). When increased duties and inflation are accounted for, such small increases in appropriations are insufficient.

CHAPTER 11

Enron-Era Economics versus Economic Democracy

Raymond J. Michalowski and Ronald C. Kramer

THROUGHOUT THE 1990s, a number of high-profile corporations such as Enron, WorldCom, Tyco, and many others engaged in "pump and dump" schemes involving creative—and often illegal—accounting practices designed to inflate the value of corporate stock (Tillman and Indergaard 2005). The economic house of cards these companies built on questionable earnings reports, however, began to collapse when Enron Corporation, the poster-child for the new economy and a leading practitioner of creative accounting, imploded under the weight of its stock manipulation schemes.

From 1997 through 2001, Enron had regularly posted spectacular earnings, for which it reaped skyrocketing stock values. On October 16, 2001, however, the financial balloon that had taken Enron to great heights burst when the company reported the first of two major restatements of earnings. These restatements revealed that Enron's reported profits were not the rewards of innovation and efficiency. They were the ill-gotten gains from gaming the stock market in ethically marginal, and frequently illegal, ways (Fox 2002; Fusaro and Miller 2002). By December, its image as a paragon of the "new economy" shattered, Enron filed the largest bankruptcy in U.S. history (Fox 2002). Within six months, over two hundred Fortune 500 companies would file similar restatements of earnings. Some, like Global Crossing, would follow Enron into bankruptcy; others suffered plummeting stock values. The era of Enron economics had come to an end, and with this ending came a new opening to reconsider how state-corporate crime is an intimate expression of the ethical frameworks that inform American capitalism.

In our view, the Enron-era scandals were particularly egregious cases of state-facilitated corporate crime. Yet as McLean and Elkind (2004) point out in their book *The Smartest Guys in the Room: The Amazing Rise and Fall of*

Enron, even in the aftermath of one of the largest corporate scandals in history, few of the people involved were willing to admit that they had done anything wrong. No one seemed to be sorry and after-the-fact rationalizations were widespread. McLean and Elkind (2004:406) go on to argue that "the larger message was that the wealth and power enjoyed by those at the top of the heap in corporate America—accountants, bankers, executives, lawyers, and members of corporate boards—demand no sense of broader responsibility." And such a demand was certainly not forthcoming from the administration of President George W. Bush or from many in the Congress.

In this chapter we suggest that the Enron case provides the occasion for serious and widespread rethinking of the purpose of corporations, the ethics that guide their relationship to the wider society, and the role of the state in guiding corporations toward a new ethic of inclusion. The current economic system, as the Enron case reveals, is fraught with unnecessary risks for both corporations and the citizens whose lives are so dependent upon them. Without a thorough reconsideration of the corporate role in society and the corporate-state relationship, however, the risks revealed by the Enron scandal and other recent cases of corporate wrongdoing will be lost to historical amnesia, just as have so many other similar moments in modern economic history. We begin our reconsideration of the corporate role in society with the following proposition: the ethics of *exclusion* on which the current form of corporate organization is founded must be replaced with a practical economic democracy based on ethics of inclusion, which recognize that the pursuit of social justice ought be the primary purpose of both corporations and the governments that authorize them.[1]

This proposal is not a condemnation of the corporate form in toto. Even capitalism's most pointed critic, Karl Marx, recognized the stock corporation as a powerful engine for organizing economic energy. The historical record shows that much of the economic and social progress that accompanied industrialization was made possible by the ability of stock corporations to pursue large-scale development by both pooling economic resources and reducing economic risk (Sklar [1988] 1991). Nor do we mean to suggest that corporate managers are the cause of the problem. Our analysis of the behavior of corporate leaders is guided not by the conservative ideology of individualism but by organizational theory that recognizes that the majority of good and bad choices made by corporate managers reflect institutional forces operating inside and structural forces operating outside the firm, rather than just their personal moral choices (Clinard and Yeager 1980; Kramer 1984). It is this organizational perspective that leads us to the conclusion that strategies for avoiding a future filled with corporate-caused human suffering must give at least as much attention to reforming corporate structures as it does to reforming those who inhabit them.[2]

THE PROBLEM: CORPORATE DOMINATION
AND NEOLIBERAL POLICY

The current trajectory of corporate concentration and centralization is generating increasingly sharp economic and social class inequalities (Greider 1997; Hertz 2001; Wolff 1995). This is not necessarily the intention of those who operate today's global corporations. Yet it is, nevertheless, the collective consequence of their individual endeavors to ensure corporate survivability and growth through maximization of profits and stock value in an increasingly globalized economy. Does this mean we are doomed to a future of increasingly stark gaps between the haves and have-nots both within and among nations, with all of the attendant social problems, unrest, and conflict such inequalities inevitably create? Or are there other ways to build an economic future for the global economy and the nations within it?

Barring serious social cataclysm, it is likely that ever-larger global corporations will continue to be the dominant form of economic organization for the foreseeable future. Given the likely longevity of the corporate form, we suggest there is a growing need to restore the corporation to its proper place in society. Specifically, the for-profit corporation must be recognized as a socially constructed form of economic organization, authorized by governments, for the purpose of maximizing human welfare. The current form of the corporation and the "rights" it claims are neither inherent nor inevitable. The corporate form is neither more nor less than the accumulation of social, political, and legal choices that have been made—or so it is claimed—for the benefit of society. These choices can also be unmade or altered when they fail to provide those promised benefits, or when those benefits can be provided in less destructive ways.

As Toombs and Whyte (2003) note, defenders of the status-quo economic order frequently argue that "there is no alternative" to the current form of business practice. Such claims, however, are not statements of fact. They are rhetorical moves designed to foreclose serious consideration of how corporations might produce and distribute material and social well-being in less destructive and more socially just ways. At times what is good for a corporation *is* good for society. At other times what is good for corporations is harmful for the human and natural environment. Instead of claims that there are no alternatives to the present relationship between corporations, the state, and society, what is needed is careful consideration of which elements and practices of the current corporate form produce genuine social welfare and which do not.

The need to reconstitute the corporate form so it serves human needs, rather than having humans serve only corporation needs, arises from significant political-economic changes during the last quarter century. The 1980s ushered in a new era of centralization, concentration, and globalization of

Depression," growing at "half the rate that they had achieved during the previous two decades" (Weisbrot 2002:27). The answer to how good people can tolerate such outcomes lies in the way ethics of exclusion provide frameworks governing when and where ethical mandates are presumed to be operative.

Ethics of exclusion are beliefs and practices that facilitate the creation of boundaries around our community of responsibility (Diaz 2001). By "community of responsibility" we mean those whose well-being we believe we must take into account when selecting a course of action. In some cases, ethics of exclusion foster exceptionally narrow boundaries limited to oneself and one's immediate family or clan. More typically, the boundaries drawn by ethics of exclusion are somewhat broader. These may extend beyond one's immediate relations, perhaps to all the middle-class people in my neighborhood, or to the members of my ethnic group, or to "people like me" in general.[4] But in all cases, ethics of exclusion encourage us to see the great majority of the human species as outside our community of moral obligation, thereby freeing us—consciously or unconsciously—from a sense of responsibility for the consequences our actions may visit upon them.

By design, corporations are instruments for drawing ownership boundaries, and as such they are well suited in their present form for practicing ethics of exclusion. Corporations comprise sets of boundaries governing to whom corporations owe legal and moral obligations. These boundaries define a group of insiders for whom the corporation is responsible, and a group of outsiders whose well-being is beyond the formal responsibility of the corporation.[5] This vision of the corporation is rooted in a set of highly exclusionary nineteenth-century laws and practices that limited the moral community of corporations to their "owners," that is, to their stockholders (Kelly 2001).

As just noted, the boundaries created by ethics of exclusion can be drawn more or less narrowly. Historically, the U.S. corporate form has encountered periodic challenges to its tendency to promote narrow moral boundaries. By law and custom, the early-nineteenth-century stock corporation had few obligations other than to stockholders and managers. The industrial safety movement of the late nineteenth century and the successful social movement for unionization during the Great Depression of 1929–1942 forced a reluctant expansion of corporate moral boundaries to include a limited responsibility for the well-being of workers. The need for revenue and military machinery during World Wars I and II inserted the nation-state and its tax base inside the moral boundaries of the twentieth-century corporation. The post–World War II era of capital-labor accords and welfare-state policies further increased the scope of corporate obligations by creating conditions through which corporations would share a portion of productivity-related profit growth with workers, through indexed wages and benefits, and with society in general, through progressive taxation. In the last decades of the century, movements for equal employment opportunities and environmental protection made some headway in defining women, minorities, and the ecosystem as part of the moral community of corporations.

Although the moral community of the corporation experienced significant (and often forced) expansion during much of the twentieth century, the core political-economic theme since the "Reagan revolution" that began in the 1980s has been focused on reconstituting a narrower corporate moral topography that more closely resembles the nineteenth-century corporation. This is what Ronald Reagan meant when he promised that he would "get government off the back of corporate America" (Manheim 2000:7). Reagan was promising to reduce the range of stakeholders empowered to define the meaning of responsible corporate behavior. The Reagan administration and the laissez-faire movement of which it was a part achieved spectacular success in promoting ethics of exclusion. By the end of the twentieth century, this movement had achieved a significant retrenchment of the boundaries that define the corporate community of responsibility. And it was this retrenchment—including a now deeply ingrained governmental reluctance to closely scrutinize how corporations become profitable—that made 1990s era of corporate "pump and dump" scandals behavior possible.

The Ethics of Inclusion

As a result of history and practice, business corporations have a strong tendency to operate according to ethics of exclusion that promote narrow moral boundaries. If we are to move beyond the current crisis of corporate morality, we need to explore how it might be possible for corporations to begin to adopt ethics of inclusion. Ethics of inclusion are beliefs and practices that promote the idea that our community of responsibility extends to all those who might be affected by our actions, our choices and our intentions (Diaz 2001). Ethics of inclusion encourage us to see larger portions of the human species as belonging to our community of moral obligation. The more that ethics of inclusion guide corporate practices, the more corporate boundaries will encompass stakeholders beyond the traditional focus on stockholders.

To move corporations toward the adoption of ethics of inclusion will require us to confront a number of significant cultural and structural obstacles. Under the current corporate form, moral boundaries are defined by a combination of profit potential and law, not the personal morality of corporate leaders. As economic institutions, corporations have little incentive to serve the well-being of any moral community unless doing so either serves the interest of its small society of "owners" or is mandated by government. We are not suggesting that corporations never consider the needs of other stakeholders. Corporations will often consider the needs of workers in times of labor shortage or when meeting these needs will increase worker productivity. Similarly, corporate philanthropy is often used to earn public "goodwill" or to increase corporate name recognition in ways that will ultimately improve corporate revenues. Corporations will also respond to the appeals for socially responsible behavior where they find that they can "do well by doing good." Thus, for instance, many modern corporations have adopted "green" recycling strategies because they have proved to be cost effective. The problem is that, in their current form, corporations have little structural motivation to expand their moral horizons without either government compulsion or perceived economic benefit.

We are not suggesting that corporate managers are inherently unconcerned with broader issues of human social welfare. Rather, we contend that the structure of capitalist competition makes it foolhardy, if not fatal, for any corporation to undertake profit-reducing extensions of moral obligations unless mandated to do so by laws, which, if enforced uniformly, will ensure that no company suffers a competitive disadvantage by behaving responsibly. Thus certain features of the current political economy must be restructured if corporations are ever to move toward ethics of inclusion.

THE DOCTRINE OF SHAREHOLDER VALUE AND THE DEREGULATION MOVEMENT

Two features of the current political economy of corporate capitalism that stand as obstacles to the movement toward ethics of inclusion are the legal doctrine of shareholder primacy and the weakened government regulatory structure. Both must be significantly restructured if corporate moral boundaries are to be expanded and corporate harms reduced.

As we noted above, since the nineteenth century by law and custom the corporation has limited its moral boundaries to its stockholders. Despite a variety of twentieth-century social movements for greater corporate social responsibility, the prevailing cultural view as espoused by Milton Friedman and other gurus of neoliberal economics is that the only real obligation a corporation has is to make as much money for its stockholders as possible (Cassidy 2002). This perspective is sustained and reinforced by legal obligation. Various writers have recently pointed out that corporate law as enforced by state courts requires that corporations maximize returns for stockholders (Greider 2002b; Hinckley 2002; Kelly 2002; Mitchell 2001). As Marjorie Kelly, editor and founder of *Business Ethics* magazine and a central figure in the corporate social responsibility movement, notes; "when we speak of a corporation doing well we mean that its shareholders did well. The company's local community might be devastated by plant closings. Employees might be shouldering a crushing workload. Still we will say, 'The corporation did well' " (Kelly 2002:2).

The legal doctrine and cultural weight of shareholder primacy was significantly reinforced by a wave of takeovers and "whitemail" in the 1970s.[6] The threat of hostile takeovers prompted many corporate managers and major investors to see increasing share value (along with increasing corporate debt-revenue ratio) as an important shield against having the corporation deemed to be "undervalued" and therefore ripe for a leveraged takeover (Levitt 2002). At the same time a "shareholder rebellion" emerged with the goal of linking the interests of corporate managers more closely to those of stockholders. A central strategy of this movement was increasing the use of stock options as a part of compensation packages for corporate managers. The consequence was that growth in stock value came to be seen, by both managers and stockholders, as the primary goal of corporations and the key measure of managerial success. This created both motivations and methods among corporate managers to make gaming the stock market an important operational goal (see Fox 2002; Fusaro and Miller 2002; Greider 2002b; Kelly 2003; K. Phillips 2002; Tillman and Indergaard, 2005).

The widespread practice of gaming the market to increase stock value cannot be explained as the idiosyncratic behavior of greedy and corrupt executives, as the Bush administration and conservative pundits contend. In the first six months of 2002 alone, 112 companies issued financial restatements because they had engaged in Enron-like accounting practices designed to maximize stock price (Sloan and Roberts 2002:28).[7] Organizational deviance on this scale can only be explained by institutional pressures, the central one being the doctrine of stockholder primacy. Thus we agree with William Greider, one of the more trenchant social analysts of economic practices in recent years, when he says that "the 'shareholder value' doctrine" must be replaced with "a broader understanding of the corporation's purpose, its obligations to the other constituencies like employees, communities, and society at large, and their right to be heard on major policy decisions" (Greider 2002a:14).

The second major obstacle to the adoption of ethics of inclusion by business corporations is the success of the laissez-faire movement in weakening state and federal regulatory systems. Neoliberalism is the view that the best—some would say the "only"—way to provide for economic growth and ameliorate societal problems both domestically and worldwide is to allow economic markets to operate free of governmental or community regulation that would interfere with private profit-making in those markets. This market fundamentalism repudiated one of the central tenets of the New Deal—learned through the hard experience of the Great Depression—that markets cannot be trusted to regulate themselves and that one of the fundamental roles of government is to keep capitalism efficient and honest.

Neoliberalism came to dominate the thinking of political elites in the United States starting in the late 1970s, and it resulted in a full-scale assault on the federal regulatory system in the 1980s and 1990s. In particular during these years we witnessed the systematic dismantling of financial regulation that enabled the economy to revert to a laissez-faire system more reminiscent of the nineteenth century than an extension of the twentieth. This financial deregulation led directly to the state-facilitated corporate crimes of the Enron era, as Robert Kuttner (2002:24) points out in a passage worth quoting at length:

> If the regulation of options-trading and electricity had not been undermined, Enron would have had to make its money in the old-fashioned way: selling real products and services and reporting honest earnings. If the Glass-Stegall Act had not been gutted by regulatory indulgence and then formally repealed, banks could not have enriched themselves by making profit-sharing deals with dishonest partners such as Enron. If the Congress and the SEC had not undercut the regulation of accountants, corporate books could not have been cooked to artificially inflate profits. If SEC oversight had held corporate directors personally accountable for their decisions and their lapses, corporate boards would never have approved many rotten deals. If stock options had been more tightly regulated, insiders would not have had an incentive to artificially pump up share prices in order to cash them in.

Nevertheless, revelations of and prosecutions for pump and dump schemes produced little political will to institute a serious system of accounting oversight. Instead, the accounting industry managed to control the process of appointing a director to the accounting oversight board established by the Sarbanes-Oxley Act, and the U.S. House of Representatives was unwilling to fund the $338 million-dollar increase in the SEC's budget called for by this act (Weisman 2002:25). This lack of political will to establish a firm regulatory climate is a crucial element in creating the conditions for a continuation of Enron-like state-corporate crime.

The combination of performance pressure to maximize profits and stock value under the doctrine of shareholder primacy, along with the absence of normative controls due to the dismantlement of the federal regulatory system, has resulted in a climate consistent with what criminologists Steven Messner and Richard Rosenfeld (2001) term "institutional anomie." In the corporate context, institutional anomie arises when there is a gap between the goals of a corporation and the means available to achieve them. Thus if an intense emphasis on maximization of profits and stock value is combined with relatively weak controls in the form of regulatory laws or other institutional counterbalances, those striving to achieve the culturally defined success goals will experience anomie, that is, a state of normlessness. Under these conditions, corporate managers will become more likely to employ legally and ethically questionable strategies to achieve their corporate success goals. To put it in the language of corporate ethics, given the current form of the corporation, institutional anomie strengthens exclusionary corporate moral boundaries and weakens inclusionary ones.

TOWARD ECONOMIC DEMOCRACY

If institutional anomie is the product of intensified success goals combined with weakened controls, then the route to a less anomic corporate form is through redefining the success goals and creating a more effective regulatory climate. We suggest that redefining corporations as partners in building economic democracy rather than as exclusively profit-making entities will create less destructive and more socially responsible corporate forms. Combined with an attentive and well-funded regulatory structure, this change of vision can help reverse the harms done by corporations acting as independent, exclusionary entities with few obligations to the wider world within which they are permitted to operate.

We suggest the following key principles as the basis for genuine economic democracy.

First, corporations are politically authorized public entities. Thus the corporate form is both an appropriate topic for public debate and rightfully subject to change through the legitimate exercise of political power.

Second, as social and political constructions, corporations are not persons and should not be granted constitutional rights as natural persons despite legal opinions to the contrary. In his book *Unequal Protection: The Rise of Corporate Dominance and the Theft of Human Rights* (2002), Thom Hartmann not only criticizes the idea of corporate personhood and corporate rights but demonstrates that these ideas are a legal fiction that arose through an error in the casebook headnote for the 1886 *Santa Clara County v. Southern Pacific Railroad* decision by the U.S. Supreme Court. Thus the rights of natural persons should prevail over alleged rights of corporations.

Third, in a world dominated by global capitalism, corporate actions affect the well-being of employees and communities of location more than those of any other entity, including governments. Thus the rights of employees and communities affected by corporate actions must be understood as equivalent to the financial rights of stockholders in those corporations.

Four, because corporations control the most significant production and distribution system in contemporary societies, they must be understood as having broad responsibilities to foster general social welfare.

Five, corporations are human communities. As such, they are best governed through democratic processes, operating both inside and outside the firm (Kelly 2002:15).

While these principles provide a general framework for replacing the current exclusionary corporate form with a more inclusive economic democracy, like all broad frameworks they also require specific strategies for implementation.

The development and deployment of actual strategies to advance economic democracy can only result from widespread public debate and concerted political action. Thus we cannot specify here the exact corporate form that would be compatible with economic democracy everywhere, and we recognize that the specificity of such forms would need to vary from culture to culture. We can, however, offer some general stratagems (some of which were first offered by Christopher Stone over thirty years ago) that we feel are necessary to make corporations partners in creating economic democracy for the twenty-first century. The first four deal with the corporate structure itself, while the last two involve the creation of effective systems of external control.

First, the current form of stockholder corporations governed through highly interlocked systems of financial directorates must be replaced by stakeholder corporations governed by boards of directors comprising of a balanced representation of stakeholders. At a minimum these "general public directorships" would include representatives of employees, communities of location, and the operating ecosystem (Stone 1975).

Second, boards of directors should be elected, with 50 percent chosen by stockholders and 50 percent selected by stakeholder groups.

Third, membership on a board of directors should be full-time, paid employment with specified functions and special powers to enable them to engage in a full-time analysis of corporate operations (Stone 1975). In addition, no person should serve on more than one corporate board at a time.

Fourth, one of the responsibilities of stakeholder members of corporate boards should be to ensure that the development plans and financial strategies of corporations are rendered wholly transparent to the corporation's expanded community of moral obligation, which includes employees, community, and environment (Stone 1975). This transparency will create the conditions for broad and open public discourse and public input into corporate decisions and practices, further democratizing the process of corporate decision making.

Fifth, citizens should be empowered to challenge corporate actions under civil law if corporations cause direct injury or act in a socially irresponsible manner. This would involve two strategies. One is the protection, rather than the curtailment, of existing legal rights of individuals to sue under civil law for substantive and punitive damages for injuries caused by corporate wrongdoing (Nader and Smith 1996). As Greider (2002b) points out, the trial lawyers who help bring these suits seem to be the only successful corporate reformers who are able to consistently win significant public interest victories over powerful business interests. He goes on to suggest that "conceivably, their influence could help revive serious arguments about the nature of the corporation and of financial markets, making public space for fundamental critiques of the system that for many decades have been confined to academic conferences or kitchen-table conversations about who runs America" (Greider 2002b:12).

The other strategy to empower citizens to challenge power through civil law would be the creation of legally binding codes of corporate responsibility. One such code is Robert Hinckley's Model Code of Corporate Citizenship, which would enable citizens to sue corporations in state courts for acting in ways that harm the environment, human rights, the dignity of employees, public health, or the safety of communities in which they operate (Hinckley 2002). To make these strategies truly effective, however, the legal fiction of corporate personhood and corporate rights would need to be replaced with a vision of corporations as human creations subservient to the rights and needs of human persons (Hartmann 2002).

Sixth, specific forms of corporate activity (for example, financial, environmental, and commercial) should be scrutinized by professionally staffed state and federal regulatory agencies whose employees and leaders are chosen through civil service procedures, not through appointment by elected officials. This modest step would help reduce the level of "regulatory capture" that has turned many agencies into advocates for, rather than regulators of, the industries covered in their portfolio (Ayres and Braithwaite 1991). Reducing regulatory capture, reversing deregulation, and strengthening the reach of regulatory controls will be vital in the struggle to prevent future manipulations of financial and stock markets. As John Braithwaite and Peter Drahos (2000:629) note, "when the strong have wanted regulation, very often it has been to protect their monopoly; when they have wanted deregulation it has been to save them paying for the burdens they inflict on ordinary citizens. Consequently, most citizens of the world . . . rightly want the opposite: deregulation of monopoly privilege and strengthened regulation to protect the community from the abuse of corporate power. The struggle for the sovereignty of citizens is an uphill battle to effect that reversal."

CONCLUSION

Despite the enormous impact of the state-facilitated corporate pump and dump crimes, the idea that we could (or should) re-create business corporations as partners in the project of creating an economic democracy guided by ethics of inclusion will be seen as fanciful by those faced with immediate obligations to increase the corporate bottom line. Such a transformation would certainly involve social change on a grand scale, and it would be neither quick nor painless. Rather, it would take a concerted campaign to create solidarity rather than antagonism between corporations and all those stakeholders whose lives these corporations now control. We suggest, however, that far from being fanciful and unrealistic, such a significant restructuring of corporate purpose is the only hope we have to avoid not only many more state-facilitated corporate tragedies in the future but a globe plagued by a devastating growth in economic disparity and the attendant wars and terrorism such a world is likely to breed.

NOTES

Updated, adapted, and revised from Raymond Michalowski, "Beyond Enron: Exclusion, Inclusions, and the Ethics of Corporate Responsibility," paper presented to the Center for Social Ethics, Western Michigan University, November 2002.

1. I want to thank Dr. Elena Diaz of Facultad Latino Americana Ciencas Sociales (FLACSO) at the University of Havana for introducing me to the dichotomy between ethics of inclusion and exclusion, through both her years of example and her 2001 paper "Inclusion and Exclusion in Cuba."—R.M.

2. Full consideration of the theoretical debates surrounding how organizations can be said to be something more than agglomerations of the individual choices of their members is beyond the scope of this chapter. It is widely accepted in sociology and economics, however, that the culture and institutional framework of a corporation can increase or decrease the likelihood that individuals operating within them will treat the law with scrupulous respect, calculating manipulation, or outright disrespect.

3. We do make a distinction here between levels of consumption necessary for health and human dignity and consumption that is above and beyond these basic needs. Thus while we are critical of expanding material consumption in developed nations, we also support economic development to achieve basic levels of health and human dignity in the less-developed areas of the world.

4. Although modern nation-states frequently utilize an inclusive rhetoric that suggests all members of a nation bear common ethical responsibilities toward one another, actual practices typically differentiate among those who are full beneficiaries of the best the nation-state has to offer and others who are treated as though they are not part of the general moral community.

5. Corporations will sometimes flex these boundaries through charitable or philanthropic donations. These, however, are voluntary acts, and do not arise from any sense of formal obligation. As corporations become larger and more global, their charitable and philanthropic giving tends to become a smaller proportion of their wealth.

6. "Whitemail" occurs when a corporation agrees to buy back a significant portion of its stock from takeover artists at inflated prices in order to get them to withdraw their takeover bids.

7. Although there are over thirty thousand registered corporations in the United States, a mere two hundred control over 80 percent of American market share (Korten 1995:23). Insofar as the majority of those corporations filing financial restatements in the aftermath of the Enron collapse are among the largest in the country, this suggests that Enron-like financial manipulations have blanketed the bulk of economic activity in corporate America.

CHAPTER 12

Violations of Treaty Rights

Linda Robyn

There can be no moral agreement with injustice, even though one may agree voluntarily to what is unjust.

Winston A. Van Horne (1991:vii)

SINCE THE FOUNDING OF THE UNITED STATES, the question of land and land ownership has played a central role in economic and political processes. Those who control the land are in control of the fundamental resources for human survival and societal growth. Land ownership, social control, and all the other aggregate components of power are fundamentally interrelated (Churchill and LaDuke 1992). The creation of treaties between the United States government and American Indian tribes was the primary method used by the United States government to acquire "legal" title to the lands formerly inhabited by American Indians. In this chapter I examine Indian relocation through treaties as a state crime and the violation of those same treaty rights to benefit corporate interests as a form of state-corporate crime.

BACKGROUND

In 1778 President George Washington negotiated the first treaty with the Delaware Indians; it essentially established a legal-political relationship with all Indian tribes in the United States. Over the next hundred years, more than six hundred treaties and agreements were made with native tribes and nations of North America. Every one of these agreements was, at some point, broken (Deloria and Lytle 1983). As Van Every has noted, "the interminable history of diplomatic relations between Indians and white men had before 1832 recorded no single instance of a treaty that had not been presently broken by the white parties to it ... however solemnly embellished with such terms as 'permanent,' 'forever,' 'for all time,' 'so long as the sun shall rise' " (quoted in Zinn [1980] 2003:142).

These treaties, and those that followed, were designed to ensure peaceful relations with the Indian tribes, a claim that appears to be innocent enough. However, treaties were also the mechanism that was used to secure a peaceful transfer of land ownership from the tribes to the United States government (Deloria and Lytle 1983). These vast areas of land were considered unowned, underutilized, and open to exploitation. The transfer of land meant that Indian tribes would have to live somewhere else, and the best way to achieve this was to move most American Indian people to reservations set aside for them by the U.S. government. Indian people and the regions in which they lived were shaped and changed forever through these land transfers. These land transfers, in and of themselves, would advance the economic interests of the state and certain multinational corporations. But eventually, these powerful state-corporate entities would also come to realize that even on the set-aside reservations, American Indians were sitting on resources the rest of the world wanted, and wanted at the lowest possible cost.

This history between Europeans and American Indians has led to the perception that indigenous people are an exploitable, disposable resource. Many American Indians have been forced to live within a nation whose mainstream culture is so different from their own that they have had to abandon or distort their culture in order to survive. Sometimes they are successful, but all too often they suffer from the consequences of economic extortion and dependence on the white culture.

Through treaties with the United States, many Indian tribes were victimized into giving up their lands, or allowing the use or development of their lands, in return for economic relief. More times than not, this economic relief has led to the failure of capitalism to work to the advantage of many Indian tribes and has led to other problems, such as alcohol and drug abuse. Until recently, many tribes were politically weak and physically isolated. Most of their power had been stripped away, making resistance to state and corporate greed by indigenous people relatively ineffective.

INDIAN REMOVAL

One of the images of government is that it is there to protect every citizen from crime and wrongdoing. With regard to American Indians, however, that has not always been the case. Most history books read by children do not portray the United States government as being the perpetrator of serious crimes, involving physical harm to people, loss of total sovereignty, and the economic devastation of hundreds of Indian tribes. However, these crimes were inherent in the very first treaty and all those that followed. These crimes, committed by officials acting for the state, have been renamed; and have been politely called "Indian removal." Indian people, also known as obstacles to progress, were not needed and could be dealt with by sheer force, occasionally glossed by language such as "paternalism" and "relocation" preceding the burning of villages (Zinn [1980] 2003:123).

Zinn ([1980] 2003) points out that the outcome of treaties, or Indian removal, cleared the land for white occupancy between the Appalachians and the Mississippi, to grow cotton in the South and grain in the North, for expansion, immigration, canals, railroads, new cities, and the building of a large continental empire across to the Pacific Ocean. The cost in human life cannot be accurately measured, in suffering not even roughly measured, but yet U.S. children read a different history. Most of them grow up not realizing that their history is a social construction always written by the winners, and that their history books have left out the important facts that in the quest for resource acquisition and profit maximization, some of the most powerful institutions in the industrial global economy have been defined by genocide, social hierarchy, and out-of-control technology. The results of nonrenewable resource addiction, life-threatening pollution, massive habitat destruction, endless material growth, dominance of indigenous peoples by powerful institutions, and the suppression of indigenous knowledge are social harms that ultimately hurt us all.

BEFORE TREATIES

In reality, thousands of generations of peoples indigenous to the western hemisphere lived out their lives, practiced their cultures, and perpetuated their societies through time. These societies were rich and diversified and universally marked by being natural in the sense that they lived in relative harmony with nature and the natural environment. When the Europeans arrived, they proclaimed the land a wilderness needing to be brought under human control. The settlers relied on the land and its riches to provide life. In the same manner, while defining the Indian as savage, the framers of the U.S. constitution borrowed the form of the Iroquois Confederacy to organize the new U.S. government. Farming methods of the Pequot, Pennobscott, Passamaquoddy and Wampanoag were adopted as the basis of the new settlers' agriculture. In order to meet the needs of a new and growing country, the best way for settlers to subsume the wilderness and the Indian into their own culture was to form treaties.

Interestingly, Canassatego, one of the Haudenosaunee leaders, first suggested during a meeting between colonists and British officials in 1744 that the thirteenth English colonies be organized into a federation similar to that created by his own people. Ideas drawn from Greece and Rome and, thinkers such as Voltaire and Rousseau were intermingled with those of the Iroquois, resulting in a blending of Haudenosaunee libertarianism within its Euro-American counterpart (Jaimes 1992). Various founding fathers of the United States, such as Benjamin Franklin, Tom Paine, John Adams, and Thomas Jefferson acknowledged in their personal papers that in their pursuit to establish the first modern republic much of their visionary inspiration came from the Haudenosaunee. (Jaimes 1992).

WHAT TREATIES ARE ABOUT

Treaties are legally binding agreements made between two nations, and they are powerful documents because they are recognized in the U.S. Constitution as being the supreme law of the land. As legally binding agreements, they are respected within the framework of federal law, and federal courts have therefore upheld treaty rights of tribes in many significant court decisions across the nation (Great Lakes Indian Fish and Wildlife Commission 1993). The U.S. government, however, has yet to keep even one treaty agreement made with Indian tribes despite the fact that over four hundred such treaties and agreements have been entered into (Deloria 1989).

Indian Governance before Treaties

That North America's indigenous societies traditionally organized themselves into tribes ruled by chiefs is a common misperception. An examination of the Five (later Six) Nations Iroquois Confederacy dispels this fallacy. Jaimes (1992) points out that the Iroquois Confederacy, or the Haudenosaunee, was located in present-day New York State and southeastern Canada and was based on the Kaianerekowa (Great Law of Peace) brought about by Deganwida three centuries before Columbus. This method of governance may have been the first functioning model of real democracy and a precursor to the modern-day aspirations for international harmony expressed through the United Nations (Jaimes 1992).

The Haudenosaunee were living under a highly effective form of representative government for hundreds of years while even the most sophisticated European nation-states were still plagued with the belief in the divine rights of kings. And in contrast to bias against females displayed by European nations to this day, the Haudenosaunee created gender balance by vesting all power to select delegate government officials in women. This gender balance carried over to other socioeconomic areas such as property relations, age-based organizational mandates, and the matrilineal/matrilocal nature of kinship bonding (Jaimes 1992).

The Iroquois Confederacy did not use this form of government because they were a small, backwoods, and powerless people. On the contrary, records show that they were accomplished diplomats, entering on an even footing into the bilateral agreements with European powers. The Iroquois Confederacy held the balance of military power in their area for almost two hundred years after first contact with Europeans, and they were instrumental in tipping the scales of victory to Great Britain during the French and Indian Wars (Jaimes 1992).

The Creek Confederacy is another example of successful indigenous governance. Beginning around 1350, the Creek Confederacy, in what are now the southern states of Georgia, Florida, and Alabama, also adopted an elected council structure of governance. They too were successful in dealing with high-level diplomacy over an extended period with European nation-states. Other examples exist that might be used to illustrate the political effectiveness of indigenous peoples on the North American continent before contact with Europeans. During its westward expansion, the U.S. government formally recognized the pre-existing full national sovereignty of many native peoples at least 371 times between 1778 and 1871 (Jaimes 1992).

Disease as a Political Tool

Because the U.S. government could not totally eradicate the continent's indigenous population through warfare or disease, treaties became the vehicle through which Indian people could be removed from their lands. But disease played a part. Contrary to popular beliefs, the Europeans were well versed in the practice of spreading disease and had been doing so since 1385 (Churchill 1997). Even though early efforts at biological warfare were often unsuccessful, military leadership of the Old World had learned the rudimentary mechanics of epidemiology well before 1492.

Churchill (1997) notes that in North America, many episodes of epidemics and pandemics killed scores of native populations. Often these epidemics were very convenient for those who had set out to conquer or eradicate these peoples; the first occurrence was in 1636 (Churchill 1997). The Narragansetts believed that Captain John Oldham, officer for the Massachusetts Colony, had deliberately infected them with smallpox in 1633, probably by dispensing contaminated "gifts," causing an epidemic that claimed the lives of more than seven hundred of their people and allies. Oldham was brought before the council of Narragansett sachems on Block Island, tried for this offense, and executed (Churchill 1997).

This was by no means a singular incident, and from 1513 until the turn of the twentieth century approximately 99 percent of the continent's indigenous population was eradicated. As of 1900 the U.S. Bureau of Census reported barely over 237,000 native people surviving within the country's claimed boundaries, and the Smithsonian Institution reported less than a third of a million for all of North America including Greenland (Thornton 1987). Thornton (1987) argues that the aboriginal population of the western hemisphere circa 1492 numbered at least seventy-two million and probably slightly more. By falsifying and minimizing estimates of how many people there actually were, the extent of the native population reduction seemed much less severe than it had actually been (Thornton 1987).

of the United States, to join the present confederation, and to form a state whereof the Delaware nation shall be the head, and have a representation in Congress: Provided, nothing contained in this article to be considered as conclusive until it meets with the approbation of Congress.

In order to manipulate the Delawares into aiding the colonists during the Revolution, the United States held out equality and statehood to them and any other tribes from whom they could gain support. But ultimately the promises made to the Delawares and others were forgotten in the rush to steal their land (Deloria 1989).

There are countless examples of Indian nations entering into various peaceful compromises with the United States in order to be considered their equal. The United States guaranteed tribes peaceful enjoyment of their lands and has broken that promise over and over again. When treaties were first made, tribes could punish whites entering their lands in violation of treaty provisions. But punishment of whites became the purview of the army, and shortly after that the government gave up all pretense of enforcing provisions set out in the treaties. However, many years would pass before the tribes were "shocked into awareness that the United States had silently taken absolute power over their lands and lives" (Deloria 1989:37). Deloria (1989:37) observes that not only was it a shock, "but a breach of common decency when Congress decided that it had absolute power over the once-powerful tribes."

VIOLATIONS OF TREATIES AS STATE-CORPORATE CRIME

In addition to the state crime of coercively and deceptively using treaties to remove Indian tribes from lands desired by whites, American governments (state and federal) have also violated the treaties themselves in order to advance the economic interests of large corporations. These violations have most often occurred when multinational corporations desire to extract scarce resources from Indian reservations. The use of state power, in violation of treaty rights, to assist in the corporate plunder of Indian lands is a type of state-corporate crime.

These state-corporate crimes take several forms. Sometimes the government attempts to eliminate those who would protest and call attention to the violation of treaty rights. The case of American Indian Movement leader Leonard Peltier provides an example. The American Indian Movement was instrumental during the 1970s in siding with traditional Lakota Sioux people who were trying to keep their corrupt tribal chairman from leasing away tribal lands to the U.S. government and various multinational corporations for strip-mining operations. In an effort to advance the leasing of tribal lands, the U.S. government began a paramilitary operation to eliminate the American

Indian Movement that was a threat to this corporate activity (see Baer 1991; Churchill and VanderWall 1990, 2002; Matthiesen 1983, 1991, 1992; and Messerschmidt 1983).

We are a neocolonial society in which the state and multinational corporations are skilled at setting one group against another to advance their interests. This form of state-corporate crime has been occurring in South Dakota over much of the last hundred years. As far as the Lakota are concerned, under the provisions of the Fort Laramie Treaty of 1868, the land on which they live is Lakota land. Since the early 1970s, however, the federal government has argued that under the Homestead Act of 1868 this land is white land, and it has told both peoples, indigenous and white, that the other is trying to take their land (Churchill 1997). Both Indian and white people now point accusing fingers at each other over who owns land and who is trying to steal land. Meanwhile multinational corporations are quietly coming into the region and claiming the area for themselves. Multinational corporations that came in the early 1970s include Union Carbide, Exxon, Westinghouse, Burlington Northern, Chevron, Conoco, and Decker Coal.

Approximately four million acres could be mined in the Black Hills region, illustrating the magnitude of the profits to be had. Brohm Mining Company is one of the gold companies currently strip mining the northern hills region. This company has requested an expansion of eight-hundred acres onto what the government calls Forest Service land. According to corporate records and announcements, this eight-hundred acre expansion will yield approximately three-and-one-half billion dollars' worth of gold. If a mere eight-hundred acres of the Black Hills can yield three-and-one-half billion dollars' worth of gold, consider the enormous profit potential from gaining access to the entire two million acres of Black Hills gold country. The incentive to displace Indians from this land is thus also enormous. This reality helps explain why the Pentagon had become directly involved with an isolated area of the country inhabited by a small group of impoverished people—people whom corporate interests recognize as a threat to their multibillion dollar operations.

The treaties are important because they could potentially be used to block corporate activity on Indian land. In 1992, at a Mining Resource Meeting in Tomahawk, Wisconsin, Mike Sturdevant (1992), leader of the Menominee Warrior Society asked, "Why should we help whites [in fighting mining corporations]? Because Indians have treaties and treaties protect the land." His statement sums up why treaties have come back into the picture today. Treaties outline the issue of ownership as well as the value of resources and who has the right to manage them. Native people are on the frontlines of the battles over mining and other projects because their lands are directly threatened.

The Chippewa of Wisconsin have defended themselves using their very limited resources against giant multinational corporations. Few people were aware of their struggle until recently, when a growing concern prompted resistance to the ecologically destructive projects proposed by the multinational corporations. Key to this resistance is the role played by native assertion of treaty rights. Once the Chippewa asserted their rights to control the resources within their territories as outlined in the treaties, the question shifted from how projects would be developed to who will be involved in the decision-making process.

Multinational corporations rarely make provisions for public participation in their resource development decisions. Usually they make their plans and then present their proposed projects to the public as inevitable. This tactic discourages potential opposition until it is too late to stop the project.

Once native people assert their treaty rights and become participants in the decision-making process, the state-corporate entity is slowed down, giving natives and their environmental allies time to research and share their concerns about the wide-ranging social, economic, and environmental impacts of these projects with a larger audience.

A good example of this process is the Great Lakes Indian Fish and Wildlife Commission (GLIFWC), formed by the Chippewa tribes in 1984. This commission provides coordination services for the implementation of their treaty rights in ceded territories and represents tribal interests in natural resource management. An important part of GLIFWC's mission is to provide environmental protection, "recognizing that fish, wildlife, and wild plants cannot long survive in abundance in an environment that has been degraded" (Gedicks 1993:185). It is in this area that treaty rights have the greatest potential to protect the environment, highlighting their importance today. Treaty rights have enormous potential to protect the environment for Indian and non-Indian communities as well as to provide knowledge about the colonization practices of multinational corporations. If governments violate treaty rights in order to assist corporations in the extraction of resources for profit, their actions provide a clear example of state-corporate crime.

LEGACY OF U.S. TREATIES WITH INDIAN NATIONS

There was a time when the United States depended on Indian people for its very existence. When Europeans first set foot on the North American continent, tribes kept them alive during times of famine, drought, and blizzard. Tribes cared for these people, who were uneducated in the ways of surviving harsh winters, as they cared for their own members. Not surprisingly, many Indian people harbor deep resentment toward the U.S. government for the exploitation they have suffered from 1492 until the present day.

State-corporate actors and their interactions with Indian tribes are historically situated in colonial-style treaties. The psychological impact of the wording of treaties, which fostered removal of Indian people from their homelands and placed them on reserves in particular groups, became a mode of domination. People who grew up on reservations many years ago and the generations that followed had unequal access to power. The unequal access to power, which kept Indian people in a subordinate position, allowed those privileged by power to engage in colonial-type practices that continue today. But today, as Indian people increase their base of knowledge, they are becoming more powerful and are challenging the power structures of resource colonialism. Resistance by tribes to the environmentally destructive forces of mining is seen as an action that challenges state-corporate notions of what business is and what it should be.

American society and the policies of the U.S. government have caused grave problems by their malignant indifference to native peoples. Broken treaties and broken promises have led to poverty and the moral destruction of Indian people for the benefit of the state and multinational corporations, a state-corporate crime. The world is watching the United States with a close eye. The U.S. government would do well to redeem itself by relinquishing cultural and economic imperialism and realistically facing and rectifying the injustices done to Indian people in the name of state-corporate greed.

CHAPTER 13

The Invasion of Iraq

Ronald C. Kramer and Raymond J. Michalowski

IN THE WORDS OF THE Nuremberg Charter, wars of aggression—the most destructive and destabilizing of all state-initiated harms—are "the supreme international crime." Elsewhere, we and others have provided extensive legal analyses demonstrating that the invasion of Iraq, instigated and led by the United States, was a clear violation of the United Nations Charter and other forms of public international law, making it a state crime of the highest order (Boyle 2004; Falk 2004; Kramer and Michalowski 2005; Kramer, Michalowski and Rothe 2005; Mandel 2004; Sands 2005; Weeramantry 2003). It is only the power of the United States on the world stage that has kept this crime from being named as such and its authors being condemned as war criminals. If any small state had behaved with as much wanton disregard for the sovereignty and citizens of another nation as did the United States in Iraq, it would have been condemned and its leaders—if possible—taken before the International Criminal Court for crimes against humanity. Consistent with the foundational arguments of this book, we contend that the absence of formal, international condemnation of the U.S. invasion of Iraq, just like the lack of condemnation of many elite crimes, does not render it legal. It remains a violation of international law whether or not the international community has the ability to enforce that law. To reason otherwise is to agree that there is no standard of right in the international arena other than might.

This chapter examines the ways in which the U.S. invasion of Iraq, in violation of all legitimate international principles of self-defense, was not a single, isolated act of international criminality, but rather a logical expression of a nexus of forces involving the long- and short-term interests of corporate capital on the one hand, and the imperial designs of the U.S. government under the administration of George W. Bush on the other. Our primary goal is to provide a critical narrative of the historical and contemporary forces that came together in the days after the Al Qaeda attacks against the United States on September 11, 2001. In developing this critical analysis of the Iraq war we also demonstrate how the integrated model for the study of organizational deviance central to this volume can be applied to the problematic of large-scale international crimes as well as those that are more contained within national arenas.

ANALYZING STATE CRIME: AN INTEGRATED APPROACH

There are three major theoretical approaches to the study of organizational wrongdoing: political-economic analyses (Barnett 1981; Michalowski 1985; Quinney 1977; Young 1981), organizational analyses focusing on defective standard operating procedures and/or maladaptive emphases on performance within organizations (Braithwaite 1989b; Finney and Lesieur 1982; Gross 1978; Hopkins 1978; Kramer 1982; Passas 1990; Vaughan 1982, 1983, 1996), and analyses of the role of grounded human interaction in the process toward deviant organizational activities informed by Sutherland's (1940, 1949) theory of differential association. Despite their different foci, the theoretical and actual intersections suggested by these different approaches provide a sensitizing, integrated framework for analyzing specific cases of organizational deviance (see chapter 2).

The historical contours of the political-economic arrangements and dominant ideologies of the capitalist world system are reflected differentially, but reflected nonetheless, in the positions, procedures, goals, means, and constraints that define concrete organizations of governance, production, and redistribution in contemporary nation-states. At the same time, direct and indirect communications among people within and across specific political, economic, and social organizations, that is, differential association, translates the formal elements of organizations into the work-related thoughts and actions of the people in them. At every moment in time, each of these levels is manifest in the others, with organizations serving as the site in which large-scale political-economic arrangements and small-scale human actions intersect in ways that generate either conformity or deviance.

Our approach to the invasion of Iraq links these three levels of analysis with the three catalysts for action discussed in chapter 2: motivation, opportunity, and social control. Our goal is to highlight the key factors that contributed to or restrained the war on Iraq at each intersection of a catalyst for action and a level of analysis. The underlying theoretical premise guiding this analysis is the proposition that organizational deviance is most likely to occur when pressures for goal attainment and/or faulty operating procedures in corporate and governmental organizations intersect with attractive and available illegitimate means in the absence or neutralization of effective social control.

MOTIVATION AND OPPORTUNITY:
AMERICAN IMPERIALISM IN HISTORY

The U.S. decision to invade Iraq was the product of a presidential administration embedded in a history and ideology of U.S. imperial designs that found itself faced with opportunities and constraints created by the end of the Cold War, the attacks of September 11, 2001, and a bizarre electoral outcome in November 2000. These forces intersected in ways that allowed the new administration to deploy a messianic vision of a "New American Century" in which U.S.-style neoconservative economics and electoral democracy would rule the world, with the United States as the imperial power overseeing the ongoing maintenance of this world order. It was this vision, given powerful impetus by the September 11th attacks, which served as the trigger for the commission of state crimes against the people of Iraq.

America as Imperial Project

America has been an imperial project from its earliest years (Ferguson 2004; Garrison 2004). In the late eighteenth century and throughout the nineteenth century, U.S. leaders sought to expand America's economic horizons through both acute and chronic applications of force, including enslavement of Africans, expropriation of Native lands in the name of "manifest destiny" (see chapter 12), the invasion of North African states to protect U.S. trade interests in that region, claiming North and South America as an exclusive American sphere of economic and political influence (the Monroe Doctrine), expansionist war with Mexico, and using American warships to ensure Asian trading partners (Beard and Beard 1930; Kolko 1984; Sewall [1905] 1995; W. A. Williams 1959, 1969). Perhaps nothing better symbolizes this link between imperialism and militarism in U.S. history than the opening words of the Marine hymn. "From the Halls of Montezuma to the shores of Tripoli" speaks not about the defense of the U.S. homeland against foreign aggressors, but about U.S. wars of aggression aimed at projecting and/or protecting U.S. economic power beyond the country's borders.

As the nineteenth century drew to a close, structural contradictions in American capitalism provoked an intensification of America's imperial reach. With the frontier expansion stalled at the Pacific Ocean and the economic infrastructure fully capitalized, surplus productive capacity in the United States began to generate significant pressures for new markets and cheaper sources of material and labor (Sklar 1991). In 1898, increased pressures for new economic frontiers motivated an imperialist war against Spain. Although it was publicly justified as bringing "freedom" to Spain's remaining colonies, instead of liberation the people of the Philippines, Hawaii, and Puerto Rico were annexed and colonized by the United States, while those in Cuba were subject to a virtual colonization that did not end until the Cuban revolution of 1959 (Thomas 1971). In a foreshadowing of future American imperialism, the acquisition of these territories was construed not as expansionism but rather as a moral duty to uplift and civilize other races by spreading the American system of business and government, what Ferguson (2004:54) calls "the paradox of dictating democracy, of enforcing freedom, of exporting emancipation." In this there was nothing novel. As Hardt and Negri (2004) have observed, this is the way of imperialism; economic expansion under the protection of powerful guns is always justified in terms of delivering civilizing benefits to the conquered, never in the name of what it is—ethnic hubris mixed with the lust for national power and private wealth.

The United States would soon abandon its brief experiment with formal colonization as too economically and politically costly. Moreover, America's political and ideological roots were more purely commercial than those of European mercantile nations, whose feudal history was rooted in the control of land. As a result, U.S. leaders were quicker to recognize that in the emerging commercial era "what mattered was not ownership or even administrative control but commercial access" (Bacevich 2002:25).

Hints of this change are found in the 1899 Open Door Notes of Secretary of State John Hay. Hay promoted what W. A. Williams (1959) termed "Open Door" imperialism, based on diplomacy among the major capitalist powers to keep foreign markets open to trade, rather than dividing the world into the closed trading blocs typical of mercantile capitalism since the British and Dutch East India trading companies of the eighteenth century. Although the strategy of controlling without owning was based on considerable military might (by 1905 the U.S. Navy was second only to that of Great Britain), it became the basic design of American foreign policy in the twentieth century (W. A. Williams 1959).

American Imperialism in the Twentieth Century

Despite this early imperial history, the United States has always been, in Ferguson's (2004) apt phrase, "an empire in denial." Through a rhetorical move that equated capitalist markets with "freedom," two centuries of American leaders have established a political habit of mind that comprehends any war or invasion as noble sacrifice rather than self-interest. By conveniently limiting the conception of imperialism to the direct colonization of physical territory, for more than a century the Open Door ideology has enabled Americans to avoid recognizing that market imperialism is imperialism nonetheless.

As the United States rose to ever greater power after World War I and then World War II, it clung to its self-image as a "reluctant superpower," a master narrative claiming that the United States involved itself in world affairs only under duress, and then always for selfless reasons (Bacevich 2002). President

Woodrow Wilson's famous claim that the United States must enter World War I "to make the world safe for democracy" exemplifies this narrative in action. The need to ensure that the United States could play a significant role in creating a new political and economic order out of the collapse of the Ottoman and Austro-Hungarian empires was carefully crafted as selflessness rather than as self-interest (Johnson 2004:48).

In the years between World War I and World War II, America's strategy of securing the benefits of imperialism by dominating an open trade system was threatened by the Great Depression and by the economic expansionism of Nazi Germany and imperial Japan (Kolko 1986; Zinn 1980). World War II, however, lifted the United States out of economic depression and established it as both the world's dominant military power and the economic hegemon in charge of the key institutions of global capitalism such as the International Monetary Fund (IMF), the World Bank, and the General Agreement on Tariffs and Trade (Derber 2002; Friedrichs 1996a).

There were two challenges to the U.S. imperial project in the post–World War II era: the threat of independent nationalism and the Soviet Union. Nations on the periphery and semiperiphery of the world system, many of them former colonies of the world's wealthy capitalist nations, were limited to service roles in the global capitalist economy, providing resources, cheap labor, and retail markets for consumer products and finance capital (Frank 1969; Wallerstein 1989). U.S. planners were concerned that "radical and nationalistic regimes," more responsive to popular pressures for immediate improvement in the living standards of the masses than to advancing the interests of foreign capital, could become a "virus" infecting other countries and threatening the "overall framework of order" that Washington had constructed (Chomsky 2003).

Although never as powerful as American leaders made it out to be, the Soviet Union nonetheless, with its rival ideology, its own imperialistic goals, and its atomic weapons also threatened American domination to some extent. However, neither the United States nor the Soviet Union seriously challenged the overall framework of power sharing established at Yalta near the end of World War II. Instead, the two "superpowers" pursued their global interests through client states in the less-developed world, with the Soviet Union frequently courting the favor of independent nationalist movements and the United States working with local elites to limit the expansion of such movements. In this struggle, the Soviet Union and the United States were also able to periodically stalemate one another's interests by exercising their veto powers in the United Nations Security Council.

Although it represented constraints, the Cold War was consciously recognized by growth-oriented government and corporate leaders in the United States as an opportunity to justify expanding military budgets, establish a "permanent war economy," and strengthen the military-industrial complex (Elliot 1955). America's post–World War II imperial project began with a far-flung empire of military bases justified as necessary tools in the fight against communism, thereby linking America's imperial project to a rhetoric of liberation rather than one of geopolitical expansion (Johnson 2004). Or in Ferguson's words (2004:78): "For an empire in denial, there is really only one way to act imperially with a clear conscience, and that is to combat someone else's imperialism. In the doctrine of containment, born in 1947, the United States hit on the perfect ideology for its own peculiar kind of empire: the imperialism of anti-imperialism."

MOTIVATION AND OPPORTUNITY: THE UNIPOLAR MOMENT

The fall of the Berlin Wall in 1989 and the collapse of the Soviet Union in 1991 brought the Cold War to an end, presenting the United States with a new set of opportunities and challenges. With the Soviet Union out of the way and American military supremacy unrivaled, the "unipolar moment" had arrived (see Krauthammer 1989, 1991). The goals of Open Door imperialism never seemed more realizable. According to the unipolarists, American military power, a primary tool at Washington's disposal to achieve global hegemony, could now be used with relative impunity, whether it was punishing small neighbors such as Panama and Grenada for their failure to fall in line with U.S. interests or using Iraq's 1990 incursion into Kuwait to establish a more permanent U.S. military presence in the oil-rich Persian Gulf region (Bacevich 2005; Klare 2005).

The unipolar moment was not without its challenges, however. The fall of the Soviet Union removed the primary ideological justification for the suppression of independent nationalism, and it weakened domestic political support for expanding military budgets and a permanent war economy, so much so that many Americans expected that the end of the Cold War would produce a "peace dividend" that could be directed toward correcting pressing domestic social problems such as health care and social security (Zinn 1980).

Economic and political elites linked to the military-industrial-petroleum complex, however, did not acquiesce to the reduction in their power that would have resulted from such a realignment of American goals. Instead, they were soon searching for new "enemies" and, with them, new justifications for continued imperial expansion. A sharp struggle soon emerged between rival factions over how to capitalize on the opportunities offered by the fall of the Soviet Union while deflecting threats presented by the possibility of a new isolationism. One group supported a globalist and internationalist approach typical of the administrations of George H. W. Bush and Bill Clinton. The other, often referred to as "neoconservatives," argued for a more nationalist, unilateralist, and militarist revision of America's Open Door imperialism. It was this latter group that would, surprisingly, find itself in a position to shape America's imperial project for the twenty-first century.

Neoconservatives and the New American Century

The term "neoconservative" (often abridged as "neocon") was first used by the American democratic socialist leader Michael Harrington in the early 1970s to describe a group of political figures and intellectuals who had been his comrades in the U.S. Socialist Party, but who were then moving politically to the right. Many of this original neoconservative group, such as Irving Kristol and Norman Podhoretz, had been associated with the Henry "Scoop" Jackson wing of the Democratic Party, but in reaction to the cultural liberalism and anti-Vietnam war stance associated with the 1972 Democratic presidential candidate, George McGovern, they moved to the right, eventually joining the Republican Party (Dorrien 2004).

A number of neoconservatives affiliated with the Reagan administration, often providing intellectual justification for that administration's policies of military growth and rollback of, rather than coexistence with, the Soviet Union. While the first generation of neoconservatives also addressed economic and cultural issues, their primary foreign policy goal was confronting what they claimed to be the globe-girdling threat of the Soviet Union's "evil empire." As the Soviet Union began to weaken, neocons in the administration of George H. W. Bush began forcefully promoting an aggressive post-Soviet neo-imperialism. Their first concern, shared by many within the military-industrial complex, was to stave off cuts in the military budget in response to the weakened Soviet threat and popular expectations for a peace dividend.

In order to justify continued high levels of military spending, General Colin Powell, chairman of the Joint Chiefs of Staff, and Secretary of Defense Dick Cheney both prepared plans to fill in the "threat blank" vacated by the Soviet Union (Armstrong 2002). Although the first Gulf War temporarily reduced the pressure to cut the defense budget, the swift victory in Kuwait and the complete disintegration of the Soviet Union in 1991 reinvigorated calls for a peace dividend and with them the threat of cuts to critical military-industrial budgets.

In 1992 aides to Secretary Cheney, supervised by neocons Paul Wolfowitz and I. Lewis (Scooter) Libby, prepared a draft document titled *Defense Planning Guidance (DPG)*, a classified, internal Pentagon policy statement used to guide military officials in the planning process. The draft 1992 *DPG* provides a first look at the emerging neoconservative imperialist agenda. As Armstrong (2002:78) notes, the *DPG* "depicted a world dominated by the United States, which would maintain its superpower status through a combination of positive guidance and overwhelming military might. The image was one of a heavily armed City on a Hill."

The draft *DPG* stated that the first objective of U.S. defense policy should be to prevent the reemergence of a new rival. It also endorsed the use of pre-emptive military force to achieve its goal. The document called for the United States to maintain a substantial arsenal of nuclear weapons and to develop a missile-defense shield. The *DPG* was a clear statement of the neoconservative vision of unilateral use of military supremacy to defend U.S. interests any-where in the world, including protecting U.S. access to vital raw materials such as Persian Gulf oil (Armstrong 2001; Bacevich 2005; Halper and Clarke 2004; Klare 2004; J. Mann 2004). The aggressive tone of the *DPG* generated a firestorm of criticism when a draft was leaked to the press. President George H. W. Bush and Secretary Cheney quickly distanced themselves from the *DPG*, and ordered a less obviously imperialist version prepared.

The surprisingly rapid collapse of the Soviet Union ultimately revealed that the "neocons" had been wrong on almost every issue concerning the Soviet threat. As a consequence, neoconservatism lost much of its legitimacy as a mainstream political ideology, and these early neocons would eventually find themselves in political exile as part of a far-right wing of the Republican Party.

The election of President Bill Clinton removed the neocons from posi-tions within the U.S. government, but not from policy debates. From the side-lines they generated a steady stream of books, articles, reports and op-ed pieces in an effort to influence the direction of U.S. foreign policy. In 1995, second-generation neoconservative William Kristol (son of Irving Kristol) founded the right-wing magazine *The Weekly Standard,* which quickly became a major outlet for neocon thinking. Many of the neoconservatives also joined well-funded conservative think tanks to advocate for their agenda.

Throughout the Clinton years, the neocons continued to warn about new threats to American security, repeatedly calling for greater use of U.S. military power to address them (Bacevich 2005; J. Mann 2004). One persistent theme in their writings was the need to eliminate Saddam Hussein's government from Iraq, consolidate American power in the Middle East, and change the political culture of the region (Dorrien 2004).

In many ways Clinton administration foreign policy was consistent with that of the previous administration. Clinton shared the elder Bush's views of America as a global leader that should use its economic and military power to ensure openness and integration in the world economic system (Bacevich 2002). In this sense, Clinton-era foreign policy remained consistent with the Open Door system of informal imperialism practiced by the United States since the beginning of the twentieth century, stressing global economic inte-gration through free trade and democracy (Dorrien 2004).

Where Iraq was concerned, the Clinton administration developed a pol-icy of "containment plus regime change" (Rai 2003). Despite the devastating human costs of the comprehensive economic sanctions that had been imposed on Iraq following the 1991 war, Clinton continued these restrictions, pursued low-level warfare against Iraq in the form of unauthorized "no fly zones," and used UN weapons inspections (UNSCOM) as a way of spying on the Iraqi military (Rai 2003; Ritter 2003; Simons 2002). Although the Clinton administration hoped to provoke regime change in Iraq, it did not consider doing so without UN authorization.

Neoconservatives subjected the Clinton administration to a barrage of foreign policy criticism, particularly with respect to Clinton's handling of the Middle East and Iraq. In early 1998 the Project for the New American Century (PNAC), a key neoconservative think tank, released an open letter to President Clinton urging him to forcefully remove Hussein from power (Halper and Clarke 2004; J. Mann 2004). In September of 2000, PNAC issued a report entitled *Rebuilding America's Defenses: Strategy, Forces, and Resources for a New Century.* This report resurrected core ideas in the controversial draft *Defense Planning Guidance* of 1992, calling for massive increases in military spending, the expansion of U.S. military bases, and the establishment of client states supportive of American economic and political interests. The imperial goals of the neocons were clear. What they lacked was the opportunity to implement these goals. Two unanticipated events gave them the opportunity to do so.

Motive, Happenstance, and Opportunity

In December 2000, after a botched election put the question in their lap, the Supreme Court of the United States awarded the U.S. presidency to George W. Bush, despite his having lost the popular vote by over half a million ballots. This odd political turnabout would soon restore the neocons to power, with more than twenty neoconservatives and hard-line nationalists being awarded high-ranking positions in the new administration (Dorrien 2004). In a classic demonstration of the creation of shared understandings through differential association, the Pentagon and the vice president's office became unipolarist strongholds, reflecting the long-standing working relationship between neoconservatives and Vice President Dick Cheney and the new Secretary of Defense, Donald Rumsfeld (M. Moore 2001).

Even though a stroke of good luck had placed them near the center of power, neoconservative unipolarists found that the new president remained more persuaded by "pragmatic realists" in his administration such as Secretary of State Colin Powell, than by their aggressive foreign policy agenda (Dorrien 2004). This was to be expected. The PNAC report *Rebuilding America's Defenses* had predicted that "the process of transformation is likely to be a long one, absent some catastrophic or catalyzing event—like a new Pearl Harbor." The neoconservatives needed another stroke of good luck.

The 9/11 attacks presented the neocons with the "catalyzing event" they needed to transform their agenda into actual policy. The terror attacks were a "political godsend" that created a climate of fear and anxiety that the unipolarists mobilized to promote their geopolitical strategy to a president who lacked a coherent foreign policy, as well as to the nation as a whole (W. Hartung 2003). As former Treasury secretary Paul O'Neill revealed, the goal of the unipolarists in the Bush administration had always been to attack Iraq and oust Saddam Hussein (Suskind 2004). This, they believed, would allow the United States to consolidate its power in the strategically significant Middle East and to change the political culture of the region (Dorrien 2004).

On the evening of September 11, 2001, and in the days following, unipolarists in the Bush administration advocated attacking Iraq immediately, even though there was no evidence linking Iraq to the events of the day (Clarke 2004; Woodward 2004). After an internal struggle between the "pragmatic realists" led by Secretary of State Powell and the unipolarists led by Vice President Cheney and Secretary of Defense Rumsfeld, the decision was eventually made to launch a general "war on terrorism," and to begin it by attacking Al Qaeda's home base in Afghanistan and removing that country's Taliban government (J. Mann 2004). The unipolarists were only temporarily delayed, because they had achieved agreement that as soon as the Afghanistan war was under way, the United States would begin planning an invasion of Iraq (Clarke 2004; Fallows 2004). By November, barely one month after the invasion of Afghanistan, Bush and Rumsfeld ordered the Department of Defense to formulate a war plan for Iraq (Woodward 2004). Throughout 2002, as plans for the war on Iraq were being formulated, the Bush administration made a number of formal pronouncements that demonstrated that the goals of the unipolarists were now the official goals of the U.S. government. In his State of the Union address on January 29, 2002, Bush honed the focus of the "war on terrorism" by associating terrorism with specific rogue states such as Iran, Iraq, and North Korea (the "axis of evil") who were presented as legitimate targets for military action (Callinicos 2003). In a speech to the graduating cadets at West Point on June 1, the president unveiled a doctrine of preventative war, a policy that many judged as "the most open statement yet made of imperial globalization" (Falk 2004:189), soon to be followed by the Bush administration's new National Security Strategy. Not only did this document claim the right to wage preventative war, as previously discussed, but it also claimed that the United States would use its military power to spread "democracy" and American-style laissez-faire capitalism around the world as the "single sustainable model for national success" (Callinicos 2003:29). As Roy (2004:56) notes: "Democracy has become Empire's euphemism for neo-liberal capitalism."

In the campaign to build public support for the invasion of Iraq, the Bush administration skillfully exploited the political opportunities provided by the fear and anger over the 9/11 attacks. By linking Saddam Hussein and Iraq to the wider war on terrorism, the government was able to establish the idea that security required the ability to attack any nation believed to be supporting terror, no matter how weak the evidence. This strategy obscured the more specific geopolitical and economic goals of creating a neoconservative Pax Americana behind the smokescreen of fighting terrorism. In Falk's (2004:195) words, "the Iraq debate was colored by the dogs that didn't bark: oil, geopolitical goals in the region and beyond, and the security of Israel."

Messianic Militarism

The final factor to consider in understanding the Bush administration's war on Iraq is the fusion of a neoconservative imperial agenda with the fundamentalist Christian religious convictions of George W. Bush, a convergence that has been variously referred to as "messianic militarism" (*The Progressive* 2003), "political fundamentalism" (Domke 2004) or "fundamentalist geopolitics" (Falk 2004). Bush's evangelical moralism creates a Manichaean vision which views the world as a struggle between good and evil, a struggle that requires him to act on behalf of the good. In his West Point speech, for instance, Bush (2002) insisted that "we are in a conflict between good and evil, and America will call evil by its name. By confronting evil and lawless regimes we do not create a problem; we reveal a problem. And we will lead the world in opposing it."

George W. Bush is not the first U.S. president to justify his foreign policy on ideological or moral grounds. As we noted above in our historical overview of the American imperial project, many presidents have rationalized the pursuit of empire on the basis of ideological claims such as "white man's burden" or "making the world safe for democracy." But George W. Bush presents himself as more explicitly motivated by a specific religious doctrine than past presidents, as well as apparently more willing to act on those convictions. As Domke (2004:116) observes, "the Bush administration . . . offered a dangerous combination: the president claimed to know God's wishes and presided over a global landscape in which the United States could act upon such beliefs without compunction." Thus, at this moment, the leader of the global hegemon claims to be "divinely inspired to reshape the world through violent means," a "messiah complex" that conveniently fuses with the unipolarist dream of American global imperial domination (*The Progressive* 2003:8).

THE FAILURE OF SOCIAL CONTROLS

Motivations and opportunities alone are not sufficient to generate organizational deviance. Although policy planners who supported aggressive American unilateralism as a route to global dominance have enjoyed insider positions in a presidential administration willing to embrace just such a strategy, this alone is not a sufficient explanation of how the United States found itself on the pathway to committing state crime against Iraq and the Iraqi people.

Despite the desire of Bush administration unipolarists to invade Iraq, the military power of the United States, and the political opportunities provided by the 9/11 attacks, strong social control mechanisms could have blocked the march to war. No such mechanisms emerged, however. Our integrated approach to crimes at the intersection of business and government requires that we also consider the social-control context of the Iraq war, and explain why these mechanisms failed to prevent the state crime of aggressive war against Iraq. Specifically, the model directs us to examine potential controls at the intersections of the structural, organizational, and interactional levels of analysis.

At the level of the international system, the United Nations failed to provide an effective deterrent to a U.S. invasion of Iraq largely because it has little ability to compel powerful nations to comply with international law if they choose to do otherwise. There are two reasons for this. First, the use of sanctions or force to compel compliance requires a Security Council vote, and the world's most powerful nations, as permanent members of the Security Council, can and do veto any action against their own interests, just as the United States would have in this situation. It could be said that the UN Security Council "served the purpose of its founding by its refusal to endorse recourse to a war that could not be persuasively reconciled with the U.N. Charter and international law" (Falk 2004:201). Although this may be true, it is also true that the assembled nations of the world, most of whom opposed the invasion of Iraq, had no structural power to prevent the United States from violating the UN Charter. Falk (2004) goes so far as to suggest that the United Nation's inability to deter the war on Iraq calls into question the very future of the Charter system.

Second, much of the power of the United Nations rests with its ability to extract a price in terms of negative world opinion against those who would violate international law. When a nation enjoys a hegemonic economic and military position, as did the United States in 2003, it can easily believe it need not be overly concerned with world opinion. This is precisely the understanding that informed the neoconservative vision underlying the move to invade Iraq. Whether the United States is, in fact, free to do just what it wants with no cost in the world community remains to be seen. At this point, however, potential world opinion appears to exert little social control over the neoconservatives shaping U.S. foreign policy.

Like the United Nations, world public opinion, including massive antiwar protests, had little impact on the Bush administration's decision to invade Iraq. As the unipolarists pushed for the invasion of Iraq, a global antiwar movement came to life. On February 15, 2003, as U.S. military forces were poised for the invasion, over ten million people across the globe participated in antiwar demonstrations. These protests "were the single largest public political demonstration in history" (Jensen 2004:xvii). The next day the *New York Times,* seemingly in agreement with Hardt and Negri's (2004) view of the importance of "multitude" in the new global order, editorialized that there were now two superpowers in the world: the United States and world public opinion. The "superpower" of world public opinion, however, proved to be a paper tiger, exerting no deterrent effect on U.S. plans to invade Iraq. As Jensen (2004:xviii) notes, "the antiwar movement had channeled the people's voices" but it had not "made pursuing the war politically costly enough to elites to stop it." Indeed, it is unlikely, given U.S. economic and military power, that world public opinion is capable of altering U.S. government policies unless this opinion is translated into consequential actions such as a global boycott on U.S. products.

While world public opinion was overwhelmingly against the Bush administration's war plans, within the United States, public opinion shifted from initial opposition to a preventative attack without UN sanction to majority support for the war, despite a substantial U.S. antiwar movement. Two interrelated factors appear to explain the U.S. public's support for the invasion of Iraq. First, the Bush administration engaged in an effective public relations campaign that persuaded many Americans of the necessity of a war in Iraq (Rutherford 2004). As noted, this propaganda campaign rested mainly on false claims about Iraqi weapons of mass destruction (WMD), ties to Al Qaeda, and complicity in the 9/11 tragedy (Corn 2003; Rampton and Stauber 2003; Scheer, Scheer, and Chaudhry 2003). It was also undertaken at a time when many Americans were in a wounded, vengeful, and hyperpatriotic mood as a result of the 9/11 terrorist attacks. Public opinion polls taken on the eve of the war show that the government's public relations blitz had successfully convinced a majority of the American polity that Saddam Hussein was threatening the United States with weapons of mass destruction, and had also convinced an astounding 70 percent of its American audience that Iraq was directly involved with the 9/11 attacks (Berman 2003; Corn 2003). As Rutherford (2004:193) concludes in his study of the marketing of the war against Iraq, "democracy was overwhelmed by a torrent of lies, half-truths, infotainment, and marketing." Later it was learned from British government officials through the famous "Downing Street Memo" that in early 2002 the Bush administration was already planning for an invasion of Iraq and that "the intelligence and facts were being fixed around the policy" (Danner 2005). This was not the first time in American history that a "big lie" repeated frequently enough from a high enough platform had created public support for war. What is significant, however, is that it could do so even in the face of large-scale counterefforts and in the face of mounting evidence that many of its claims were in fact false.

An important factor explaining public support for the invasion of Iraq was the failure of the media in the United States to perform its critical role as "watchdog" over government power (Schell 2004). It is one thing to have evidence that government claims are weak. It is another to be able to insert those claims into the same high-profile media through which the government is promoting its public relations message. A number of studies document that the media failed to provide the American public with an accurate assessment of Bush administration claims about Iraq; nor did they provide any useful historical or political context within which the public could assess those claims (Alterman 2004; Friel and Falk 2004; Kellner 2005; Massing 2004; Moeller 2004a,b; D. Miller 2004; Solomon and Erlich 2003; Western 2005). Most news reports promoted the administration's official line and marginalized dissenters (Rendall and Broughel 2003). As Moeller (2004:3) concluded, most "stories stenographically reported the incumbent administration's perspective on WMD, giving too little critical examination of the way officials framed the events, issues, threats, and policy options." Both the *New York Times* and the *Washington Post* would later acknowledge that they should have challenged the administration's claims and assumptions more thoroughly (Kurtz 2004; *New York Times* 2004). As Orville Schell (2004:iv) points out, an independent press in a "free" country, allowed itself "to become so paralyzed that it not only failed to investigate thoroughly the rationales for war, but also took so little account of the myriad other cautionary voices in the on-line, alternative, and world press." The performance of the media in the period leading up to the invasion is a near-perfect illustration of Herman and Chomsky's (1988) "propaganda model."

In addition to the institutional failure of the media, the U.S. Congress also failed to provide an effective constraint on the Bush administration's war plans. This represented a significant institutional failure of the formal system of checks and balances among the three branches of government built into the U.S. Constitution. Article I, section 8, clause 11 of the U.S. Constitution grants the power to declare war to the Congress alone. The framers of the Constitution explicitly stated their desire that the power to take the country to war not rest on the shoulders of the president, but should be reserved to the people through their representatives in Congress.

On October 16, 2002, immediately before the midterm elections, Congress abdicated its responsibility to determine when the country would go to war by passing a resolution that authorized President Bush "to use the Armed Forces of the United States as he determines to be necessary and appropriate in order to 1) defend the national security of the United States against the continuing threat posed by Iraq; and 2) enforce all relevant United Nations Security Council resolutions regarding Iraq" (Bonifaz 2003:11). As Congressman John Conyers (2003:xi) pointed out, by taking this action, "Congress had unconstitutionally delegated to the president its exclusive power to declare war." Thus, in the aftermath of the 9/11 tragedy, Congress (including many members of the Democratic Party) voluntarily removed itself as a significant player in the unfolding events leading to the invasion and occupation of Iraq.

Sources of organizational and interactional control within the Bush administration were also ineffective. The pragmatic realists within the administration, led by Secretary of State Colin Powell, were not in full support of the unipolarist agenda. But in a struggle for control of the administration's foreign policy, Powell and the pragmatists lost out to neoconservatives pushing for war against Iraq (Dorrien 2004; Halper and Clarke 2004; J. Mann 2004).

Among the unipolarists there is a strong "subculture of resistance" to international law and institutions (Schell 2004). According to Braithwaite (1989b:346), such organizational subcultures "neutralize the moral bond of the law and communicate knowledge about how to create and seize illegitimate opportunities and how to cover up offending."

The group dynamics involved in the decision making of the unipolarists also demonstrate classic characteristics of "groupthink" as described by Janis (1982). The unipolarists were a highly cohesive group with a strong commitment to their assumptions and beliefs about America's role in the world. They valued loyalty, believed in the inherent morality of their position, had an illusion of invulnerability, and shared stereotypes of out-groups. But most important for this analysis, the unipolarists within the Bush administration were highly selective in gathering information; ignored, discounted or ridiculed contrary views; engaged in self-censorship; and protected the group from examining alternatives to their war plans (Dorrien 2004; Halper and Clarke 2004; J. Mann 2004).

Finally, the administration used a variety of "techniques of neutralization" (Sykes and Matza 1957) in an effort to rationalize its criminal acts in Iraq. It denied responsibility (the war was Saddam's fault), denied the victims (most were terrorists), denied injury (there was only limited "collateral damage"), condemned the condemners (protesters were unpatriotic and the French were ungrateful and cowardly), and appealed to higher loyalties (God directed Bush to liberate the Iraqi people).

CONCLUSION

The invasion and occupation of Iraq by the United States and its allies violated international law in a climate where there were powerful economic and political motives to wage war, no effective social control before the fact, and very little obvious potential for sanctions after the fact. We suggest that the invasion of Iraq provides an excellent opportunity to observe the complex interactions among historical and contemporary political and economic forces, as well the need for analysts to recognize the "butterfly effect" as both chaos theorists and moviemakers term it. History is neither linear nor teleological. Although there are clearly tendencies in social systems—for example, the tendency in capitalist systems both to pursue expansion and to suffer declining rates of profit—those tendencies will be given concrete direction by a variety of exogenous forces, some of them entirely unpredictable, such as the election of 2000. In the case of Iraq, fewer than six hundred votes in the 2000 presidential election, combined with the external events of 9/11, made the difference between no invasion and one of the most significant acts of illegal aggression in recent times.

At the same time, neither 9/11 nor the selection of George W. Bush as U.S. president are adequate in themselves to explain the state crimes encompassed by the invasion and occupation of Iraq. The fuller explanation resides in the relationship between U.S. economic interests as resident in the structure of corporate capital and the long-standing will to empire these economic interests have forged as a key characteristic of the U.S. political establishment.

Unlike many analyses of state-corporate crime, which focus on harms caused by the relationship between specific corporate and political organizations at a single moment in time, our inquiry into the origins of the Iraq war has surveyed both historical and contemporary intersections within the grand contours of U.S. economic and political interests. Within these grand contours there exist a number of specific intersections between business and government that, as the analysis of private military corporations in chapter 14 demonstrates, transform grand historic and political-economic contours into concrete, criminogenic collaborations. We suggest that criminological analyses of state crimes in the international arena need to be alert to both of these levels of analysis—large-scale tendencies and specific intersections. Specific state-corporate crimes, particularly international ones, do not occur in a historic vacuum, but at the same time, historic tendencies always have more than one possible outcome. It is in the dialogue between past and present, between structure and happenstance, that the reality of international state-corporate crimes is born.

NOTE ON SOURCE

Updated, adapted, and revised from Ronald Kramer and Raymond Michalowski, "War, Aggression, and State Crime: A Criminological Analysis of the Invasion and Occupation of Iraq," *The British Journal of Criminology* 46, no. 4 (July 2005): 446–469.

CHAPTER 14

Iraq and Halliburton

Dawn Rothe

THE INTERSECTION OF STATE and corporate interests during times of war is a fundamental part of the war-making process. Every capitalist country must rely on private-sector production to produce the weapons of war. In the United States, for example, major auto manufacturers such as Chrysler, Ford, and Chevrolet retooled to produce tanks, guns, and missiles instead of cars during World War II, while many other companies refocused some or all of their production to serve the war effort. With the introduction of a permanent wartime economy after the end of World War II, amid concerns that the United States was coming to be dominated by a military-industrial complex (Melman 1974), major providers of weapons and logistical support such as General Electric, Boeing, Bechtel Group, and Lockheed Martin became regular recipients of government contracts. They were also repeatedly at the center of controversies concerning cost overruns and questionable charges (Johnson 2004; Greider 1998).

The close alignment of corporate and government interests in the production and procurement of the weapons of war is a vivid example of the "revolving door" effect as described by C. Wright Mills (1954) in *The Power Elite*. As executives from major military contractors fill elected or appointed government positions, the interests of the state become increasingly entangled with prior corporate loyalties.

In recent years the integration of state interests with those of the private corporation has intensified. This integration began with efforts to adapt to a downsized military through increased reliance on just on time privatized logistic contracts. The move to an active war footing following the attacks of 9/11, including the wars in Afghanistan and Iraq and the permanent "war on terror," further cemented the private-public strategy for war making in the United States.

The controversy surrounding links between Vice President Dick Cheney and Halliburton, the company he formerly headed, provides a demonstration of the potential for state-corporate crime embedded in this new policy of war by subcontract. There have been claims that the association between Cheney and Halliburton resulted in no-bid, cost-plus contractual work without competitive pricing or oversight. According to some, the affiliation between Cheney and Halliburton has established war profiteering as an acceptable and systematic practice within the Bush administration by rewarding "corporations for who they know rather than what they know, and a system in which cronyism is more important than competence" (W. Hartung 2003:26).

This chapter examines the relationship between Halliburton, the current Bush administration, the "war on terrorism," and war profiteering.[1] In doing so, I incorporate themes from previous state-corporate crime literature, particularly the concepts of state-facilitated and state-initiated forms of state-corporate crime in delineating the relationships between Halliburton and the U.S. government. On the one hand, I suggest that war profiteering in the form of overcharges is state-facilitated crime insofar as the government was aggressive in it refusal to take appropriate and available regulatory action. On the other hand, the Bush administration's repeal of the Clinton administration ruling regulating state contracts can be analyzed as state-initiated crime to the extent that these repeals allowed Halliburton to attain state contracts for which it would have not qualified previously.

I suggest that the relationship between Cheney and Halliburton has resulted in specific acts of both state-facilitated and state-initiated crime. I offer a criminological analysis of the relationship between Cheney and Halliburton and the subsequent acts of war profiteering, and in doing so I utilize Kauzlarich and Kramer's (1998) integrated model of state-corporate crime to explore the etiological elements of these crimes on the macro (historical-structural), meso (organizational), and micro (individual-interactional) level. This model provides a useful framework for discussing how motivation, opportunity, and control work within these dimensions.

BRIEF HISTORY OF HALLIBURTON

Halliburton was first established in 1919. Since that time the company has purchased several subsidiaries that include Brown and Root (including the consortium of Devonport Management Ltd.), Dresser Industries (known as KBR after the purchase of M. W. Kellogg by Dresser), Landmark Graphics Corporation, Wellstream, Well Dynamics, Eventure, and Subsea 7 (Halliburton 2004). The success of the Halliburton Corporation is the consequence of a range of strategic practices. Since the mid-1990s, however, many of Halliburton's corporate actions have come under the scrutiny of several U.S. governmental oversight organizations (such as the Securities and Exchange Commission, U.S. General Accounting Office, and congressional leaders), criminologists, and international critics. More specifically, the GAO charged Halliburton with improper billing for questionable expenses associated with its logistical work in the Balkans and the Defense Department charged fraudulent claims were submitted for work at Fort Ord, California. Among these corporate actions are a series of Halliburton's practices that can be classified as corporate crime. Halliburton's actions of systematically overcharging the U.S. government for contracted work, utilizing bribes to attain foreign contracts, and using subsidiaries and foreign joint ventures to bypass U.S. law restricting trade embargos have a long history.

Foreign Trade Barred under International Sanctions

Halliburton's participation in the practices of overcharging, bribing, and utilizing "loopholes" in general to bypass U.S. trade law or international sanctions cannot be traced solely to the 2003 invasion and subsequent occupation of Iraq. The company's business practices of corruption and corporate crime were evident during the 1990s when Dick Cheney was chief executive officer. For example, in 2001 the Treasury Department opened an inquiry into whether Halliburton had used transnational trade loopholes that allowed the company to circumvent sanctions on Iran by doing business with that country through foreign subsidiaries. In another instance, Halliburton's subsidiary, Dresser Inc., did substantial business with Iraq from 1997 through the summer of 2000, closing $73 million in deals with Saddam Hussein at a time when such dealings were prohibited by international trade sanctions (United Nations 2001). Many of these contracts occurred under the United Nation's oil-for-food program through joint ventures with the Ingersoll-Rand Company via subsidiaries known as the Dresser-Rand and Ingersoll Dresser Pump companies. Although Cheney claimed that Halliburton divested itself of the subsidiaries in 1998 as soon as it learned of the trading in violation of U.S. legislation prohibiting business ventures while Iraq was under sanctions by the United States and the United Nations (Kristof 2001), the firms continued trading with Baghdad for over a year past the time of Cheney's initial "awareness." Cheney signed nearly $30 million in contracts before he sold Halliburton's 49 percent stake in Ingersoll Dresser Pump Company in December 1999 and the 51 percent stake in Dresser-Rand in February 2000 (United Nations 2001).

International Bribery Charges

In 2004 Halliburton came under investigation by the French government, the United States Department of Justice, and the Securities and Exchange Commission for international bribery. The U.S. Department of Justice conducted a criminal investigation into an alleged $180 million bribe paid by Halliburton and three other companies to the government of Nigeria. The alleged bribe was paid in exchange for awarding a contract to the companies to build a $4 billion natural gas plant in Nigeria's southern delta region. France is also investigating a former Halliburton executive for his role in the scheme. Investigators said

$5 million of the bribes intended for Nigeria were deposited into the Swiss bank account of former KBR chairman Jack Stanley, who retired from the company on December 31, 2003. In 2002, the U.S. Securities and Exchange Commission investigated a second bribery case involving Nigeria. Halliburton admitted that its employees paid a $2.4 million bribe to a government official of Nigeria in order to receive favorable tax treatment, in violation of the U.S. Foreign Corrupt Practices Act and the convention adopted by the Organization for Economic Cooperation and Development prohibiting making bribes in the course of commercial transactions. At this writing the cases remain ongoing.

History of Fraud and Overcharges

In 1997 the U.S. General Accounting Office charged Halliburton with billing the U.S. Army for questionable expenses associated with its logistical work in the Balkans. These charges included billing $85.98 per sheet of plywood that cost Halliburton $14.06 and "cleaning" offices up to four times a day. A 2000 follow-up report by the GAO regarding Halliburton's contract in the Balkans found continuous systematic overcharges via inflated costs submitted in its billing to the army. Halliburton paid $2 million in fines to resolve the fraudulent overcharges.

In a separate inquiry, the Defense Department inspector general and a federal grand jury had investigated allegations that a subsidiary of Halliburton, KBR, defrauded the government of millions of dollars through inflated prices for repairs and maintenance for work at Fort Ord in California. In February 2002 Halliburton paid an additional $2 million in fines to resolve the fraud claims.

As these examples show, Halliburton has a history of corporate criminality and questionable organizational practices. However, it is the recent intermingling of Halliburton and Vice President Cheney that makes its corporate practices a case of state-initiated and/or state-facilitated corporate crime.

HALLIBURTON–CHENEY CONNECTIONS

The connections between Halliburton and Cheney date back to the early 1990s. Dick Cheney, as Ronald Reagan's secretary of defense, assigned Halliburton subsidiary Brown & Root the task of conducting a classified survey detailing how private corporations such as itself could provide logistical support for U.S. military forces scattered around the world. At that time Halliburton prepared a report to implement the privatization of everyday military activities and logistical planning, for which it earned $3.9 million. During the latter part of 1992, Halliburton received an additional $5 million for a follow-up study to outline how private firms could supply the logistical needs of several contingency plans at the same time. This led to "a five-year contract to be the U.S.

Army's on-call private logistics arm," what was known as the Logistics Civil Augmentation Program (LOGCAP) (Singer 2003:142–143). Halliburton held this contract until 1997, when Dyncorp, another private firm specializing in providing military logistical support, beat Halliburton's competitive bid.

When Cheney's term as secretary of defense ended in 1993, he and his deputy secretary of defense, David Gribbin, were hired by Halliburton: Cheney as acting CEO and Gribbin as the official go-between to obtain contracts from the U.S. government. Cheney gave Halliburton "a level of access that no one else in the oil sector could duplicate" (Dean 2004:43). Between 1995 and 2000 intense lobbying efforts paid off with a doubling of the value of Halliburton's government contracts (Institute for Southern Studies 2004). During 1999 and 2000, Halliburton reported spending \$1.2 million on lobbying efforts while obtaining approximately \$1 billion in defense contracts (Beelman, 2004). The pattern of paying lobbyists to represent and to obtain future contracts quickly diminished once Cheney took office as vice president. As will be seen, the ratio of money spent on lobbying declined significantly while the value of contracts awarded to Halliburton increased notably.

The Cheney–Halliburton marriage, as with all marriages, incorporated distant family members that include some members of the Bush family tree. William H. (Bucky) Bush, the uncle of George W., is a trustee on the board of Lord and Abbott, one of Halliburton's top shareholders. Indeed, this relationship may have played a role in prime contracts recently awarded to Lord Abbott in Iraq.[2] The purchase of Dresser Inc. (1998) by Halliburton further enhanced the family tree of the Halliburton–Cheney marriage. Prescott Bush, father of George H. W. Bush, was the bank representative who financed Dresser and a member of the company's board for several years. The former president of Dresser Industries, Neil Mallon, was a close family friend and mentor to George H. W. Bush, and it was Mallon who was responsible for getting Bush into the oil industry.

Republican Party presidential nominee George W. Bush hired Cheney to oversee the selection process for a vice-presidential candidate. Just as Cheney was finding the right candidate (May–June 2000) to run on Bush's ticket, he sold 100,000 shares of Halliburton stock for 50.97 dollars a share for an approximate value of \$5.1 million (Dean 2004). The first week of July 2000 the news was official: it would be a Bush-Cheney ticket. Cheney resigned from Halliburton in August 2000 with a retirement package on a future contract worth \$45 to \$62.2 million, which included stocks, options, and deferred income payments. Shortly after his role as CEO of Halliburton ended and he announced he was running for vice president, Cheney sold another 660,000 shares of stock (worth approximately \$36 million). However, he continued to hold 433,000 stock options. Moreover, in September 2003, Senator Frank R. Lautenberg released a congressional report stating that receiving a deferred salary and holding stock options in a corporation while serving as vice president constitutes a "financial interest" under federal ethics standards. Another issue explained in the Congressional Research Service (CRS) report is that the president and vice president are both exempt from the enforcement of the ethics laws because forcing the president or vice president to disqualify themselves from certain duties or recusing themselves from certain issues could interfere with their constitutionally required duties. Normally politicians put their stock assets into a blind trust after being elected to high office, so that someone else manages their stock portfolio. However, Cheney continued to hold 140,000 shares of unvested stock that is worth $7.6 million at 2005 stock prices. This stock could not be managed or sold by anyone until 2002, because it was unvested; thus it could not be put into a blind trust. Therefore Cheney had a direct financial interest in the value of Halliburton's stock and the financial profitability of Halliburton the first two years of his vice presidency. Cheney also owns great amounts of Halliburton stock that are safely tucked away in a blind trust for post–vice presidency personal use. As of 2004, four years into his vice presidency, Cheney still holds 433,000 Halliburton stock options, although their exercise price is above the company's current stock market price. Cheney signed an agreement to donate any profits from these stock options to charity, and pledged not to take any tax deduction for the donations. However, should Halliburton's stock price increase over the next few years, Cheney could exercise his stock options for a substantial profit, benefiting not only his designated charities but also providing Halliburton with a substantial tax deduction (Chatterjee 2004; Lautenberg 2003).

The Cheney–Halliburton relationship had indeed proved to be mutually beneficial while Cheney acted as CEO. Halliburton's revenue from state defense contracts such as LOGCAP nearly doubled (from $1.1 to $2.3 billion) under Cheney's five-year tenure as CEO compared with the five prior years (Center for Public Integrity 2004). For example, in 1995 Halliburton jumped from seventy-third to eighteenth on the Pentagon's list of top contractors, benefiting from at least $3.8 billion in federal contracts and taxpayer-insured loans, according to the Center for Public Integrity.

HALLIBURTON AND
CHENEY—POST-"RETIREMENT"

Although it may appear to many that the Cheney–Halliburton marriage ended with the selling of stocks and options, the relationship continued. During his tenure as vice president, Cheney drew income both from U.S. taxpayers and from Halliburton. As Bivens (2004:1) stated, "billions are slyly, secretively and controversially showered on the entity [Halliburton] that paid Dick Cheney 178,437 dollars this year, by the entity [the federal government] that paid him

198,600 dollars." For the previous year, 2002, Cheney received $162,392 from Halliburton and $190,134 as vice presidential pay (White House 2004).

A Halliburton financial statement of January 2, 2001, showed that $147,579 was paid to Cheney that day as payout of salary from the company's Elective Deferral Plan. This amount was a part of the salary Cheney earned in 1999 but had chosen to receive in five installments spread over five years. Another financial statement, of January 18, 2001, showed an additional $1,451,398 was paid under the company's "Incentive Plan C" for senior executives. This sum was Cheney's incentive compensation (yearly bonus based on the company's performance in 2000). Cheney's personal financial disclosure forms show that Cheney received $398,548 in deferred salary from Halliburton as vice president. Moreover, Cheney received another payment in 2004, and a final payment is to be made in 2005. As previously mentioned, Halliburton drastically reduced its lobbying for governmental contracts once Cheney took office. In the two years prior to Cheney's election as vice president, Halliburton spent $1.2 million lobbying and attained contracts worth approximately $900 million a year (U.S. Senate Lobbying Disclosure Statements 2004). During 2001–2002, Halliburton spent $600,000 dollars lobbying for contracts. In 2003 Halliburton lobbyist Charles Dominy (a retired general with the Army Corps of Engineers, which oversees contracts awarded in Iraq) spent only $300,000 lobbying Congress on behalf of Halliburton (U.S. Senate Lobbying Disclosure Statements 2004). Overall, from 2001 through 2003 Halliburton and its subsidiaries earned $6 billion in U.S. government contracts while spending only $900,000 lobbying, less than they would have spent in one year before their former CEO became vice president. As Thurber (2004:1) observed, "they are already in; they don't need to lobby any more."

Although the relationship between Cheney and Halliburton appeared to be a major factor in awarding contracts to Halliburton (Chatterjee 2004), Cheney denied any involvement in the contracting process. On "Meet the Press" he said: "As Vice President, I have absolutely no influence of, involvement of, knowledge of in any way, shape or form of contracts let by the Army Corps of Engineers or anybody else in the Federal Government" (NBC "Meet the Press" 2003). Private memos, however, proved otherwise. An internal Pentagon e-mail (March 5, 2003) sent by an Army Corps of Engineer official claimed that Douglas Feith, the Defense Department's undersecretary for policy, approved arrangements for a multibillion dollar contract for Halliburton "contingent on informing the WH tomorrow. We anticipate no issues since action has been coordinated w/VP office" (*Time* 2004:1). Within three days Halliburton received one of the first State Department contracts for Iraq worth as much as $7 billion, according to information on the Army Corps of Engineers Web site (Gongloff 2003; U.S. Army Corps of Engineers 2003).

Thus state-initiated actions put Halliburton in a favorable position to attain future multibillion-dollar contracts.

Halliburton Contracts

Immediately after September 11, 2001, the neoconservatives and many corporations seized the moment for personal, political, and economic gain.[3] The "war on terrorism" was announced, the long-sought plans to attack Iraq were jump-started, and Halliburton was ready to cash in on its relationship with its past CEO. In November 2001, Halliburton subsidiary Brown & Root received a contract worth $2 million to reinforce the U.S. embassy in Tashkent, Uzbekistan. By December 2001, Halliburton had won back the cost-plus LOGCAP contract to provide facilities, logistic support, and provisions for U.S. troops in places such as Afghanistan, Qatar, Kuwait, Georgia, Jordan, Djibouti, and Uzbekistan. The contract was originally won back through a competitive bid. However, additional no-bid contracts were awarded as the holder of the quick-response LOGCAP contract was already providing logistical help for the U.S. military and thus was ready at hand. "Halliburton was the obvious choice," said Army Corps of Engineers commander Lt. Gen. Robert Flowers. "To invite other contractors to compete to perform a highly classified requirement that KBR [Halliburton] was already under a competitively awarded contract to perform would have been a wasteful duplication of effort" (Flowers 2003). Unlike the previous LOGCAP contract, the new contract extended over a ten-year period with an estimated value of $830 million to over $1 billion (Aljazeera 2003). Halliburton (KBR) also received contracts worth $110 million to build prison cells and other facilities at Guantanamo Bay. With the recent addition of Camp 5 (a permanent addition also built by KBR), the prison capacity grew to 1,100 detainees (Higham, Stephens, and Williams 2004).

In June 2002, Halliburton (KBR) was awarded a contract worth $22 million to run support services at Camp Stronghold and the Khanabad Air Base in Uzbekistan, the main U.S. base for the "war on terrorism" in Afghanistan. This contract included serving the CIA paramilitary units, maintaining combat equipment, targeting aircraft, and providing logistical support. For example, Halliburton (KBR) employees operated the U.S. Air Force Global Hawks (unmanned surveillance planes) (Little 2002; Singer 2003).

During September 2002, 1,800 Halliburton employees were present in Kuwait and Turkey (under a contract for nearly $1 billion) to provide temporary housing (tents) and logistical support for the invasion into Iraq (Chatterjee 2003). Under the competitively bid contract, KBR provides for the support of the Reception, Staging, Onward Movement, and Integration (RSOI) process of U.S. forces as they enter or depart their theater of operation by sea, air, or rail. The post for the Halliburton employees, Camp Arifjan, includes a gymnasium and fast food outlets, including Burger King, Baskin-Robbins, and Subway, all paid for by U.S. taxpayers. While Halliburton employees are eating fast food, U.S. troops are served mess hall food and live in tents. Excessive U.S. taxpayer money is spent on cost-plus contracts allowing posh conditions for private contractors such as the one in Camp Arifjan while troops are left without the necessary equipment such as bullet-proof vests and armored vehicles. Moreover, Camp Arifjan is the same base in which a Saudi subcontractor hired by KBR billed for 42,042 meals a day on average but served only 14,053 meals a day (CNN Money 2004; Reuters 2004; *Wall Street Journal* 2004).

In the fall of 2002, Halliburton attained an additional no-bid contract to extinguish oil fires in Iraq, because "the company was the only one in a position to implement the plan on time because it designed it" (Beelman 2004:2). (It was Halliburton who had constructed the contingency plans for what would be needed under these circumstances.) Several other corporations, however, had been contracted to do similar work in Kuwait after the Persian Gulf War. For example, Cudd Pressure Control and Boots & Coots were two of three U.S. companies that extinguished hundreds of oil fires in Kuwait and were in touch with the Pentagon about similar service shortly before the war on Iraq began. Yet Halliburton was favored. Opening the bid to a competitive bidding process was thought to be a wasteful duplication (Flowers 2003). By November 2002, Halliburton (KBR) received an additional contract valued at approximately $42.5 million to service troops in Bagram and Khandahar (Chatterjee 2003). Once the invasion of Iraq occurred, Halliburton was a front-runner for even more contracts. This included a no-bid contract awarded by the Army Corps of Engineers worth up to $15.6 billion for putting out oil fires and infrastructure repairs in Iraq (Bannerjee 2003). Awarded contracts also included cooking meals, delivering mail, building bases, and delivering supplies (Chatterjee 2004). By the end of 2003 the United States had spent more than $8 billion in payments for these contracts (Chatterjee 2004).

Not only has Halliburton received billions of dollars from the state through competitive and noncompetitive contracts, but most of these were cost-plus contracts. Cost-plus contracts are essentially blank checks that ensure that Halliburton is reimbursed for whatever it bills for its services as well as an additional percentage (between 2 percent and 7 percent) for the company's profits (fees). These types of open-ended contracts are incentives to maximize expenditures to attain an increase in the total value of the contract and profits. Moreover, the larger the contract, the more valuable becomes Halliburton's stock. In October 2002, for example, Halliburton's stock was $12.62 a share. When the KBR Iraq restructure contract was awarded, its stock rose to $23.90 a share (see Halliburton stock portfolios 2001–2004). According to Henry Bunting's testimony to the Democratic Policy Committee; the Halliburton motto in Iraq is "don't worry about it, it's cost plus" (Bunting 2004).[4] In essence, no one questioned pricing. "The comment by both Halliburton buyers and

management was 'it's cost plus,' don't waste time finding another supplier"
(Chatterjee 2004:32).

To date, Halliburton has over 24,000 workers in Iraq and Kuwait alone,
11,000 more than the number of British soldiers deployed there (Chatterjee
2004; *Mother Jones* 2004a). By 2005 KBR had earned contracts worth over
$2.2 billion from work in Iraq (of this, 42 percent was spent on combating oil
fires and restoring pipelines and 48 percent for housing and transportation for
troops) (Institute for Southern Studies 2004). Overall, it has been estimated
that Halliburton has received more than $8 billion in contracts since Cheney
became vice president.

Under the Bush-Cheney administration, the profit from the war on terror
benefited those corporations that were part of the "family." [5] Few other United
States, foreign, or most significantly, Iraqi contractors benefited from U.S. government contracts resulting from the Iraq war. In May 2004, a Pentagon program management office in Baghdad reported that only 24,179 Iraqis were
employed in the postwar rebuilding efforts (less than 1 percent of Iraq's total
work force of seven million) (Chatterjee 2004:12). Meanwhile, just 25 percent
of Halliburton's employees in Iraq—6,000 out of 24,000 total—were Iraqis.

The close relationship between the administration and Halliburton constitutes a form of state-initiated war profiteering. While Halliburton may be
guilty of inflating total contract values through overcharges and/or charges for
services not provided, the opportunities for profiteering were the products of
the cozy relationship between the company and a sitting administration whose
vice president was Halliburton's former CEO.

Halliburton Overcharges, Kickbacks, and Cost Overruns

Halliburton and its subsidiaries have engaged in systematic and significant
overcharging for services for contracts awarded in Iraq. This is not new behavior for the company. Thus it is not surprising that Halliburton would use "war
on terrorism" cost-plus contracts as an opportunity for overcharging. Previously,
systemic overcharging by corporations potentially could have resulted in periods of ineligibility for new federal contracts. Specifically, some of the added language required a satisfactory record of integrity and business ethics, including
satisfactory compliance with the relevant labor and employment, environmental, antitrust, and consumer protection laws (FAR [Federal Acquisitions Regula-
tions] 9.104-1(d)). The burden of enforcement was on the contracting officers
to consider all relevant credible information, with the greatest weight given to
offenses adjudicated within the past three years. Thus it relied on the compliance
of contracting officers for enforcement (FAR part 9, no. 65 FR 80255).

During the Clinton administration, requirements for contractors bidding
on federal contracts were strengthened. New "blacklisting" regulations would
have barred contractors from future contracts if they had committed past labor,

environmental, or violations of federal trade laws. On April 1, 2001, however, the Bush administration revoked this regulation (no. 65 FR 80255) with no. 66 FR 17754, thus undoing the tightening of regulations put forth by the Clinton administration. This change made it possible for Halliburton and other corporate criminals to obtain contracts regardless of previous or current allegations of illegal practices (Federal Register 2001; White House 2004). Moreover, although payments to corporations under investigation by a federal agency are supposed to be deferred, Halliburton continued to receive its pay as investigations were being carried out, thereby facilitating Halliburton's alleged illegal activities. For example, Halliburton was under investigation by the SEC for accounting fraud that was alleged to have occurred from 1999 to 2001, and the Justice Department was conducting an investigation on charges of bribery connected with the Nigerian official to attain an oil contract in Nigeria. After contracts were awarded to Halliburton in Iraq, the company continued to come under investigations by the Congressional Oversight Committee and the Department of Defense for overcharges, as we shall see.

In 2003 a Pentagon audit found that Halliburton (KBR) had overcharged the U.S. government for approximately fifty-seven million gallons of gasoline delivered to Iraqi citizens under a no-bid contract. These overcharges totaled nearly $61 million from May through September 2003. KBR was charging from $2.27 to $3.09 a gallon to import gasoline from Kuwait, while a different contractor delivered gas from Turkey to Iraq for $1.18 a gallon (Kelley 2003). Iraq's state oil company (SOMA) was charging 96 cents a gallon for gasoline delivered to the same depots in Iraq, utilizing the same military escorts (*Southern Studies* 2003/2004).

Further exacerbating the problem, part of the money for the KBR gas service contract came from the United Nation's oil-for-food program (now the Development Fund for Iraq). Under the terms of UN Security Resolution 1483, an independent board called the International Advisory and Monitoring Board was to be created to ensure that UN oil-for-food funds were spent for the benefit of Iraqi citizens. The purpose of this agency was to be "the primary vehicle for guaranteeing the transparency of the DFI and for ensuring the DFI funds are used properly" (U.S. House 2003:6). As of the end of 2003, this body had not been created (U.S. House 2003:5). Thus the use of these funds to pay inflated prices to Halliburton ($600 million out of $1 billion in funds was transferred to Halliburton) by the U.S. Coalition Provisional Authority went uncontested. In this case the government's failure to provide the necessary oversight agency constitutes a case of state-facilitated wrongdoing.

After it won a ten-year contract worth $3.8 billion to provide food, wash clothes, deliver mail, and other basic services, Halliburton continued to systematically overcharge the government for services rendered (and unrendered). In one case Halliburton charged the government $67 million more for military dining services than the corporation had paid to the actual subcontractors who provided the service (Ivanovich 2004a). The *Wall Street Journal* reported that Pentagon auditors believed the corporation overcharged $16 million for meals served at Camp Arifjan (subcontracted to Tamimi Global Company). Moreover, the military was already paying Halliburton $28 a day per soldier. In December 2003, Halliburton had estimated it served twenty-one million meals to 110,000 soldiers at forty-five sites in Iraq. Early in 2004 military auditors suspected the corporation was cooking the numbers and overcharging the government millions of dollars (Chatterjee 2004). The fact that these overcharges occurred in at least five of Halliburton's facilities suggests they were part of a systematic effort to increase profit margin.

Not only did Halliburton overcharge the government (nearly three times the number of meals than were actually provided to soldiers in Kuwait over a nine-month period), it had been repeatedly warned and audited for its dining service conditions by the Coalition Provisional Authority's inspector general Bowen. The claims were that the food was dirty, blood was consistently found on the kitchen floors, the utensils were dirty, and meats were rotting in four of the military messes the company operates in Iraq (*Boston Globe* 2004b; CBS 2003; Chatterjee 2004; *Washington Post* 2004). Moreover, Halliburton's promises of improvement in these messes were empty as they "have not been followed through" (NBC News 2003). Regardless of the Pentagon report warning of "serious repercussions," no actions to date have been taken. The government has thus facilitated illegal and unethical profiteering by allowing charges for meals never provided and unsafe food handling and preparations (NBC News 2003).

Halliburton was also charged with improprieties surrounding a joint venture with Morris Corporation, an Australian catering company to which it has awarded a $100 million contract to supply meals to U.S. troops in Iraq. Halliburton canceled the contract six weeks after it was signed. An insider involved in the deal stated that the contract was canceled after a Halliburton employee sought kickbacks worth up to $3 million during the negotiations. A Pentagon report released in March 2004 stated that Halliburton failed to inform the military that the Morris contract to supply meals had been canceled while Halliburton continued to use the contract to estimate costs of more than $1 billion dollars for catering, including the site of Kuwait (Wilkinson 2004).

Halliburton initially agreed to credit the military $27.4 million and suspend billing on the remaining $141 million until the issue of overcharges had been satisfactorily addressed. In response to a criminal investigation by the Defense Criminal Investigation Service, in March 2004, Halliburton (while agreeing to suspend future billings to the government while under investigation) froze payments to its subcontractors totaling nearly $500 million in outstanding invoices (*Wall Street Journal* 2004). The first week of May 2004, however, Halliburton proceeded with billing the United States for the remaining $141 million.

Pentagon experts reported that this billing violated a standing rule whereby contractors bill no more that 85 percent of costs until the corporation and military reach a consensus on a fair price (Ivanovich 2004). By mid-May 2004, the Pentagon suspended an additional $159.5 million payment after finding the company submitted incomplete paperwork (Chatterjee 2004).

Halliburton also acknowledged that it accepted up to $6 million in kickbacks taken by employees in return for granting a subcontract to a Kuwaiti firm pertaining to Iraq's rebuilding. Halliburton said it would repay the government $6.2 million to cover the overbilling by an unidentified Kuwaiti firm it contracted to as well as the kickbacks given to "one or two" KBR employees (Ivanovich 2004).

The Coalition Provisional Authority (CPA) inspector general Bowen made allegations that Halliburton was claiming overexpenditures for the Hilton Kuwait Resort (where KBR houses employees while providing logistical support to U.S. military troops and while rebuilding Iraq's oil infrastructure) (Ivanovich 2004). Along with these charges, in early 2004 the CPA conducted an audit into the "unnecessary" purchase of trucks and other costs associated with KBR's services.

Beyond overcharging and purchasing unnecessary and/or excessive products, Halliburton systematically billed for labor never performed. For example, Representative Henry Waxman posted whistleblower testimony on his Web site revealing systematic practices of overpaying employees for hours of labor never performed and billed to the U.S. government (Waxman 2004b). One of the testimonials, from Mike West, stated he was hired as a labor foreman at a salary of $130,000. Moreover, he stated he was paid despite the fact that he had no work; "I only worked one day out of six in Kuwait" (West 2003:1). During his tenure at Al Asad he claimed to have worked one of every five days, although he was told by his supervisor to bill for twelve hours of labor every day (Chatterjee 2004). The failure of the House of Representatives Government Reform Committee to hear whistleblower testimony suggests that Halliburton's actions clearly fall in the category of state-facilitated corporate crime.

Halliburton's practice of billing for delivering supplies has amounted to systematic overcharges. The U.S. taxpayer has been billed nearly $327 million as of mid-2004 for these runs, and Halliburton was expecting to charge an additional $230 million more. Yet many of these runs have been unnecessary, because at least one in three trucks makes the three-hundred-mile trip empty while others may carry only one pallet of supplies (Chatterjee 2004). Moreover, of the fleet of trucks (Mercedes and Volvos), dozens have not been used (Wilson 2004). Trailers are left along the roadside when the slightest mechanical problem or flat tire occurs, or when the convoy lacks necessary maintenance items. It was also reported that one Halliburton employee took a video in January 2004 of fifteen empty trailers on the road and stated, "This is just a sample of the empty trailers we're handling called sustainers. And there's more behind me. . . . this is fraud and abuse" (Chatterjee 2004:37).

As controversy continues to shroud the Bush-Cheney administration, little to no public outcry has occurred over the blatant misuse of a political office. In part this is due to the ideology of unquestioning patriotism during times of war, and also due to the lack of attention by news media to these issues. This has led to state-facilitated profiteering by Halliburton as an agent of the state. After all, Halliburton is the "biggest contractor to the U.S. government in Iraq earning three times as much as Bechtel, its nearest competitor . . . earning $3.9 billion dollars from the military in 2003, a dizzying 680% increase from 2002 when it earned $483 million" (Chatterjee 2004:39).

The Bush-Cheney team has achieved a level of secrecy and symbolic power unlike that of any other administration (Dean 2004). Criminologists and the public must delve into understanding how and why the Cheney–Halliburton marriage has been able to remain and prosper in the White House. Not doing so increases the probability of future abuses of power, corrupt relationships, and war profiteering.

THE ALI BABA AND THE "WAR ON TERRORISM": THEORETICAL INTERPRETATION

The overall pattern of transnational globalization and military privatization that emerged from the early 1990s reinforced the already symbiotic relationship between states and corporations. It has long been acknowledged by many scholars that the state plays a major role in protecting the capitalist system and, thus, corporate interests (Chambliss and Zatz 1993; Gold, Lo, and Wright 1975; Marx 1906; Matthews and Kauzlarich 2000). The growth of the privatization of military logistics, supports, services—creating "corporate warriors"—coupled with corporate goals of profit making, may lead to crimogenic tendencies.[6]

War profiteering itself is not a new phenomenon (Clinard 1946). Yet, when the state and corporations become synonymous, the alliance of state actors and corporations is in and of itself a conflict of interest, perhaps even more so when this alliance co-produces military planning for an open-ended "war on terrorism." The opportunity and changes that this incestuous relationship portends is tectonic and has indeed led to a grand scale of war profiteering that is systematically condoned by the state by virtue of the dialectic interests of Halliburton and Cheney.

Motivations

The Halliburton–Cheney relationship and subsequent motivations cannot be analyzed without taking account of the geopolitical environment prior to the war on Iraq.[7] Prior to the Bush administration's appointment to the White House, a neoconservative agenda had been formulating for years, dating back to the pre-Reagan era (Kramer and Michalowski 2005). More recently, in 2000, documents such as *Rebuilding America's Defenses: Strategy, Forces, and Resources for a New Century*, put out by the Project for a New American Century, a key neoconservative think tank, clearly stated the ideology that would come to guide Bush's foreign policies and the war on Iraq. The report called for mass increases in the military budget and spending, the expansion of U.S. military bases, and the establishment of U.S. client states supportive of United States' economic and political interests. The imperial goals of the neocons were clear. Yet, as noted in chapter 13, what they lacked was the opportunity to implement these goals. Two unanticipated events gave them the opportunity to do so (Kramer and Michalowski 2005:26).

The primary "happenstance" was the victory of the Bush-Cheney ticket. Having Bush in the White House put the neocons in political positions near the center of power. However, at this point, Bush's political ideology remained attuned to the "pragmatic realists" in his administration, such as Secretary of State Colin Powell, than to those who sought a more aggressive foreign policy agenda (Kramer and Michalowski 2005:26).

The second "happenstance" was September 11, 2001. The atrocity acted as the kind of catalyst that the PNAC report had foreseen would speed up the process of transformation in the nation's view of the world (Kramer and Michalowski 2005:27). Conditions became favorable to swing Bush's "realistic" ideology to the far right.

Campaign attempts to build public support for the invasion of Iraq skillfully exploited the political opportunities provided by the fear and anger many felt over the 9/11 attacks (Michalowski and Kramer 2005; Rothe and Muzzatti 2004). By linking Saddam Hussein and Iraq to the wider war on terrorism, the administration established the idea that U.S. security required the ability, as a strategic unilateral defense mechanism, to attack any nation believed to be supporting terror. Yet this obscured the geopolitical and economic goals of creating a Pax Americana (Falk 2004:195). Moreover, the hidden agenda to change the political and economic culture in the Middle East was in fact to privatize whole economic structures favorable to capitalism and U.S. corporate interests.

In addition, for nearly two decades, the culture of international society has adhered to and utilized privatization of military activities (Singer 2003).[8] International society openly promotes the global market and capitalism. The role transnational corporations play within the global economy is enormous; thus the use and expansion of private U.S. corporations to supplement the U.S. military can be seen as a common trend.

After September 11, 2001, the United States received unprecedented international support to root out the terrorists responsible for the atrocity. Although the legalities of the war on terrorism remain dubious at best, it was largely supported as the United States went after Osama bin Laden in Afghanistan. The utilization of Halliburton (and other private corporations) within this climate might be seen as a "natural" role. Even as the United States alienated many other nations by taking illegal unilateral action in its attack on Iraq, the role of private corporations within a military setting remained common in the context of a global market. It is not the use of private corporations for logistical services per se that is problematic, but rather the use of corporations heavily tied to the political apparatus. As stated by Dwight Eisenhower in his 1961 farewell presidential speech, "This conjunction of an immense military establishment and a large arms industry is new in the American experience. . . . we must guard against the acquisition of unwarranted influence, whether sought or unsought, by the military-industrial complex. The potential for the disastrous rise of misplaced power exists and will persist. We must never let the weight of this combination endanger our liberties or democratic processes" (Eisenhower 1961).

Moreover, the dangers of war profiteering increase significantly when the vice president is connected to the largest LOGCAP contractor, Halliburton; Secretary of the Army Thomas White is linked to Enron; and George H. W. Bush, the current president's father, is tied to Carlyle Group.

Neoconservative state managers favor the utilization of private corporations for military purposes for several reasons. First, the neoconservative model of global economics supports the privatization (that is, outsourcing) of the provision of state services. Second, the ability to downsize the military force, thus using fewer uniform troops in a conflict or war, helps minimize public opposition. The trend to privatize state responsibilities dates, like the Halliburton–Cheney relationship, back to the early 1990s contracts that provided a schematic for the privatization of military logistic support. Yet the scope of the global privatization of the state's traditional duties greatly expanded once the George W. Bush administration took office. As President G. W. Bush's top economic advisor, Greg Mankiw (2004), has said, outsourcing is "a plus for the economy."

Beyond the promotion of privatization in general, the Bush-Cheney administration had further incentive to utilize private corporations for the war on terrorism. As has been noted most recently in the Iraq prisoner abuse scandals, private corporations are not held accountable under international criminal law, as U.S. soldiers would be. Transnational loopholes (Michalowski and Kramer 1987), which, as we will see, leave these corporations unregulated, played a role as well. The contracts awarded (and subsequent profits obtained) may also be classified for "security" reasons, further sheltering the administration from public disclosures and further increasing the potential for war profiteering.

An additional motivation for the administration to utilize corporations was the claim that private corporations are more cost effective than the military, thus saving the public's tax money. Further, the funds to pay corporations for wartime efforts were taken from funds that were unregulated by Congress. For example, contractors were originally to be paid with money approved by Congress, but the Coalition Provisional Authority decided to use Iraqi money through the DFI funds, which were subject to "fewer restrictions and less rigorous oversight" (*Mother Jones* 2004b). Contracts that used congressional funds would, by law, require rigorous oversight and an open bidding process. Using other monies gave the administration more leeway to fund its agenda without requesting additional funds for these corporations, thus alleviating the need for making requests associated with "rebuilding" costs or military support funds public.

Perhaps more significant is the desire to keep down the numbers of troops actively engaged in warfare to appease the public, while still having enough personnel to do the job. This preference is, in a part, a reaction to the public's abhorrence of the death and violence that war inevitably inflicts on U.S. soldiers. Since the end of the Vietnam War, presidents have worried that their military actions would lose support once the number of troop casualties climbed and news media began distributing pictures of the remains of U.S. soldiers on the battlefield or in draped coffins. Private contractor casualties, in contrast, are not reported or tallied by the Pentagon; the Pentagon leaves it up to the corporation to report or not. "They were afraid of turning this into another Vietnam," Larry Makinson, a senior fellow at the Center for Public Integrity, said. "They know what it's like to see casualty figures day after day. The reliance on civilian contractors in Iraq is really a different variation on the same theme that led the Pentagon to ban taking photographs of flag-draped coffins" (Ivanovich 2004c).

The use of Halliburton and subsidiaries has been a convenience because they are directly connected to the White House through their relationship with Cheney. Halliburton and its subsidiaries were also the founders of privatizing logistic support and providing plans to diffuse oil fires. Thus the use of Halliburton came easily, and no-bid contracts awarded could be justified by referring to the company's role in creating these "cost-efficient plans."

Halliburton's motivation is linked to its profit-making abilities. With the sharp decline in its stock (in the beginning of 2001), a result of the dozens of asbestos lawsuits filed against its subsidiary Dresser Ltd., Halliburton's need to regain losses coupled with its previous investment in Cheney (and his generous leave payment) represented a significant motivation to attain as many defense contracts as possible.

Opportunity

Motivation in and of itself, however, is not a sufficient catalyst. There must also be an opportunity for the state to award contracts to Halliburton and its subsidiaries. The opportunity must also be in place for Halliburton to attain state defense contracts and for it to systematically overcharge, use overrun costs, and take kickbacks.

The most palpable opportunity provided to Halliburton to attain vast state defense contracts was the direct connection to Cheney, yet the relationship itself would not have been enough without several other contingencies that had come into play to make the environment ripe for war profiteering. Specifically, opportunity began with the contested election of 2000 and the Supreme Court decision that put Bush and Cheney into office. Cheney's office put him at the core of political power. Thus his alliance with Halliburton became an even greater benefit for the company. Halliburton's ability to be in a position to bid on or accept contracts, however, is another matter.

Only three months into office, the Bush administration took steps to ensure corporate contracts would be unhindered. On April 1, 2001, the administration revoked regulation number 65 FR 80255. This regulation was the final Clinton ruling attempting to regulate corporations holding or attaining federal contracts, and it would have blacklisted Halliburton and many of its subsidiaries from qualifying for contracts. It required contracting officers to consider a prospective contractor's business record when awarding a contract and it required contractors to certify whether they had been convicted of any felonies within the past three years, or had any felony charges currently pending against them, or had otherwise been found liable in a civil proceeding. Moreover, Part 9 stated that a satisfactory record of integrity and business ethics included satisfactory compliance with the law, including tax, labor, employment, environment, antitrust, and consumer protection laws. Contracting officers were to consider all relevant information prior to granting a contract and were required to put the greatest weight on offenses adjucated within the past three years. These offenses included instances of fraud, defined as acts of corruption or attempts to defraud the government or corrupt its agencies (31.205-47).

As previously mentioned, on January 20, 2001, the Bush administration temporarily suspended the Clinton ruling (no. 65 FR 80255), followed with a second suspension on January 3, 2001, and then a permanently repealed the ruling via regulation number with 66 FR 17754 in April 2001 (Federal Register DOCID 2000, 2001). This was done in Item I, term of stay of final rule of Contractors Responsibilities published December 20, 2000, and Item II, finalizing the April 2001 proposed rule, thus revoking the December 20, 2000, rule in its entirety. Insofar as the administration facilitated Halliburton's ability to obtain future contracts, we can say that to some degree Halliburton's malfeasance was state-initiated.

The door of opportunity was further widened for U.S. corporations (mainly Halliburton) when Cheney began pushing for reviews of U.S. policy toward Libya and Iran. Cheney strongly criticized sanctions against countries like Iran and Libya, arguing that the sanctions did not work and punished U.S. companies. At an energy industry conference in 1996, Cheney said sanctions were the greatest threat to Halliburton and other American oil-related companies trying to expand overseas. The former defense secretary complained in a 1998 speech that U.S. companies were cut out of the action in Iran because of the sanctions (Kelley 2004). Moreover, in May 2001, the administration began lobbying the UN Security Council to end an eleven-year embargo on sales of civilian goods, including oil-related products, which would create future business for Halliburton subsidiaries (Dresser Ltd.) (Lynch 2001). Again, this is a case of the state acting as an initiator in setting the conditions for Halliburton.

The international arena had already been tested for expanded military privatization (see Singer 2003). Beyond this, the conditions that had been set within the international culture by the Bush-Cheney administration's unilateral approach to the "war on terrorism" with the invasion of Iraq provided further opportunities for Halliburton to obtain favorable contracts. After Russia, France, and Germany had denounced the U.S. plan to attack Iraq, the playing field for attaining contracts was limited to U.S. corporations. To ensure that the privatization of Iraq profited U.S. corporations, through the Coalition Provisional Authority the Bush administration ruled that no Iraqi state-owned companies would be eligible to bid for reconstruction contracts. Regardless of the cost-effectiveness of utilizing Iraqi companies or the negative consequences of not employing the Iraqi general population, the administration continued to hand out cost-plus contracts to Halliburton (and several other White House–connected corporations). For example, in addition to the gasoline charges already mentioned, according to the American Progress Report of 2004, "the U.S. bypassed General Co. for Water Projects, the formerly state-owned Iraqi company which knows the water system inside and out and which had already made preliminary progress on upgrading the decrepit water system. Instead, they gave a $16 million contract to Bechtel" (American Progress Report 2004b:1).

The relationship between Halliburton and Cheney further paved the way for systematic acts of war profiteering, because the relationship itself is legally dubious. It constitutes a conflict of interest that provided a level of access and opportunities for Halliburton enjoyed by no other company (Dean 2004). Beyond these opportunities, there were few controls or constraints acting against the administration or their corporate affiliates.

Controls and Constraints

At the international level, controls regulating transnational corporations are fewer and weaker than those in their home nations (Michalowski and Kramer 1987). Beyond traditional corporate activities, the privatization of the military force or support is "only subject to the laws of the market" (Singer 2003:220). Private military forces (PMF) and private logistical support teams amplify the concept of "loopholes," because their efforts involve minimal oversight, no transparency, and no standing international criminal laws to regulate them. Without some form of control, individuals are relatively free to behave as they see fit in the environments within which they operate. Hence PMFs operate with little or no controls to deter the development of deviant patterns of operation. Moreover, they are not subject to the Uniform Code of Military Justice, as soldiers are. In general they are subject to the laws of the nation-state they operate in. However, in Iraq, for example, the Coalition Provisional Authority issued an order providing immunity from Iraqi law for actions by contractors or their employees in the course of their official activities.[9] The laws under which U.S. civilian contractors might be prosecuted for actions abroad are restrictive and have never been tested (Singer 2003).

Internal controls were further weakened with the general move to privatize state defense work during the 1990s. For example, the personnel for the Defense Department's accounting and budget fell from 17,504 to 6,432. At the same time the number of workers in the defense contract audit agency of the Pentagon fell from 7,030 to 3,958 (*Financial Times* 2002). Thus most state contracts, especially with the recent surge of contracts pertaining to the war on terrorism, do not receive proper auditing or oversight.

Once the "war on terrorism" began, several congressional initiatives were taken to ensure federal contracts were receiving some form of monitoring. These initiatives included an amendment to the Iraq Appropriations Bill that would have criminalized war profiteering and required ongoing audits for submitted bills by the General Accounting Office for contracts over $25 million. Such measures, however, were derailed by the administration (and the House Republican Leader). The former head of the defense Energy Support Center stated, "The fact that those measures were defeated signaled, we don't agree oversight is necessary" (Jones 2003). This lack of oversight further ensured an organizational culture of resistance and crimogenic tendencies by providing unlimited opportunities for corporations to partake in war profiteering. It is also an illustration of state-facilitated behavior.

When controls were in place (such as the Defense Contract Audit Agency, DCAA), they were systematically ignored. On December 31, 2003, the audit of Halliburton by the DCAA was delivered to the Army Corps of Engineers and other DOD agencies. It revealed systematic overcharges, discrepancies, and unjustified cost proposals (U.S. House 2004). The DCAA recommended the Army Corps "contact us to ascertain the status of [Halliburton's] estimating system prior to entering into future negotiations" (U.S. House 2004:4). Three days later the Army Corps granted an additional $1.2 billion contract to Halliburton for restoring the oil infrastructure in southern Iraq without complying with the DCAA's recommendation.

Although Iraq war contracts in Kuwait were supposedly monitored, the teams responsible for this oversight were U.S. reservists who had received a two-week training course on contract management. Known as the Logistics Support Units, these oversight units were supposed to prepare independent cost estimates to be compared with Halliburton's estimates. Yet many "had never heard of LOGCAP" and "were being sent to the Middle East to provide contracting advice to commanders" (U.S. House 2004:6). Therefore it should come as no surprise that when a contract worth $587 million and only six pages long was submitted by Halliburton, it was approved in less than ten minutes (Bivens 2004; Chatterjee 2004). The Bush-Cheney administration has systematically ensured that oversight and regulations for federal state contracts were nullified or ignored; it thus neglected its duties to protect the interests of U.S. taxpayers while facilitating Halliburton's abusive open-ended contracts.

The downsizing of oversight staff by the Pentagon further exacerbated the lack of internal controls. In September 2003, the Pentagon put forth a new strategy to bolster the weakened staff by outsourcing the oversight agency. The Pentagon awarded a $121 million contract to a private contractor to oversee and regulate other private contractors. Some of these oversight agencies (Parsons Energy and the URS Group) also have Pentagon logistical support contracts (Shapiro 2004). As Congressman Waxman stated, one "could easily imagine one private contractor having other business dealings with the company over which they're supposed to be conducting oversight" (Waxman 2004a in Shapiro 2004:2).

Several studies have documented the failure of the media to provide the U.S. population either with an accurate portrayal of the Bush-Cheney administration's claims about Iraq or with the historical or political context within which the public could assess those claims (Alterman 2003; Kramer and Michalowski 2005; Moeller 2004a,b; Miller 2004; Solomon and Erlich 2003). Barak (1998) addressed the role of the media's representations as being the most significant communication that the average person will come to know about the world outside his or her immediate experiences. Society's foci are commanded by media accounts of events and political dictates (Burns and Crawford 1999). The coverage of the events of September 11, 2001, the war on terrorism, and the war on Iraq promoted as sacrosanct doctrine the idea that the United States was facing additional and continuing imminent threats (Rothe and Muzzatti 2004). This continued, unquestioning reproduction of state messages by communications media reveals its structural role as an ideological state apparatus.

Moreover, the U.S. media saturated the public with state-provided info-bites surrounding the war while failing to pay close attention to growing war profiteering, particularly regarding the ways in which profiteering was facilitated by the relationship between Halliburton with Cheney. When dissent occurred or information was leaked it was often challenged by the administration. For example, Cheney, in response to allegations of his ties to Halliburton and subsequent corruption in a CNN report, responded, "Allegations of corruption stem from 'desperate' political opponents who can't find any legitimate policy differences to debate" (CNN Web site, January 22, 2004).

Another example of the general trend of administration-slanted media coverage was the congressional report released September 2003 that found Cheney still owned more than 433,000 shares of Halliburton stock options. Cheney refuted his ties to Halliburton, saying, "And since I left Halliburton to become George Bush's vice president, I've severed all my ties with the company, gotten rid of all my financial interests. I have no financial interest in Halliburton of any kind and haven't had now for over three years" ("Meet the Press," September 14, 2003). However, the Congressional Research Service report says that the deferred compensation that Cheney receives from Halliburton as well as the 433,000 stock options he possesses "is considered among the 'ties' retained in or 'linkages to former employers' that may 'represent a continuing financial interest' in those employers which makes them potential conflicts of interest." Senator Frank Lautenberg said, "The ethics standards for financial disclosure [are] clear. Vice President Cheney has a financial interest in Halliburton."

From the onset, the administration of George W. Bush acted to reverse any existing regulations or oversights. Halliburton was in an opportune position to "cash in" on its past with Cheney and attain enormous state contracts while exerting relatively little effort to obtain them. The level of secrecy and lack of transparency within the government have reached all-time highs, providing further vast opportunities for contracts to be awarded with little scrutiny.[10] Indeed, the state facilitated and initiated Halliburton's ability to illegally and unethically obtain contracts and earn profits.

CONCLUSION

The atrocity of September 11, 2001, clearly was a factor in enabling the Bush administration to gain public support for the war on Iraq. Moreover, the timing of the attacks coincided with the "right" administration being placed in the White House. Halliburton was perfectly positioned to seize the moment to attain additional state contracts. Moreover, the direct connection to Cheney provided further opportunities for Halliburton that would not have been present without the aforementioned conditions.

While war profiteering by Halliburton has been characterized by defense officials as stupid mistakes that can be made right by *nole contendere* payments, the systematic practice of over-costs, overcharges, failure to provide services charged for, and kickback profits are actually a result of the incestuous relationship between Halliburton, Cheney, and Bush. Beyond their existing empowered roles within the state, their political agendas have paved the way for further privatizing areas of the world deemed U.S. interests. More specifically, the Bush administration's imperial agenda, coupled with its private interest in fostering economic expansion through privatization for its "family" companies, has created an environment conducive to war profiteering. Thus the motive for economic gain is both personal and political, serving both administration members' individual financial situations and their neoconservative political agenda. Moreover, Cheney's ties with Halliburton "represent a continuing financial interest in those employers which makes them potential conflicts of interests" (Congressional Research Service, quoted in Chatterjee 2004:44). Hence the Supreme Court rulings appointing Bush and Cheney into the White House, coupled with the September 11, 2001, attacks, brought an explosion of opportunities for the administration, Halliburton, and war profiteering.

As the theoretical model illuminates, efforts to control these forms of state-corporate crimes must address all levels of the model: actors; the organizational, structural, and economic culture of hypercapitalism; and the international arena. As state and state-corporate crime literature suggests, there must be internal and external controls. Until measures are taken to provide international regulations for transnational corporations and accountability measures for states utilizing privatization of defense work, no external controls will exist. Currently there are little to no incentive or enforcement mechanisms for the state to adhere to any international laws. Therefore an empowered universal criminal court that is empowered to address states and corporations must be allowed to exist within the international arena.

As long as the current administration's use of secrecy and flagrant violations of checks and balances remains unchallenged by Congress, the public, and the press, little will be done to stop the practices of granting unregulated defense contracts. Internal regulations must be established to separate state from corporate interests. These must include an end to the practice of lobbying and campaign contributions. The revolving door between public and private must be closed. Without these internal and external controls, war profiteering will continue.

NOTES

1. War profiteering can be classified as immoral or unethical; however, I use "war profiteering" as a concept that includes both unethical and illegal acts, as they are often intermingled.

2. William H. T. Bush made $450,000 in war profits from Iraq via the St. Louis–based defense contractor Engineered Support Systems Inc. William, who sits on the company's board, cashed out a half-million of the company's stock options in January 2005. ESSI's stock prices had skyrocketed to record heights after the decision by the Bush administration to invade Iraq was made public. ESSI raked in millions from contracts to refit military vehicles with extra armor, build protective shelters for chemical and biological weapons worth $19 million (despite the fact that no biological or chemical weapons have been found in Iraq), and provide communications support services to the Coalition Provisional Authority (American Progress Report 2004a).

3. For more details on neocons and their ideology, see Dorrien (2004). See also chapter 13 above.

4. Bunting is one of six former employees who came forward publicly to testify and provide Congress with information about egregious overcharges by Halliburton (Waxman 2004).

5. The Bush-Cheney family includes the Carlyle Group (where the senior Bush was a board member and holds significant stock shares); Lockhead Martin (Lynne Cheney was a board member from 1994 to January 2001 as well as a director); Engineered Support Systems (William Bush is on the board of directors); and Lord and Abbott (William Bush is acting trustee).

6. For more information, on this topic see Singer (2003).

7. For a detailed analysis of the underlying motivations to go to war on Iraq, see chapter 13 above, Michalowski and Kramer (2005), and Dorrien (2004).

8. The terms "international community" and "international society" are indeed imagined, ideologically, to promote unity at the international level and are often associated with international organizations representing civil actors as well as political institutions. I prefer to use the term "international society," because it carries fewer connotations that there exists a common set of values, goals, and interactions. "International society" thus represents a collection of state and civil actors, active in the international political arena and in positions of power to impose or create international institutions, policies, or laws that affect the existing international political realm in its historical contexts.

9. The administrator of the Coalition Provisional Authority must give permission to prosecute contractors for acts performed outside of their official duties (Coalition Provisional Authority Order Number 17: Status of the Coalition, Foreign Liaison Missions, their Personnel and Contractors).

10. For more information on the secrecy and lack of transparency pursued by this administration, see Dean (2004).

CHAPTER 15

Taking Stock of Theory and Research

David Kauzlarich and Rick A. Matthews

Our experiences as state-corporate crime researchers and theorists have been a deeply rewarding part of our intellectual lives. Not only has working in the area of state-corporate crime provided us with intellectual challenges and research opportunities; it has also enabled us to be part of an energetic and growing network of scholars working closely and collaboratively in this area. A well-respected, prolific critical criminologist not involved in state-corporate crime research once told us that such a sustained body of high-quality scholarship from a network of researchers working in concert on a particular problem area was unparalleled in criminology. That the work performed by these scholars has made such a significant impact on both critical criminology and criminology was even more impressive to him. Any criminologist would be fortunate to be part of such a vibrant, devoted intellectual community. We are no exception.

The preceding chapters in this volume represent much of the research and theory on state-corporate crime to date. Several of the chapters in this book have played instrumental roles in placing the critical analysis of the harm generated by direct and indirect state and corporate collusion into the criminological consciousness. Judging by the increasing level of citation and reference to the concept of state-corporate crime in both mainstream and critical criminology textbooks, as well as in most if not all white-collar crime textbooks, we have good reason to be optimistic about the future of state-corporate crime research.

The first wave of state-corporate crime theory and research revolved around three concerns: (1) advancing the concept as a legitimate form of crime suitable for criminological analysis; (2) exposing the massive injury that can be caused by state and corporate wrongdoing; and (3) developing an integrated theoretical framework to help explain how and why state-corporate crime (and organizational crime more generally) occurs. Much of this scholarship was organized around empirical examinations of cases in which state agencies and corporations caused injuries to workers, transportation passengers, and the natural environment.

As the preceding chapters also indicate, the understanding of state-corporate crime has grown to include innovative theoretical and empirical expansions of the original concept. For example, Kramer, Michalowski, Wonders, and Danner have recently extended the inquiry to explore the ways in which the dynamics of globalization affect state-corporate crime (chapters 7 and 11); Wonders and Danner have exposed the disproportionate effects of state-corporate crime on women (chapter 7); Robyn has illustrated how state and corporate collusion can be racist (chapter 12); Matthews has shown how corporations can facilitate state crime (chapter 8); and the highly publicized pump and dump schemes by Enron and other major corporations has been shown by Michalowski and Kramer to have strong ties to both state policies and deeper questions of the structural and cultural construction of ethical relations (chapter 11).

There is much to celebrate, considering that the criminological study of state-corporate crime is barely fifteen years old. We have learned a great deal about the manner in which motivations, opportunities, and levels of social control influence the genesis and persistence of organizational crime and deviance. For instance, the identification of both explicit and implicit state-level policies and practices that lead to corporate harm have been highlighted in many of the studies. In studies of state-facilitated corporate crimes, we see how the Federal Aviation Administration's lax regulation over one of its most notorious airlines allowed the conditions under which over one hundred people died in the crash of ValuJet flight 592 (Matthews and Kauzlarich, chapter 6). In Aulette and Michalowski's (chapter 4) analysis of the Imperial Food Products fire, it becomes clear that the minuscule attention given to workers and the workplace by both state and federal OSHA offices never even approached what a reasonable person would consider to be satisfactory. In studies of state-initiated state-corporate crime, such as the one by Kauzlarich and Kramer on the environmental damage caused by U.S. nuclear weapons production (chapter 5), it is not difficult to see how the state's drive for control over global resources, hegemony, and the creation and maintenance of a friendly capitalist world order provided the larger backdrop for the crimes. In the *Challenger* case (chapter 3), the mounting pressure on NASA in the context of the Cold War and the specific desire to resurrect the U.S. space program provided paths for action by state agents that ultimately led to disaster.

Just as it has been important to state-corporate crime scholars to study the underlying economic and political motivations of the state, such analysis is by definition necessary as it pertains to corporate and organizational goals more generally. Similar forces also influence corporations, albeit in a different way, as private corporations are motivated to accumulate capital, while the state tries to find ways to facilitate this activity, either directly or indirectly. The link between corporate concerns with profit maximization and corporate indifference to actual and potential safety hazards is well documented in Mullins's analysis of the Ford and Firestone-Bridgestone tire tread separation problem (chapter 9). The same type of corporate negligence is illustrated by Cruciotti and Matthews's (chapter 10) case study of the *Exxon Valdez* oil spill, which is probably the worst avoidable environmental disaster to date. Corporate greed tends to trump health, environmental, and safety concerns in many cases of state-corporate crime. This ordering of priorities has been understood for many years in the organizational crime literature, but how and why the crimes emerge when they do can only be fully understood by examining the context of each case, especially the perceived opportunities, the level of pressure for organizational goal attainment, and the degree to which social control mechanisms are operational.

Much has also been learned about the ways in which opportunity structures the behavioral manifestations of these motivations and, in turn, how the broader regulatory climate affects opportunities. Many state-corporate crimes develop in the context of weak or nonexistent social control mechanisms. This is especially true in cases involving U.S. government involvement in crime during the Cold War, but also holds true in the new age of globalization, where the diffusion and unevenness of knowledge and power are exacerbated by geography, the fickle dynamics of international relations, the enduring desire for capitalist expansion around the globe, and the willingness of nation-states to facilitate the development of pathways for capitalist development and growth. The very existence of the political state and of corporations depends on inequality, specifically significant concentrations of economic or political power in relatively few hands. When economic and political institutions act together to reach common objectives, the consequences for those without the power to resist can be devastating. Indeed, as with the victimology of traditional street crime, the least powerful are almost always the most likely to be victimized by state-corporate crime.

Although the body of research and theorizing on state-corporate crime continues to grow, garner attention, and expand the range of inquiry, much work is still left to do. In this closing chapter we will discuss some ways in which the phenomenon of state-corporate crime could be better understood. One way is by using a greater variety of methodologies and research designs in empirical examinations of the phenomenon. Almost all of the empirical studies of state-corporate crime are qualitative case studies. Relatedly, another area in need of further development is the teasing out of some of the interactional forces at work between individuals performing their bureaucratic and professional roles. Greater attention to the "lived reality" of state-corporate crime would add more multidimensionality to our understanding of the phenomenon. We also need to continue to examine harms that occur at the international level, particularly crimes of globalization and crimes of empire. Finally, there is work to do in the area of praxis—that is, bringing the concept of state-corporate crime from academic quarters to the real world.

FUTURE THEORETICAL AND METHODOLOGICAL DIRECTIONS

The integrated theoretical framework originally developed by Kramer and Michalowski provides a meaningful way to examine the structure and process of state-corporate crime at several different levels of analysis. The theory is centered on the proposition that state-corporate crime is likely to result when the motivation for organizational goal attainment is strong, opportunities to engage in illegitimate means to achieve those goals are available, and social control is weak. The logic of the model is not dissimilar from that found in several important criminological theories, including Merton's (1938) strain theory, various structural Marxist explanations of crime, and Sutherland's differential association theory. Further, the model is consistent with the basic approach taken by several other theorists of organizational crime, including Coleman's (1998) emphases on control, opportunity, and motivation, as well as central elements of Braithwaite's theory of reintegrative shaming (1989a). As an integrated theoretical model, Kramer and Michalowski's framework reflects a larger trend in criminology over the last fifteen years of fusing disparate theories into a more powerful, general explanation of crime. Because state-corporate crime tends to be among the more complicated types of crime to explain (owing to the multitude of actors, policies, and relationships involved) weaving the most important concepts together from different theories is not only appropriate but also necessary. One of the advantages of theoretical integration is that several different levels of social reality can be included in one analysis. Most conventional theories of traditional and white-collar crime tend to privilege one level of analysis over others. With integrated theoretical models, however, an attempt is made to "cover all the bases" in order to highlight the multiple connections between individuals, organizations, structures, and processes vital to the genesis and persistence of high level deviance.

Kramer and Michalowski's original theoretical model, and subtle refinements to it by Kauzlarich and Kramer (1998), however, has never really been used to its full potential. We believe that this is due in large part to the tendency of the empirical studies of state-corporate crime to focus on the structural and organizational levels of analyses. Although one can detect some degree of interactional or individual-level analysis in these studies, inference rather than systematic data tends to be characteristic of this research. We are guilty ourselves, in that our case study of the ValuJet crash (chapter 6) highlights factors on the structural and organizational level of analysis, that is, airline deregulation and Federal Aviation Administration policies. To be sure, there are good reasons for this emphasis in our own work and in the work of others. Careful analysis at the macrosociological level of analysis is crucial for understanding how the conjoined practices and policies of states and corporations cause injury. In the 1980s and 1990s, criminology seemed to be moving farther away from structural-level approaches, as evidenced by the popularity of Gottfredson and Hirschi's self-control theory (1990) and the biosocial approach of Wilson and Herrnstein (1985). These theories are of little use in efforts to understand organizational crime, and they have been critiqued on those grounds (Reed and Yeager 1996). Still, it is important that criminologists such as those working in the area of state-corporate crime give priority to the structural level of analysis, because by definition the phenomenon cannot be understand if it is divorced from macrolevel structures. However, the theoretical framework that has been used by many of us as a guiding analytical tool calls for attention to three units of analysis: interactional, organizational, and institutional. But in most if not all of the case studies, the phenomenon is seldom as rigorously examined on the interactional level of analysis as on the others. Instead, there is a tendency to focus on the internal elements of the organizations involved and the relationships they have with other abstracted entities that produce injury. Such contextual analysis is important, but it only provides a part of the picture.

It is to be expected that studies of state-corporate crime would focus on higher-order relationships and practices. As a concept that challenges traditional criminological formulations of crime, state-corporate crime pushes the discipline into somewhat unfamiliar territory, and therefore requires its students to understand a major ontological assumption: that state and corporate organizations are real actors that can be understood as connected to, but analytically distinct from, individual employees, owners, and regulators. However, although it is true that this matter represents an enduring issue in criminology, and therefore needs to be addressed in some way (especially with students, conservative scholars in criminology, and the public in general—after all, traditional criminology and students of the field often gravitate toward atomistic perspectives and structural analysis often gets shortchanged), the body of literature on state-corporate crime seems to be developed enough to provide room to expand the parameters of study without losing the critical, humanistic edge that has become a hallmark of this body of work.

Some of the gaps in understanding state-corporate crime on the interactional level of analysis may be filled by designing studies that tap into the lived experience of the actors and victims associated with the crimes. Here we are referring to the ways in which the persons who occupy positions within state and corporate structures conceptualize their relationship to their work and their organization and how those individuals who are hurt by state-corporate crime come to grips with their victimization. The only way to get at this is by conducting qualitative interviews. Although many of us have in fact conducted interviews as part of our case studies, there may be a greater reliance on secondary interview data sources (court or congressional testimony, journalistic interviews, and watchdog group or media investigations) or the document trail (such as declassified documents, official mission statements, and memoirs) to provide this part of the picture. There is nothing wrong with using these sources as long as they are interpreted judiciously, but more can be learned if we take the plunge into full-scale interview methodology.

Let us consider for a moment EPA or OSHA regulators, those who may have some complicity in a state-facilitated corporate crime. It would be valuable to know if they think their work is important, how seriously they take their organization's mission, and whether they feel overworked, underpaid, understaffed, or alienated. Additionally we may want to interview these regulators to see if they find fault with themselves for the negative consequences of their inaction or inabilities. If not, do they rationalize their action or inaction in the same way that others do? Do they blame others? In our work on the ValuJet case, we wish we could have interviewed FAA agents and directors on these and other topics. Rather than taking away from the structural analysis, such inquiries could have only enriched our understanding of the event.

What about the victims of the crimes? Do they see themselves as *crime* victims? Do they blame themselves for their suffering? Do they even know they have been victimized? Are the same problems victims face in the wake of traditional street crime victimization found in state-corporate crime victimization, or white-collar crime victimization more generally? For example, it would be useful to know to what extent Holocaust survivors or the families of those lost conceptualize the complicity of IG Farben, General Motors, and Ford. How about Native Americans victimized by greedy corporations and state indifference? What narratives await our ears from these people and others, such as those workers who survived the fire in Hamlet or others who lost a loved one in a Ford Explorer rollover?

Finally, what do corporate officials involved in state-corporate crime have to say about their behavior? Do they, like many white-collar criminals, believe they are not really wrongdoers? Are they as personally obsessed with money and profits as much as the record might indicate? What do they really think of—and what language do they use to describe—worker safety issues, the protection of the environment, consumer safety, or the thresholds involved in taking "calculated risks"? Most important, do their definitions of their roles in space and time differ from the noncriminal bourgeoisie?

Qualitative interviews, like other forms of research, are rife with methodological problems and, as such, also need to be used judiciously and in combination with other data sources, such as those secondary and documentary sources described above. However, they might be the most important direction for state-corporate crime scholars to take, given the need for more interactional-level data in order to more directly link the theoretical framework's various parts together. One potential barrier to the development of an in-depth, qualitative studies of regulators, victims, and offenders of state-corporate crime is that, as Michalowski and Kramer note in the introduction to this volume, government funding for research into corporate and political crimes is rare. Thus, at least for the near future, state-corporate crime researchers will need to work diligently to cultivate private funding sources and develop creative low-cost research strategies.

We may also consider the lower tier of the integrated theoretical framework (see chapter 2). Under the motivational dimension of the interactional level of analysis, we find the following concepts: socialization, social meaning, individual goals, competitive materialism, and emphasis on material success. Regarding the opportunity dimension, we find the following sensitizing concepts: definitions of the situation and perceptions of the availability and attractiveness of illegal means. Finally, the control element of the interactional level of analysis would involve attention to personal morality, rationalizations/techniques of neutralization, separation from consequences, obedience to authority, groupthink, and the diffusion of responsibility.

Debating the whole subject-object conundrum in the social sciences is beyond the scope of this chapter, but if we want to develop the lower tier of the theoretical model so that it is more clearly tied into dynamics found at the other levels of analysis, energy must be invested into research on how actors internalize larger forces and pressures and then choose to act or not act within them. At the same time, to what extent do actors work to shape and possibly change organizational structures to fit their sense of what to do? These questions appear to be particularly salient when thinking about the complicit activities of offenders or parties to the often complex decision-making process that goes into, for example, launching a space shuttle or, as was the case with Enron, finding a way to defraud hundreds of investors and employees. Although we agree with Braithwaite and many other sociologists of crime that social-psychological explanations miss much of what is involved in white-collar crime, better attention to these matters, especially since they are a part of the theory of state-corporate crime itself, could contribute to the understanding of not only how structural and organizational forces are created and sustained, but also how they are navigated through, carried out, and impressed upon those with the discretion to act.

Our suggestions to more fully explore the theoretical and empirical interactional dimensions of state-corporate crime commission, omission, and victimization are intended to stimulate discussion and generate research in the future. This takes nothing away from the impressive body of research that has accumulated over the last two decades on state-corporate crime. At this point, however, despite some continuing challenges to the legitimacy of the concept itself in a few academic circles, the concept is probably as legitimate in academe as concepts ever get. If we are correct, attempts to both refine and expand the methodology to answer less-discussed theoretical issues should only reap rewards, rather than taking away from what we have accomplished or interfering with our continuing calls for more criminological attention to the problem.

FUTURE RESEARCH AT THE INTERNATIONAL LEVEL: GLOBALIZATION AND EMPIRE

Michalowski and Kramer (2006) have recently argued that criminologists need to do more research on the social harms that emanate from the intersection of business and government at the international level. Here they specifically refer to the crimes of globalization and crimes of empire. In an era of economic globalization, they note, it is important to explore the impact of neoliberalism. They observe (Michalowski and Kramer 2006:12)

> Transnational corporations (TNCs), national states and international financial institutions act together to privatize the global economy and promote free market policies. New legal frameworks favorable to TNCs and investors are adopted, business regulations are gutted, taxes are cut, and welfare services and other public interventions on behalf of social and economic equality are withdrawn. The consequences of these policies and practices are great crimes; that is, preventable social harms such as economic inequality, poverty, environmental destruction, hunger, disease and premature death. And, ironically, greater levels of what criminologists normally focus on: conventional forms of interpersonal violence and property crime.

Michalowski and Kramer (2006) also argue that given the imperial designs of the current U.S. government, it is also important to analyze what these authors term "crimes of empire." They note that as the neoconservatives who control the George W. Bush administration pursue a geopolitical strategy to project American power, secure access to and control over oil supplies, and reshape the political culture of the Middle East, turning that part of the world into a laboratory for radical free market policies, a number of serious state-corporate crimes have been committed. As they point out in chapter 13, in the pursuit of empire, the United States has engaged in wars of aggression and committed war crimes and other violations of human rights. These crimes of empire should be given close scrutiny by criminologists in the future.

A related area of concern that should receive close scrutiny from state-corporate crime researchers is the role of supragovernmental organizations such as the International Monetary Fund (IMF), the World Trade Organization

(WTO), and the World Bank in shaping both structural conditions and control regimes that may either be conducive to or restraints against state-corporate crime. To this we would also add the need to examine more carefully the role of nongovernmental organizations (NGOs) that have come to play an increasingly central role in shaping norms and treaties at the international level (Clark 2001). As globalization intensifies, it will be critical for researchers concerned with state-corporate crime to incorporate these new transnational entities in their formulations.

FUTURE POLICY IMPLICATIONS

As the current research in the area of state-corporate crime indicates, much harm has been created through regulatory neglect of corporate activities. Unfortunately, in many instances, corporations are not held legally accountable for their crimes. For example, over sixty years have passed and not a single U.S.-owned corporation has faced criminal charges for its activities in support of the Holocaust. Given the length of time that has elapsed, it would be naïve to think that they will in the future—too many documents have been destroyed, too many witnesses are no longer living. Besides, one might add, Congress seems busy with much larger and more pressing issues, like steroids in baseball.

It is easy to be pessimistic about the prospects for social change that would effectively prevent or control state-corporate crime. At the same time, there are glimpses of hope. For example, we believe that in some ways, the public is more receptive to taking a hard look at corporate wrongdoing. The collapse of Enron and Arthur Andersen brought a considerable amount of media attention. Further, corporate criminals are now making the front page of the *New York Times*, which while not good in the sense that they have caused significant harms, is good in the sense that public attention is being directed toward them. It is also interesting to note that Eliot Spitzer, attorney general of New York State and arguably the most aggressive corporate-crime fighter on the contemporary scene, appears poised to become governor of New York State in the 2006 election (Cassidy 2003). These trends suggest the potential for rolling back some of the neoliberal victories in weakening controls of corporate and state wrongdoing.

In chapter 11 Michalowski and Kramer outline the key principles of economic democracy and the ethics of inclusion. It is doubtful, however, that politicians will take the lead in the area of creating effective legislation to curb corporate crime or that corporate executives will take the lead in creating a new ethics of inclusion. Given the current system of lobbyists and the significant amounts of money that are poured into the political machinery by corporations, we are skeptical whether politicians or corporate executives can be an effective avenue for change. This is unfortunate, because until politicians decide to pass meaningful legislation and to create regulatory agencies with real teeth, and corporate officials practice ethics of inclusion, it will be difficult to protect the public from the predatory tendencies of some corporations.

At the same time, however, we do not want to paint such a rigid instrumentalist picture of the state that there is no prospect for political change. Old debates between the instrumental and structuralist Marxists are instructive here, and we recognize that the state acts to preserve the system, sometimes at the expense of the capitalist class. In addition, political creatures can be motivated by their instincts for self-preservation.

In the past fifteen years we have seen a great deal of political responsiveness to the fringe of the religious right in the United States. This didn't happen by accident. For over twenty years, its proponents have been organizing at the grassroots level, starting small by taking over (sometimes by stealth) local school boards. They parlayed their success at the local level to larger projects, and later found themselves building alliances with nonreligious social conservatives. With the election of George W. Bush, and the events of September 11th, they solidified their position, becoming a significant political force in U.S. politics at the outset of the twenty-first century. For progressives, this reality has created a grim political situation, and given the current political leanings of the country, the administration, and the iron-fisted grip corporations appear to have in the global economy, one may be inclined to submit to "business as usual."

Thus on the one hand we have a public that may be interested in corporate crimes, and perhaps is willing to turn a critical eye toward them, and on the other hand we have a conservative political atmosphere beholden to corporate interests and, to some extent, the religious right. On the surface, opportunity for progressive change appears limited.

One way to further understand this problem is by examining the dynamics and implications of topic "framing," as Lakoff (2002) has suggested. His work can help to explain how liberals and conservatives often talk past one another. If conceptualizing harm by state and corporate collusion as "criminal" may too harsh a word for some, what kinds of language shifts (for example, reference to larger justice and equality principles) could be heuristically used to move discourse toward a wider recognition of the need to control and prevent such elite crime? However, if Lakoff's (2004:37) claim that "if a strongly held frame does not fit the facts, the facts will be ignored and the frame will be kept," is true, then there is little reason to believe that exposure to the facts per se regarding the criminality of much state and corporate collusion would be very effective. For example, even though there is an airtight legal case that the latest U.S. war on Iraq violated the most basic tenets of international law, as Kramer and Michalowski note in chapter 13, such a "fact" is not meaningful to the majority of the American public, who believe the war in Iraq is both justifiable and legal (although many millions, perhaps a billion other citizens around the globe certainly believe the war to be illegal). Perhaps such a fact is dismissed as hyperbolic by those wedded to, in Lakoff's (2002, 2004) terms, the "strict father" perspective, because this alternative perspective challenges the emotional bonds some have to all that is perceived as "patriotism." Clearly this was at work in the domestic support by U.S. citizens for the disengagement of the United States from participation in the International Criminal Court, and, this frame has been relied upon for some time by a sizable proportion of the U.S. populace who oppose United Nations initiatives that are perceived not to meet the express interests of the United States. Bush and his allies, of course, have relied on the strict father perspective and capitalized on its power to argue for the appropriateness of the U.S. invasion of Iraq by proclaiming that the United States does not need a "permission slip" from others to protect its own national security.

At the same time, there are examples of successful academic and public collaborations that have framed state violence in formal legal terms. The Lawyers Committee on Nuclear Policy, for instance, worked hard with activist groups for decades to demonstrate that the use or threat to use nuclear weapons could in no way be reconciled with the spirit and substance of the international laws of war. Antinuclear groups and others used this argument to galvanize international support for this line of reasoning, and after several years, the issue finally made it to the International Court of Justice, where the court indeed found that any use of these weapons would be illegal (Kramer and Kauzlarich 1999). Although the decision has probably had little or no effect on U.S. public opinion due to the fact that the Court's finding received next to nothing in the way of press coverage, it is an excellent example of academic and nonacademic groups working together to create an institutional level definition of a form of state violence as clearly "criminal."

Whatever problems and the causes of those problems that mitigate against a more public criminology of state-corporate crime, it is clear that the framing of the injurious consequences of state and corporate collaboration as criminal is vital if criminology (both critical and otherwise) is to weigh in and have relevance to conversations about ongoing and future acts of violence by those in positions of political and corporate power. As Barak (2003) has recently noted, critical criminology must be especially aware of its obligation to search for and work with people from all walks of life to promote peace and nonviolence. While the concept of state-corporate crime is well established in academic criminology, more accessible, applied research, perhaps in the vein we have suggested, is needed to further understand the possibilities and difficulties of resisting the structures and processes that give rise to state-corporate crime.

Chambliss, W. 1988. *On the Take: From Petty Crooks to Presidents.* Revised edition. Bloomington: Indiana University Press.

―――. 1989. "State-Organized Crime." *Criminology* 27: 183–208.

―――. 1995. "Commentary by William J. Chambliss." *Society for the Study of Social Problems (SSSP) Newsletter* 26: 1–9.

Chambliss, W., and M. Zatz. 1993. *Making Law: The State, the Law, and Structural Contradictions.* Bloomington: Indiana University Press.

Charlesworth, H. 2003. "Is International Law Relevant to the War in Iraq and Its Aftermath?" Telstra Address, National Press Club, Canberra, Australia. October 29.

Charlotte Observer. 1991. "Firefighters Near Plant Not Called: Chief Cites Racism." September 6, 4A.

Chatterjee, P. 2003. "Halliburton Makes a Killing on Iraq War." CorpWatch, Independent Media Institute. http://www.alternet.org/print/html?StoryID=15445 (accessed March 21, 2004).

―――. 2004. *Iraq Inc.: A Profitable Occupation.* New York: Seven Stories Press.

Chatterjee, P., and Herbert Docena. 2003–2004. "Occupation, INC." *Southern Studies* (Winter).

Cheney, Dick. 2002. Meet the Press. Interviewed on NBC's Tim Russert, September. Archive. Transcript available from NBC News. http://www.mtholyoke.edu/acad/intrel/bush/meet.htm.

Chiricos, T., K. Padgett, and M. Gertz. 2000. "Fear, TV News, and the Reality of Crime." *Criminology* 38 (August): 755–785.

Chomsky, N. 1987. *On Power and Ideology.* Boston: South End Press, 1987.

―――. 1988. *The Culture of Terrorism.* Boston: South End Press, 1988.

―――. 2003. *Hegemony or Survival: America's Quest for Global Dominance.* New York: Metropolitan Books.

Chronicle. 2004. "Silence Surrounds Fate of Contractors," by David Ivanoch. November 21. http://www.chron.com/cs/CDA/ssistory.mp1/metropolitan/2911419.

Churchill, W. 1997. *A Little Matter of Genocide: Holocaust and Denial in the Americas, 1942 to Present.* San Francisco: City of Lights Books.

Churchill, W., and W. LaDuke. 1992. "Native North America: The Political Economy of Radioactive Colonialism." In *The State of Native America: Genocide, Colonization, and Resistance,* ed. M. A. Jaimes. Boston: South End Press.

Churchill, W., and J. VanderWall. 1990. *The Cointelpro Papers: Documents from the FBI's Secret Wars against Dissent in the United States.* Boston: South End Press. Reprinted 2002.

Clarfield, G., and W. Wiecek. 1984. *Nuclear America: Military and Civilian Power in the United States.* New York: Harper and Row.

Clark, A. M. 2001. *Diplomacy of Conscience: Amnesty International and Changing Human Rights Norms.* Princeton, NJ: Princeton University Press.

Clarke, R. 2004. *Against All Enemies: Inside America's War on Terror.* New York: Free Press.

Clarkson, F. 1997. *Eternal Hostility: The Struggle between Theocracy and Democracy.* Boston: Common Courage Press.

Clinard, M. 1946. "Criminological Theories of Violations of Wartime Regulations." *American Sociological Review* 2: 258–270.

―――. 1990. *Corporate Corruption: The Abuse of Power.* New York: Praeger.

Clinard, M., and R. Quinney. 1973. *Criminal Behavior Systems: A Typology.* 2nd ed. New York: Holt, Rinehart, and Winston.

Clinard, M., and P. Yeager. 1980. *Corporate Crime.* New York: Free Press.

Cloward, R., and L. Ohlin. 1960. *Delinquency and Opportunity: A Theory of Delinquent Gangs.* New York: Free Press.

CNN. 2000. CNN News. October 6. http://www.cnn.com/2000?ALLPOLITICS/ stories/10/05/vp.debate (accessed October 6, 2000).

———. 2003a. *Iraq Rebuilding Contracts.* March 25. http://money.cnn.com/2003/ 03/25/news/companies/war_contracts/ (accessed March 25, 2003).

———. 2003b. News. "*Congressional Report.*" (September 9).

CNN Money. 2004. "Pentagon Puts Hold on Halliburton Pay." March 17. http://money. cnn.com/2004/03/17/news/companies/halliburton/index.htm.

CNN Report. 2004. January 22. http://www.cnn.com/2004/ALLPOLITICS/ 05/30/cheney.halliburton/. Also available at www.americanprogress.org/ AccountTempFiles/cf/%7BE9245FE4-9A2B-43C7-A521-5D6FF2E06E03%7D/ halliburton.rtf.

Cochran, T. B. 1988. "U.S. Nuclear Weapons Production: An Overview." *Bulletin of the Atomic Scientists* (January–February): 12–17.

Cohen, M. G. 1996. "Women, Democracy, and the Future of Nations." In *States against Markets: The Limits of Globalization,* ed. R. Boyer and D. Drache, 383–414. London: Routledge.

Cohen, M. J. 1997. "Economic Impacts of the Exxon Valdez Oil Spill." In *The Exxon Valdez Disaster: Readings on a Modern Social Problem,* ed. J. S. Picou, D. A. Gill and M. J. Cohen, 133–164. Dubuque, IA: Kendall/Hunt.

Cohen, S. 1972. *Folk Devils and Moral Panics.* London: Routledge.

———. 1985. *Visions of Social Control: Crime, Punishment, and Classification.* New York: Blackwell.

Cohn, M. 2004. "Torturing Hearts and Minds." *Truthout.* http://truthout.org/docs 04/050404A.shtml.

Coleman, J. W. 1987. "Toward an Integrated Theory of White-Collar Crime." *American Journal of Sociology* 93: 406–439.

———. 1998 [1985]. *The Criminal Elite: The Sociology of White Collar Crime.* 4th ed. New York: St. Martin's Press.

Coll, Steve. 2004. *Ghost Wars: The Secret History of the CIA, Afghanistan, and Bin Laden.* New York: Penguin.

Colmenarez, A. C. 2000. Internal Bridgestone-Firestone Venezuela memo. May 9.

Congressional Budget Office. 1994. *Cleaning Up the DOE's Nuclear Weapons Complex.* Washington, DC: Congressional Budget Office.

Connors, J. 1999. "NGOs and the Human Rights of Women at the United Nations." In *"The Conscience of the World": The Influence of Non-governmental Organizations in the UN System,* ed. P. Willetts, 147–180. Washington, DC: Brookings Institution.

Conyers, J. 2003. "Foreword." In *Warrior-King: The Case for Impeaching George W. Bush,* by J. Bonifaz, ix–xii. New York: Nation Books.

Cook, R. 1985. "Problem with SRB Seals." Internal NASA memo, July 23.

———. 1986. "The Rogers Commission Failed: Questions It Never Asked, Answers It Didn't Listen To." *Washington Monthly,* November, 1321.

———. 1988. Personal communication [interview]. January 29.

Corn, D. 2003. *The Lies of George W. Bush: Mastering the Politics of Deception.* New York: Crown Publishers.

Corporate Watch. 2004. http://www.corporatewatch.org.uk/ (accessed October 28, 2004).

Cressey, D. 1953 [1971]. *Other People's Money: A Study in the Social Psychology of Embezzlement.* Belmont, CA: Wadsworth.

Crow, J. 1984. "Cracking the Solid South: Populism and the Fusionist Interlude." In Watson, *The North Carolina Experience: An Interpretive and Documentary History*, ed. L. Butler and A. Watson, 41–60. Chapel Hill: University of North Carolina Press.

Cullen, F. T., W. J. Maakestad, and G. Cavender. 1987. *Corporate Crime under Attack: The Ford Pinto Case and Beyond*. Cincinnati: Anderson Publishing.

Danner, M. 2004. *Torture and Truth*. New York: New York Review of Books.

———. 2005. "The Secret Way to War." *New York Review* 52, no. 10 (June 9): 70–74.

Danner, M., L. Fort, and G. Young. 1999. "International Data on Women and Gender: Resources, Issues, Critical Use." *Women's Studies International Forum* 22: 249–259.

Davidson, A. 1990. *In the Wake of the Exxon Valdez*. San Francisco: Sierra Club Books.

Davis, M. 1991. "Inspector: Managers Were Warned." *Charlotte Observer*, November 13, A6.

Dean, J. 2004. *Worse than Watergate: The Secret Presidency of George W. Bush*. New York: Little, Brown and Company.

Deloria, V., Jr., 1989. *Custer Died for Your Sins: An Indian Manifesto*. Norman: University of Oklahoma Press.

Deloria, V., Jr., and C. M. Lytle. 1983. *American Indians, American Justice*. Austin: University of Texas Press.

Demers, D. P., and K. Viswanath, eds. 1999. *Mass Media, Social Control, and Social Change: A Macrosocial Perspective*. Ames: Iowa State University Press.

Dempsy, P., and A. Goetz. 1992. *Airline Deregulation and Laissez-Faire Mythology*. Westport, CT: Quorum.

Derber, C. 1998. *Corporation Nation: How Corporations Are Taking Over Our Lives and What We Can Do about It*. New York: St. Martin's Press.

———. 2002. *People before Profit: The New Globalization in an Age of Terror, Big Money, and Economic Crisis*. New York: St. Martin's Press.

Diaz, Elena. 2001. "Ethics of Inclusion in 21st-century Cuba." Unpublished paper. Facultad de Ciencias Sociales Latinoamerica (FLACSO), University of Havana, Havana, Cuba.

Ditlow, C. 2000. *Testimony before the Senate Committee on Commerce, Science and Transportation*. Washington, DC. September 12.

Domke, D. 2004. *God Willing? Political Fundamentalism in the White House, the "War on Terror," and the Echoing Press*. London: Pluto Press.

Dorrien, G. 2004. *Imperial Designs: Neo-Conservatism and the New Pax Americana*. New York: Routledge.

Drescher, J. 1991a. "In Hamlet Fire Government Safety Nets Gave way." *Charlotte Observer*, September 22, A1, 7.

———. 1991b. "USDA Inspector OK'd Locking of Door in Hamlet Plant." *Charlotte Observer*, November 13, 1991c. A1, 6.

———. 1991c. "Hamlet Plant Violated Code." *Charlotte Observer*, November 15, A1, 9.

Drescher, J., and K. Garfield. 1991. "Workers: Doors Kept Locked." *Charlotte Observer*, September 5, 1A.

Drescher, J., and D. Perlmutt. 1991. "USDA Inspector Checked Food; Safety Not 'Our Responsibility.'" *Charlotte Observer*, September 12, A1, 11.

Duffy, J. 1997. "The Social Impact of Disease in the Late Nineteenth Century." In *Sickness and Health in America: Readings in the History of Medicine and Public Health, 3rd ed.*, ed. J. Leavitt and R. Numbers. Madison: University of Wisconsin Press.

Easterbrook, G. 1987. "Big Dumb Rockets." *Newsweek*, August 17, 46–60.

Edelman, M. 1985. *The Symbolic Uses of Politics*. 2nd. edition. Champagn-Urbana: University of Illinois Press.

Eisendrath, C., and M. Goodman. 2004. *Bush League Diplomacy: How the Neoconservatives Are Putting the World at Risk.* Amherst, NY: Prometheus Books.

Eisenhower, Dwight. 1961. Presidential Farewell Speech. *Public Papers of the Presidents,* 1035–1040. http://coursesa.matrix.msu.edu/~hst306/documents/indust.html.

Elliot, W., ed. 1955. *The Political Economy of American Foreign Policy: Its Concepts, Strategy, and Limits.* New York: Henry Holt and Company.

Ellsburg, D. 1981. "Fall to Mutiny." In *Protest and Mutiny,* ed. F. P. Thompson and D. Smith, i–xxviii. New York: Monthly Review Press.

Ermann, M. D., and R. J. Lundman. 1982. *Corporate Deviance.* New York: Holt, Rinehart and Winston.

———. 1987. *Corporate and Governmental Deviance: Problems of Organizational Behavior in Contemporary Society.* 3rd ed. New York: Oxford University Press.

Everrest, L. 2004. *Oil, Power, and Empire: Iraq and the U.S. Global Agenda.* Monroe, ME: Common Courage Press.

Ewen, S. 2001. *Captains of Consciousness: Advertising and the Social Roots of the Consumer Culture.* New York: Basic Books.

Exxon Valdez Oil Spill Trustee Council. 1999. "The Settlement at a Glance." http://www.oilspill.state.ak.us/setlment/setlment.htm (accessed April 9, 2001).

Eyles, D. 1986. "At NASA Where Was 'What If'?" *New York Times,* March 12.

Falk, R. 1993. "Rethinking the Agenda of International Law." In *National Sovereignty: International Communication in the 1990s,* ed. K. Nordenstreng and H. Schiller, 418–431. Norwood, NJ: Ablex.

———. 2004. *The Declining World Order: America's Imperial Geopolitics.* New York: Routledge.

Fallows, J. 2004. "Bush's Lost Year." *Atlantic Monthly,* October, 68–84.

Federal Register. 2005. United States Government Printing Office. http://wais.access.gpo.gov [DOCID:fr27de01-31] (accessed March 12, 2005).

Feminist Majority Foundation. 1999. "Gender Apartheid in Afghanistan Fact Sheet, 1999." http://www.feminist.org/afghan/facts.html (accessed June 27, 2000).

Ferguson, N. 2004. *Colossus: The Price of America's Empire.* New York: Penguin Press.

Ferrell, J., and N. Websdale, eds. 1999. *Making Trouble: Cultural Constructions of Crime, Deviance, and Control.* New York: Aldine.

Finney, H. C., and H. R. Lesieur. 1982. "A Contingency Theory of Organizational Crime." In *Research in the Sociology of Organizations,* vol. 1, ed. S. B. Bacharach, 255–299. New York: Random House.

Flowers, General Robert, 2003. Memo Response to House of Representative Waxman. http://www.house.gov/waxman/. Also available in testimony of Senate Democratic Policy Committee Hearing, http://democrats.senate.gov/dpc/hearings/hearing24/transcript.pdf.

Flynn, D. J. 2002. *Why the Left Hates America: Exposing the Lies That Have Obscured Our Nation's Greatness.* New York: Prima Publishing.

Ford Motor Company. 1997. "Explorer P235/75R15 Tire Separation in Malaysia and Thailand." Internal report.

Fox, L. 2002. *Enron: The Rise and Fall.* New York: Wiley.

Franck, T. 2003. "What Happens Now? The United Nations after Iraq." *American Journal of International Law* 97: 607–620.

Frank, A. G. 1969. *Capitalism and the Underdevelopment of Latin America.* New York: Monthly Review Press.

Frankel, M. 1989. *Out of the Shadows of Night: The Struggle for International Human Rights.* New York: Delacorte Press.

Jaimes, M. A. 1992. "Re-Visioning Native America: An Indigenist View of Primitivism and Industrialism." *Social Justice* 19: 5–23.

Janis, I. 1982. *Groupthink.* Boston: Houghton Mifflin.

Jennings, F. 1975. *The Invasion of America: Indians, Colonialism, and the Cant of Conquest.* New York: W. W. Norton.

Jensen, R. 2004. *Citizens of the Empire: The Struggle to Claim Our Humanity.* San Francisco: City Lights Books.

Johns, C., and J. Borrero. 1991. "The War on Drugs." In *Crimes by the Capitalist State: An Introduction to State Criminality,* ed. G. Barak, 67–100. Albany: State University of New York Press.

Johnson, C. 2004. *The Sorrows of Empire: Militarism, Secrecy, and the End of the Republic.* New York: Metropolitan/Holt.

Jones, J. 2003. "Iraq Reconstruction." *Public Radio Newswire,* April 19.

Jorgensen, N. 2000. *The Responsibility of States for International Crimes.* Oxford: Oxford University Press.

Juhasz, A. 2004. "Ambitions of Empire: The Bush Administration Economic Plan for Iraq (and Beyond)." *Left Turn Magazine,* January 20.

Karliner, J. 1997. *The Corporate Planet: Ecology and Politics in the Age of Globalization.* San Francisco: Sierra Club Books.

Kauzlarich, D. 1995. "A Criminology of the Nuclear State." *Humanity and Society* 19: 37–57.

Kauzlarich, D., and R. C. Kramer. 1993. "State-Corporate Crime in the U.S. Nuclear Weapons Production Complex." *Journal of Human Justice* 5: 4–28.

———. 1998. *Crimes of the American Nuclear State: At Home and Abroad.* Boston: Northeastern University Press.

Kauzlarich, D., R. Kramer, and B. Smith. 1992. "Toward the Study of Governmental Crime: Nuclear Weapons, Foreign Intervention, and International Law." *Humanity and Society* 16: 543–563.

Kauzlarich, D., R. A. Matthews, and W. J. Miller. 2002. "Toward a Victimology of State Crime." *Critical Criminology* 10: 1–22.

Keeble, J. 1997. "The Imaginary Journey of Captain Joseph Hazelwood." In *The Exxon Valdez Disaster: Readings on a Modern Social Problem,* ed. J. S. Picou, D. A. Gill and M. J. Cohen, 23–38. Dubuque, IA: Kendall/Hunt.

Kelley, M. 2003. "Halliburton May Have Overcharged By Millions." Associated Press, December 12.

———. 2004. "Cheney Once Pushed to Lift Iran Sanctions." Associated Press, October 10.

Kelly, M. 2001. *The Divine Right of Capital: Dethroning the Corporate Aristocracy.* San Francisco: Berrett-Koehler.

———. 2002. "Property Privileges (Not Rights)." *Business Ethics,* November.

———. 2003. "The Next Step for CSR: Economic Democracy. *Business Ethics,* August.

Keller, W. 1995. *Arm in Arm: The Political Economy of the Global Arms Trade.* New York: Basic Books.

Kelman, H., and L. Hamilton. 1989. *Crimes of Obedience: Toward a Social Psychology of Authority and Responsibility.* New Haven, CT: Yale University Press.

Kellner, D. 2005. *Media Spectacle and the Crisis of Democracy: Terrorism, War, and Election Battles.* Boulder, CO: Paradigm Publishers.

Kempadoo, K., and J. Dozema. 1997. *Global Sex Workers: Rights, Resistance, and Redefinition.* London: Routledge.

Kennan, G. F. 1967. *Memoirs, 1925–1960.* Boston: Atlantic Monthly Press.

Key, V. O. 1950. *Southern Politics in State and Nation*. New York: Alfred A. Knopf.

Klare, M. 2004. *Blood and Oil: The Dangers and Consequences of America's Growing Dependency on Imported Petroleum*. New York: Owl Books.

Klare, M., and P. Kornbluh. 1989. *Low Intensity Warfare: Counterinsurgency, Proinsurgency, and Antiterrorism in the Eighties*. New York: Pantheon Books.

Klein, N. 2003. "Bring Halliburton Home." *The Nation*, November 24, 10.

Koeppel, B. 1976. "Something Could Be Finer Than to Be in Carolina." *The Progressive* 40 (June): 21–22.

Kolko, G. 1984. *Main Currents In Modern American History*. New York: Pantheon Books, 1984.

———. 1986. *The Politics of War: The World and United States Foreign Policy, 1943–1945*. New York: Random House.

Korten, D. 1995. *When Corporations Rule the World*. San Francisco: Berrett Koehler.

———. 1996. *Globalizing Civil Society: Reclaiming Our Right to Power*. New York: Seven Stories Press.

Kramer, R. C. 1982. "Corporate Crime: An Organizational Perspective." In *White Collar and Economic Crime*, ed. P. Wickman and T. Dailey, 75–94. Lexington, MA: Lexington Books.

———. 1984. "Corporate Criminality: The Development of an Idea." In *Corporations as Criminals*, ed. E. Hochstedler, 13–37. Beverly Hills, CA: Sage Publications.

———. 1989. "Criminologists and the Social Movement Against Corporate Crime." *Social Justice* 16: 146–164.

———. 1990a. "State-Corporate Crime." Paper presented at a meeting of the North Central Sociological Association and the Southern Sociological Association, Louisville, KY.

———. 1990b. "State-Corporate Crime: A Case Study of the Space Shuttle Challenger Explosion." Paper presented at the Edwin Sutherland Conference on White Collar Crime: 50 Years of Research and Beyond, Indiana University.

———. 1992. "The Space Shuttle *Challenger* Explosion: A Case Study of State-Corporate Crime." In *White-Collar Crime Reconsidered*, ed. K. Schlegel and D. Weisburd, 214–243. Boston: Northeastern University Press.

———. 1995. "Exploring State Criminality: The Invasion of Panama." *Journal of Criminal Justice and Popular Culture* 3: 43–52.

Kramer, R. C., and D. Kauzlarich. 1999. "The Opinion of the International Court of Justice on the Use of Nuclear Weapons: Implications for Criminology." *Contemporary Justice Review* 2(4): 395–413.

Kramer, R. C., and R. J. Michalowski. 1990. "Toward an Integrated Theory of State-Corporate Crime." Paper presented at a meeting of the American Society of Criminology, Baltimore, MD, November.

———. 1991. "State-Corporate Crime: Case Studies in Organizational Deviance." Unpublished manuscript.

———. 2005. "War, Aggression, and State Crime: A Criminological Analysis of the Invasion and Occupation of Iraq." *British Journal of Criminology* 45, no. 4 (June): 446–469.

Kramer, R. C., R. J. Michalowski, and D. Kauzlarich. 2002. "The Origins and Development of the Concept and Theory of State-Corporate Crime." *Crime and Delinquency* 48: 263–282.

Kramer, R. C., R. Michalowski, and D. Rothe. 2005. "The Supreme International Crime: How the U.S. War in Iraq Threatens the Rule of Law." *Social Justice* 32, no. 2 (July).

Krane, J. 2004. "Bush, Allawi Say Most of Iraq Is Stable; Map, however, Is Dotted with Violence." Associated Press. http://www.boston.com/dailynews/268/world/.

Krater, J. 1991. Personal communication [interview]. January.

Krauthammer, C. 1989. "Universal Domination: Toward a Unipolar World." *National Interest* 18 (Winter): 48–49.

———. 1991. "The Unipolar Moment." *Foreign Affairs* 70: 23–33.

Kristof, N. 2002. "Revolving-Door Master." *New York Times,* October 11, A33.

Krugman, P. 2004a. "Battlefield of Dreams." *New York Times*, May 4.

———. 2004b. "What Went Wrong?" *New York Times*, April 23.

Kugler, A. 2000. "Airplanes for the Führer: Adam Opel AG as Enemy Property, Model War Operation, and General Motors Subsidiary, 1939–1945." In *Working for the Enemy: Ford, General Motors, and Forced Labor in Germany during the Second World War*, ed. R. Billstein, R., K. Fings, A. Kugler and N. Levis. New York: Berghahn Books.

Kurtz, H. 2004. "The *Post* on WMDs: An Inside Story; Prewar Articles Questioning Threat Often Didn't Make Front Page." *Washington Post*, August 12, A01.

Kuttner, R. 1996. *Everything for Sale*. New York: Alfred Knopf.

———. 2002. "Can Liberals Save Capitalism (Again)?" *American Prospect* 13 (August 12): 22–26.

Lakoff, G. 2002 [1996]. *Moral Politics: How Liberals and Conservatives Think*. 2nd ed. Chicago: University of Chicago Press.

———. 2004. *Don't Think of an Elephant!* White River Junction, VT: Chelsea Green Publishing.

Lambert, C., S. Pickering, and C. Alder. 2003. *Critical Chatter: Women and Human Rights in South East Asia*. Durham, NC: Carolina Academic Press.

Lamperti, J. 1984a. "Government and the Atom." In *The Nuclear Almanac: Confronting the Atom in War and Peace*, ed. J. Dennis, 67–79. Reading, Mass.: Addison-Wesley.

———. 1984b. "Nuclear Weapons Manufacture." In *The Nuclear Almanac: Confronting the Atom in War and Peace*, ed. J. Dennis, 69–81. Reading, Mass.: Addison-Wesley.

Lane, R. E. 1953. "Why Businessmen Violate the Law." *Journal of Criminal Law, Criminology and Police Science* 44 (July): 151–165.

Lash, C. 1995. *The Revolt of the Elites and the Betrayal of Democracy*. New York: W.W. Norton.

Lautenberg, F. 2003. "Constituting a Financial Interest in Halliburton." Press release, September 25.

Levin, I. 1999. *The Last Deposit: Swiss Banks and Holocaust Victims' Accounts*. London: Westport.

Levinson, M., A. Underwood, and B. Turque. 1996. "A New Day at the FAA?" *Newsweek*, July 1, 46.

Levis, N. 2000. "Memory and Liability." In *Working for the Enemy: Ford General Motors and Forced Labor in Germany during the Second World War*, ed. R. Billstein, K. Fings, A. Kugler and N. Levis, 229–247. New York: Berghahn Books, 2000.

Levitt, A. 2002. *Take on the Street: What Wall Street and Corporate America Don't Want You to Know*. New York: Pantheon Books.

Lewis, N. A. 2005. "Document Say Detainees Cited Abuse of Koran." *New York Times*, May 26, A1.

Lewis, R. S. 1988. *Challenger: The Final Voyage*. New York: Columbia University Press.

Lindbergh, K., and B. L. Provorse. 1977. *The Trans-Alaska Pipeline. Vol. 3, Emerging Alaska*. Seattle: Scribe.

Lindee, S., and D. Nelkin. 1986. "Challenger: The High Cost of Hype." *Bulletin of the Atomic Scientists* (November): 16–17.

Litchblau, E. 2002. "Bush Officials Vowing to Seek Tough Penalties in Wall St. Cases." *New York Times*, December 19.

Little, R. 2002. "American Civilians Go Off to War, Too." *Baltimore Sun,* May 26.

Lichter, L., and S. Lichter. 1983. *Prime Time Crime.* Washington, DC: Media Institute.

Lord, N. 1997. "Oil in the Sea: Initial Biological Impacts of the Exxon Valdez Oil Spill." In *The Exxon Valdez Disaster: Readings on a modern social problem,* ed. J. S. Picou, D. Gill and M. J. Cohen, 95–110. Dubuque, IA: Kendall/Hunt.

Lorentzen, L.A., and J. Turpin. 1996. "Introduction: The Gendered New World Order." In Turpin and Lorentzen, *The Gendered New World Order: Militarism, Development, and the Environment,* 1–11. London: Routledge.

Luebke, P. 1990. *Tar Heel Politics: Myths and Realities.* Chapel Hill: University of North Carolina Press.

Lynch, C. 2001. "Halliburton's Iraq Deals Greater than Cheney Has Said: Affiliates Had $73 Million in Contracts." *Washington Post,* June 23, A01.

———. 2004a. "U.S. Allies Dispute Annan on Iraq War." *Washington Post,* September 17, A18.

———. 2004b. "Annan Faults Both Sides of Terror War for Eroding Rule of Law." *Washington Post,* September 21, A02.

Lynch, M., and R. Michalowski. 2005. *Crime, Power, and Identity: The New Primer in Radical Criminology.* 4th edition. Washington, DC: Criminal Justice Press.

Lyons, G., and J. Mayall, eds. 2003. *International Human Rights in the 21st Century: Protecting the Rights of Groups.* Lanham, MD: Rowman and Littlefield.

Madeley, J. 1999. *Big Business, Poor Peoples: The Impact of Transnational Corporations on the World's Poor.* London: Zed.

Mahajan, R. 2003. *Full Spectrum Dominance: U.S. Power in Iraq and Beyond.* New York: Seven Stories Press.

Makhijani, A., H. Hu, and K. Yih, eds. *Nuclear Wastelands: A Global Guide to Nuclear Weapons Production and Its Health and Environmental Effects.* Cambridge: MIT Press.

Mandel, M. 2004. *How America Gets Away with Murder: Illegal Wars, Collateral Damage, and Crimes against Humanity.* London: Pluto Press.

Mander, J., and E. Goldsmith. 1996. *The Case against the Global Economy.* San Francisco: Sierra Club Books.

Manheim, J. 2000. *Corporate Conduct Unbecoming: Codes of Conduct and Anti-Corporate Strategy.* Baltimore: Tred Avon Institute Press.

Mankinson, Larry. 2004. Quoted in David Ivanoch, "Silence Surrounds Fate of Contractors" November 21, 2004. *Houston Chronicle.* http://www.chron.com/cs/CDA/ssistory.mpl/metropolitan/2911419.

Mankiw, Greg. 2004. Quoted in Sarah Anderson and John Cavanagh, "Toward a Progressive View on Outsourcing." *The Nation,* March 22, 2004. www.thenation.com/doc/20040322/cavanagh-45k.

Mann, J. 2004. *Rise of the Vulcans: The History of Bush's War Cabinet.* New York: Viking.

Mann, P. 1986. "The NASA Story We Missed." *Bulletin of the Atomic Scientists* (November): 18.

Mark, H. 1987. *The Space Station: A Personal Journey.* Durham, NC: Duke University Press.

Markle, G. 1995. *Meditations of a Holocaust Traveler.* Albany: SUNY Press.

Marx, K. 1906. *Capital.* New York: Charles H. Kerr and Company.

Massing, M. 2004. *Now They Tell Us: The American Press and Iraq.* New York: New York Review of Books.

Mathew, R. 2001. *Effects of Declining Oil prices on Oil Exporting Countries.* http://www.stanford.edu/class/e297...de_environment/energy/heffect.html (accessed February 9, 2001).

Matthews, R. A., and D. Kauzlarich. 2000. "The Crash of ValuJet flight 592: A Case Study in State-Corporate Crime." *Sociological Focus* 3: 281–298.

Matthews, R. A., and W. J. Miller. 2001. "Ordinary Business: State-Corporate Crime in Nazi Germany." Paper presented at a meeting of the American Society of Criminology, Atlanta.

Matthiesen, P. 1983. *In The Spirit of Crazy Horse.* New York: Penguin Books. Reprinted 1991 and 1992.

Mayer, A. E. 1995. "Cultural Particularism as a Bar to Women's Rights: Reflections on the Middle Eastern Experience." In *Women's Rights, Human Rights: International Feminist Perspectives,* ed. J. Peters and A. Wolper, 176–188. New York: Routledge.

McConnell, M. 1987. *Challenger: A Major Malfunction.* Garden City, NY: Doubleday.

McDougall, W. A. 1985. *The Heavens and the Earth.* New York: Basic Books.

McLean, B., and P. Elkind. 2004. *The Smartest Guys in the Room: The Amazing Rise and Scandalous Fall of Enron.* Updated paperback ed. New York: Portfolio.

McMullan, J. 1992. *Beyond the Limits of the Law: Corporate Crime and Law and Order.* Halifax: Fernwood Press.

———. 1996. "Toxic Steel: State Corporate Crime and the Contamination of the Environment in Atlantic Canada." Presented at a meeting of the American Criminology Society, Chicago. November.

MDC. 1986. *Shadows in the Sunbelt: Developing the Rural South in an Era of Economic Change.* A Report for the Ford Foundation. Chapel Hill: MDC, 1986.

Meet the Press, NBC. 2003. Interview with Tom Russert. September 14. Transcript Available NBC News. http://www.mtholyoke.edu/acad/intrel/bush/meet.htm

Melman, S. 1974. *The Permanent War Economy: American Capitalism in Decline.* New York: Simon and Schuster, 1991.

Menn, J. 1991. "North Carolina Official Puts Blame on Legislature." Charlotte Observer, September 6, A1, 4.

Merrick, G. B. 1987. *Statement before the U.S. Congress, House of Representatives.* Committee on Energy and Commerce. Subcommittee on Transportation and Hazardous Materials. Environmental Crimes at DOE's Nuclear Weapons Facilities. 101st Cong., 1st sess. Washington, DC: U.S. Government Printing Office, 1987.

Merton, R. K. 1938. "Social Structure and Anomie." *American Sociological Review* 3: 672–682.

———. 1957. *Social Theory and Social Structure.* Glencoe, IL: Free Press.

Messerschmidt, J. 1983. *The Trial of Leonard Peltier.* Boston: South End Press.

Messner, S., M. Krohn, and A. Liska. 1989. *Theoretical Imagination in the Study of Deviance and Crime: Problems and Prospects.* Albany: SUNY Press, 1989.

Messner, S., and R. Rosenfeld. 2001. *Crime and the American Dream.* 3rd ed. Belmont, CA: Wadsworth.

Michael, J., and M. J. Adler. 1933. *Crime, Law, and Social Science.* New York: Harcourt, Brace.

Michalowski, R. J. 1985. *Order, Law, and Crime.* New York: Random House.

Michalowski, R. J., and K. Bitten. 2005. "Transnational Environmental Crime." In *Handbook of Transnational Crime and Justice,* ed. P. Reichel, 139–159. Thousand Oaks, CA: Sage Publications.

Michalowski, R. J., and R. C. Kramer. 1987. "The Space between the Laws: The Problem of Corporate Crime in a Transnational Context." *Social Problems* 34: 34–53.

———. 2005. "Beyond Enron: Toward Economic Democracy and a New Ethic of Inclusion." *Risk Management: An International Journal* 5, no. 2: 37–47.

———. 2006. Michalowski, R., and R. Kramer. 2006. "State-Corporate Crime and Criminological Inquiry." In International Handbook of White Collar Crime, ed. G. Geis and H. Pontell. Dordrecht: Kluwer Academic/Plenum Publishers.

Milgram, S. 1963. "Behavioral Study of Obedience." *Journal of Abnormal and Social Psychology* 67: 371–378.

Millen, J. V., and T. H. Holtz. 2000. "Dying for Growth, part I: Transnational Corporations and the Health of the Poor." In *Dying for Growth: Global Inequality and the Health of the Poor,* ed. J. Yong Kim, J. V. Millen, A. Irwin, and J. Gershman, 177–223. Monroe, ME: Common Courage Press.

Miller, D., ed. 2004. *Tell Me Lies: Propaganda and Media Distortion in the Attack on Iraq.* London: Pluto Press.

Miller, R. S. 2003. *Collateral Damage from U.S. Depleted Uranium Munitions in Iraq.* Winter Springs, FL: ZOR Foundation.

Mills, C. W. 1956. *The Power Elite.* New York: Oxford University Press.

Mitchell, L. E. 2001. *Corporate Irresponsibility: America's Newest Export.* New Haven, CT: Yale University Press.

Mobilization for Survival. 1989. *Banning the Bombmakers: Challenging Nuclear Weapons Production.* New York: Mobilization for Survival Fund.

Moeller, S. 2004a. *Media Coverage of Weapons of Mass Destruction.* College Park, MD: Center for International Studies at Maryland, University of Maryland.

Moeller, S. 2004b. "Weapons of Mass Destruction and the Failure of the Media." Yale Global, April 14. http://yaleglobal.yale.edu/display.article?id=3703-31k.

Mokhiber, R. 1988. *Corporate Crime and Violence: Big Business Power and the Abuse of the Public Trust.* San Francisco: Sierra Club Books.

Moore, J. 2004. *Bush's War for Reelection: Iraq, the White House, and the People.* New York: John Wiley.

Moore, M. 2001. *Stupid White Men.* New York: Harper Collins.

Moro, J., and D. Lapierre. 2002. *Five Past Midnight in Bhopal: The Epic Story of the World's Deadliest Industrial Disaster.* New York: Warner Books.

Mother Jones. 2004a. "Halliburton." http://motherjones.com/ (accessed October 28, 2004).

———. 2004b. "Iraq Reconstruction: How Not to Do It." August 10.

Mueller, S. 2004. *Media Coverage of Weapons of Mass Destruction.* College Park, MD: Center for International Studies at Maryland, University of Maryland.

Mullins, C., D. Kauzlarich, and D. Rothe. 2004. "The International Criminal Court and the Control of State Crime: Problems and Prospects." *Critical Criminology: An International Journal* 12: 285–308.

Multinational Monitor. 1999. "Controlling Corporate Scofflaws or Blacklisting?" July/August.

———. 2001. "Defending Contractor Irresponsibility." May.

Myerson, M. 1982. *Nothing Could Be Finer.* New York: International Publishers.

Nader, R. 2000. *Cutting Corporate Welfare.* New York: Seven Stories Press.

Nader, R., and W. J. Smith. 1996. *No Contest: Corporate Lawyers and the Perversion of Justice in America.* New York: Random House.

Nasser, J. 2000. Prepared Statement of Jac Nasser, Ford Motor Company, before the Committee on Commerce, Science and Transportation. United States Senate, Hearing on Firestone Tire Recall Action, September 12, 2000.

The Nation. 1986. "The Lethal Shuttle." February 22, 193.

National Academy of Sciences. 1987. *Safety Issues at the Defense Production Reactors: A Report to the Department of Energy.* Washington, DC: National Academy Press.

National Highway Traffic Safety Administration. 2001. *Engineering Analysis Report and Initial Decision Regarding EA00-023: Firestone Wilderness AT Tires.* Washington, DC.: U.S. Department of Transportation.

National Institute of Justice. 2005. "Funding Opportunities, 2005." http://ojp.usdoj.gov/nij/funding.htm.

National Response Team. 1997. "The Exxon Valdez Oil Spill and Response Preparedness: A Report to the President." In *The Exxon Valdez Disaster: Readings on a Modern Social Problem*, ed. J. S. Picou, D. Gill, and M. J. Cohen, 39–53. Dubuque, IA: Kendall/Hunt.

National Transportation Safety Board. 1990. *Grounding of the U.S. Tank Ship Exxon Valdez on Bligh Reef, Prince William Sound, near Valdez, Alaska, March 24, 1989.* Washington, DC: U.S. Government Printing Office.

———. 1997. *Aircraft Accident Report: In-Flight Fire and Impact with Terrain. ValuJet Airlines Flight 592.* Washington, DC: U.S. Government Printing Office.

NBC News. 2003. Pentagon Report News Coverage. September 14. Archived Transcripts. http://www.nbc.com.

Needleman, M., and C. Needleman. 1979. "Organizational Crime: Two Models of Criminogenesis." *Sociological Quarterly* 20: 517–528.

Nelson, B. 1986. *Making an Issue of Child Abuse: Political Agenda Setting for Social Problems.* Chicago: University of Chicago Press.

Neumann, F. 1944. *Behemoth: The Structure and Practice of National Socialism, 1933 to 1944.* New York: Oxford University Press.

New York Law Journal. 2000. Today's News. Lexis-Nexis database, October 3. http://www.lexis-nexis.com (accessed April 17, 2001).

New York Times. 2004. "From the Editors; The *Times* and Iraq." *New York Times,* May 26, A10.

Nieburg, H. L. 1966. *In the Name of Science.* Chicago: Quadrangle Books.

Nikolić-Ristanović, V. 1996. "War and Violence against Women." In *The Gendered New World Order: Militarism, Development, and the Environment*, ed. J. Turpin and L. A. Lorentzen, 195–210. New York: Routledge.

Noble, C. 1986. *Liberalism at Work: The Rise and Fall of OSHA.* Philadelphia: Temple University Press.

Normand, R. 2003. *Tearing Up the Rules: The Illegality of Invading Iraq.* Brooklyn: Center for Economic and Social Rights.

———. 2004. "Presentation on Crimes Committed during the Ongoing Occupation." *World Tribunal on Iraq.* New York, May 8. http://worldtribunal-nyc.org/Document/index.htm.

NTSB. *See* National Transportation Safety Board.

O'Connor, J. 1973. *The Fiscal Crisis of the State.* New York: St. Martin's Press.

Offe, C., and V. Ronge. 1982. "Theses on the Theory of the State." In *Classes, Power, and Conflict*, ed. A. Giddens, and D. Held, 249–256. Berkeley: University of California Press.

Office of Technology Assessment. 1991. *Complex Clean-Up: The Environmental Legacy of Nuclear Weapons Production.* Washington, DC: U.S. Government Printing Office.

Oliver, Mary Beth. 1994. "Portrayals of Crime, Race, and Aggression in Reality-Based Police Shows." *Journal of Broadcasting and Electronic Media* 38(2): 179–192.

Olsen, J. M. 2001. "Oil Spill Threatens Danish Beaches." Copenhagen, Denmark. Associated Press, April 2. http://dailynews.yahoo.com/h/ap/20010402/wl/denmark_tanker_accident_3.html (accessed April 9, 2001).

Olshansky, S. J., and R. G. Williams. 1988. "Culture Shock at the Weapons Complex." *Bulletin of Atomic Scientists* (September): 29–33.

O'Shaughnessy, N. J. 2004. *Politics and Propaganda: Weapons of Mass Seduction.* Ann Arbor: University of Michigan Press.

Oster, C., J. Strong, and K. Zorn. 1992. *Why Airplanes Crash: Aviation Safety in a Changing World.* New York: Oxford.

Otto, D. 1997. "Rethinking the Universality of 'Human Rights' Law." *Columbia Human Rights Law Review* (1997): 291–46.

———. 1999. "Subalternity and International Law: The Problems of Global Community and the Incommensurability of Difference." In *Laws of the Postcolonial,* ed. E. Darian-Smith and P. Fitzpatrick, 145–180. Ann Arbor: University of Michigan Press.

Packer, G. 2004. "Letter from Baghdad: War after War, What Washington Doesn't See." *New Yorker,* November 24, 58–85.

Parker, J., J. Menn, and K. O'Brien. 1991. "North Carolina Inspection Program Ranks Last in U.S." *Charlotte Observer,* September 5, A1.

Passas, N. 1990. "Anomie and Corporate Deviance." *Contemporary Crises* 14: 157–178.

Pearce, F. 1976. *Crimes of the Powerful: Marxism, Crime, and Deviance.* London: Pluto Press.

Perrow, C. 1984. *Normal Accidents: Living with High-Risk Technologies.* New York: Basic Books, Reprinted 1999, Princeton, NJ: Princeton University Press.

———. 1986. "Risky Systems: The Habit of Courting Disaster." *The Nation* 242 (October 11): 347–356.

Peterson, V. S., and A. S. Runyan. 1999. *Global Gender Issues.* Boulder, CO: Westview Press.

Phillips, K. 2002. *Wealth and Democracy: A Political History of the American Rich.* New York: Broadway Books.

Phillips, N. 1996. "Spillionaires." *Anchorage Daily News,* March 17. http://www.sirs.com (accessed April 18, 2001).

Pietilä, H., and J. Vickers. 1990. *Making Women Matter: The Role of the United Nations.* 2nd ed. London: Zed.

Pike, J. 1988. Personal communication [interview]. January 29.

Pilger, J. 2001. "The Truths They Never Tell Us: Behind the Jargon about Failed States and Humanitarian Interventions Lie Thousands of Dead." *New Statesman* 130, (no. 4565 (November 26): 14–16.

Piper, E. 1997. "The Exxon Valdez Oil Spill Government Settlement and Restoration Activities." In *The Exxon Valdez Disaster: Readings on a Modern Social Problem,* ed. J. S. Picou, D. Gill and M. J. Cohen, 255–270. Dubuque, IA: Kendall/Hunt.

Pitt, W. R. 2002. *War on Iraq.* New York: Context Books.

Piven, F., and R. Cloward. 1982. *The New Class War: Reagan's Attack on the Welfare State and Its Consequences.* New York: Pantheon Books.

Pontell, H., and K. Calavita. 1993. "White Collar Crime in the Savings and Loan Scandal." *Annals of the American Academy of Political and Social Sciences* 525: 31–45.

Pope, L. 1942. *Millhands and Preachers.* New Haven, CT: Yale University Press.

Porter, J. W. 1986. Statement before the U.S. Congress, House of Representatives. Committee on Government Operations. Subcommittee on Environment, Energy and Natural Resources. Review of DOE's Compliance with Environmental Laws in Managing Its Hazardous and Mixed Radioactive-Hazardous Wastes. 99th Cong., 2nd sess. Washington, DC: U.S. Government Printing Office.

Poveda, T. 1990. *The FBI in Transition.* Pacific Grove, CA: Brooks/Cole Publishing Company.

Powaski, R. E. 1987. *March to Armageddon: The United States and the Nuclear Arms Race, 1939 to Present.* New York: Oxford University Press.

Power, S. 2003. *A Problem from Hell: America and the Age of Genocide.* New York: Perennial.

Prados, J. 2004. *Hoodwinked: The Documents That Reveal How Bush Sold Us a War.* New York: New Press.

Presidential Commission on the Space Shuttle Challenger Accident. 1986. *Report of the Presidential Commission on the Space Shuttle Challenger Accident.* Vols. 1–4. Washington, DC: U.S. Government Printing Office.

Priest, D., and W. Pincus. 2004. "U.S. 'Almost All Wrong' on Weapons: Report on Iraq Contradicts Bush Administration Claims." *Washington Post,* October 7, A01.

The Progressive. 2003. "Comment: Bush's Messiah Complex." February, 8–10.

Project for the New American Century. 2000. *Rebuilding America's Defenses: Strategy, Forces, and Resources for a New Century.* Washington, DC: Project for the New American Century.

Prügl, E., and M. Meyer. 1999. "Gender Politics in Global Governance." In *Gender Politics in Global Governance,* ed. M. K. Meyer and E. Prugl, 3–16. New York: Rowman and Littlefield.

Public Citizen. 2001. "Chronology of Firestone/Ford Knowledge of Tire Safety Defect." November 6. http://dev.citizen.org/print_article.cfm?ID=5336.

Public Radio Newswire. 2004. "Spoils of War." Marketplace Series, April 20–23.

Quinney, R. 1977. *Class, State, and Crime: On the Theory and Practice of Criminal Justice.* New York: David McKay Company.

Rabin, D., and A. Cusac. 2002. "Graphic Comment: Changing the Subject." *The Progressive* 66 (November): 10.

Radioactive Waste Campaign. 1988. *RWC Report.* New York: Radioactive Waste Campaign.

Rai, M. 2002. *War Plan Iraq: Ten Reasons against War on Iraq.* London: Verso.

———. 2003. *Regime Unchanged: Why the War on Iraq Changed Nothing.* London: Pluto Press.

Rampton, S., and J. Stauber. 2003. *Weapons of Mass Deception: The Uses of Propaganda in Bush's War on Iraq.* New York: Jeremy P. Tarcher/Penguin.

Randolph, B. 1990. "Exxon's Attitude Problem." *Time* 135 (January 22): 51.

Rao, A. 1995. "The Politics of Gender and Culture in International Human Rights Discourse." In *Women's Rights, Human Rights: International Feminist Perspectives,* ed. J. Peters and A. Wolper, 167–175. New York: Routledge.

Ratner, M. 2002. "The United Nations Charter and the Use of Force against Iraq." [Online]. *Lawyers against the War.* http://www.lawyersagainstthewar.org/legalarticles/ratner.html.

Ratner, M., J. Green, and B. Olshansky. 2003. *Against War with Iraq.* New York: Seven Stories Press.

Ratner, M., and E. Ray. 2004. *Guantanamo: What the World Should Know.* Boston: Chelsea Green Publishing Company.

Rauner, A. 1999. Internal Ford Email sent to Stuart Schafrick and John Behr. August 19.

Rebovich, D., and J. L. Kane. 2002. "An Eye for an Eye in the Electronic Age: Gauging Public Attitude toward White Collar Crime and Punishment." *Journal of Economic Crime Management* 1, no. 2. Viewed at http://www.jecm.org/02_fall_art1.htm (accessed June 6, 2005).

Reed, G., and P. C. Yeager. 1996. "Organizational Offending and Neoclassical Criminology: Challenging the Reach of a General Theory of Crime." *Criminology* 36: 357–382.

Reich, S. 1996. "Fascism and the Structure of German Capitalism: The Case of the Automotive Industry." In *Quest For Empire: European Strategies of German Big Business in the Twentieth Century,* ed. V. R. Berghahn. New York: Berghahn Books.

Reicher, D. W., and S. J. Scher. 1988. "Laying Waste to the Environment." *Bulletin of Atomic Scientists* (January–February): 29–31.

Reiman, J. 2003. *The Rich Get Richer and the Poor Get Prison: Ideology, Class, and Criminal Justice.* 7th ed. New York: Allyn & Bacon.

Reinarman, C., and H. G. Levine, eds. 1997. *Crack in America: Demon Drugs and Social Justice.* Berkeley: University of California Press.

Rendall, S., and T. Broughel. 2003. "Amplifying Officials, Squelching Dissent." *Extra* 16 (May–June): 12–14.

Reuters. 2002. "G.A.O. Investigation Finds Broad Failures at S.E.C." *New York Times*, December 19.

———. 2004. Reuters News Service. 2004. "Halliburton in $16 Million Food Probe" February 2. http://www.independentmedia.tv/item.cfm?fmedia_id=5420& fcategory_desc=Dick%20Cheney%20and%20Halliburton.

Rhodes, R. 1986. *The Making of the Atomic Bomb.* New York: Simon and Schuster.

———. 2002. *Masters of Death: The SS Einsatzgruppen and the Invention of the Holocaust.* New York: Alfred Knopf.

Ridha, J. 2004. "Presentation on The Use of Incendiary Weapons." *World Tribunal on Iraq,* New York, May 8. http://worldtribunal-nyc.org/document/index.htm.

Rifkin, J. 1995. *The End of Work: The Decline of the Global Labor Force and the Dawn of the Post-Market Era.* New York: Putnam.

———. 2000. *The Age of Access: The New Culture of Hypercapitalism Where All of Life Is a Paid-For Experience.* New York: Jeremy P. Tarcher/Putnam.

Ritter, S. 2003. *Frontier Justice: Weapons of Mass Destruction and the Bushwhacking of America.* New York: Context Books.

Ritzer, G. 1988. *Contemporary Sociological Theory.* New York: Knopf.

Rodda, A. 1991. *Women and the Environment.* London: Zed Books.

Roebuck, J., and S. Weber. 1978. *Political Crime in the United States.* New York: Praeger.

Ross, J. 1995. *Controlling State Crime.* New York: Garland.

Rossi, P. H., E. Waite, C. E. Bose, and R. E. Berk. 1974. "The Seriousness of Crime: Normative Structure and Individual Differences." *American Sociological Review* 39: 224–237.

Roth, K. 2004. *War in Iraq: Not a Humanitarian Intervention.* New York: Human Rights Watch.

Rothe, D., and S. Muzzatti. 2004. "Enemies Everywhere, Terrorism, Civil Society, and Moral Panic." *Critical Criminology: An International Journal* 12: 327–350.

Roy, A. 2004. *An Ordinary Person's Guide to Empire.* Boston: South End Press.

Rummel, R. J. 1994. *Death by Government.* New Brunswick, NJ: Transaction Publishers.

Rutherford, P. 2004. *Weapons of Mass Persuasion: Marketing the War against Iraq.* Toronto: University of Toronto Press.

Sagan, S. D. 1993. *The Limits of Safety: Organizations, Accidents, and Nuclear Weapons.* Princeton, NJ: Princeton University Press.

Saleska, M., and I. Makhijani. 1990. "Hanford Clean-Up: Explosive Solution." *Bulletin of Atomic Scientists* (October): 14–20.

Sands, P. 2005. *Lawless World: America and the Making and Breaking of Global Rules.* London: Allen Lane.

Sassen, S. 1998. *Globalization and Its Discontents: Essays on the New Mobility of People and Money.* New York: New Press.

Schafer, S. 1974. *The Political Criminal: The Problems of Morality and Crime.* New York: Free Press.

Schapiro, M. 2004. "Spoils of War." *Public Radio Newswire.* Marketplace Series, report 4. April 21.

Scheer, C., R. Scheer, and L. Chaudhry. 2003. *The Five Biggest Lies Bush Told Us about Iraq.* New York: Seven Stories Press and Akashic Books.

Schehr, R. 2005. "Conventional Risk Discourse and the Proliferation of Fear." *Criminal Justice Policy Review* 16, no. 1: 38–58.

Schell, J. 2004. *A Hole in the World: An Unfolding Story of War, Protest, and The New American Order.* New York: Nation Books.

Schell, O. 2004. "Preface." In *Now They Tell Us: The American Press and Iraq,* by M. Massing. New York: New York Review of Books.

Schiavo, M. 1997. *Flying Blind, Flying Safe.* New York: Avon Books.

Schmitt, E. 2005. "No Criminal Charges for Officer at Abu Ghraib Interrogations." *New York Times,* May 12, A1.

Schoepf, B. G., C. Schoepf, and J. V. Millen 2000. "Theoretical Therapies, Remote Remedies: SAPs and the Political Ecology of Poverty and Health in Africa." In *Dying for Growth: Global Inequality and the Health of the Poor,* ed. J. Yong Kim, J. V. Millen, A. Irwin, and J. Gershman, 91–125. Monroe, ME: Common Courage Press.

Schrager, L., and J. Short. 1978. "Toward a Sociology of Organizational Crime." *Social Problems* 25 (June): 407–419.

Schrecker, E. 1986. *No Ivory Tower: McCarthyism and the Universities.* New York: Oxford University Press.

Schultz, W. 2003. *Tainted Legacy: 9/11 and the Ruin of Human Rights.* New York: Nation Books.

Schwendinger, H., and J. Schwendinger. 1970. "Defenders of Order or Guardians of Human Rights?" *Issues in Criminology* 5: 123–157.

Seager, J. 1993. *Earth Follies: Coming to Feminist Terms with the Global Environmental Crisis.* New York: Routledge.

Sebok, A. 2000. *Unsettling the Holocaust (Part I): The Strange Legal Status of the Agreement Regarding Victims of Forced Labor.* Findlaw's Legal Commentary and Writs. http://writ.findlaw.com/sebok/20000828.html.

Sellin, Thorsten. 1938. *Culture, Conflict and Crime.* New York: Social Science Research Council.

Sethi, S. P., and P. Steidlmeier. 1997. *Up against the Corporate Wall: Cases in Business and Society.* 6th ed. Upper Saddle River, NJ: Prentice Hall.

Sewall, J. 1995 [1905]. *The Log Book of the Captains Clerk.* Chicago: R. R. Donnelly and Sons.

Shapiro, Mark. 2004. "Spoils of War." April 21. Report for the *Marketplace,* National Public Radio. http://marketplace.publicradio.org/features/iraq/index.html.

Sharkey, J. 1988. "The Contra-Drug Trade Off." *Common Cause,* September/October, 22–33.

Sherman, L. 1980. "Three Models of Organizational Corruption in Agencies of Social Control." *Social Problems* 27 (April) 478–491.

Shields, J. 2000. "Getting Corporations off the Public Dole." In *Crisis in American Institutions,* 11th edition, ed. J. Skolnick and E. Currie, 21–27. Boston: Allyn and Bacon Press.

Shover, N., G. Fox, and M. Miller. 2001. "Consequences of Victimization by White-Collar Crime." *Crimes of Privilege: Readings in White-Collar Crime,* ed. N. Shover and J. P. Wright, 74–87. New York: Oxford University Press.

Silverstein, K. 2000. "Ford and the Führer: New Documents Reveal the Close Ties between Dearborn and the Nazis." *The Nation,* January 24, 11–16.

Simon, D. R., and D. S. Eitzen. 1982. *Elite Deviance.* Boston: Allyn and Bacon.

Simons, G. 2002. *Targeting Iraq: Sanctions and Bombing in U.S. Policy.* London: Saqi Books.

Singer, P. W. 2003. *Corporate Warriors: The Rise of the Privatized Military Industry.* Ithaca, NY: Cornell University Press.

Singh, R., and C. Kilroy. 2003. "In the Matter of the Legality of the Use of Force against Iraq and the Alleged Existence of Weapons of Mass Destruction." *Campaign for Nuclear Disarmament,* June 6. http://www.cnduk.org/pages/campaign/opn3.html.

Sinha, M., D. Guy, and A. Wollacott. 1999. *Feminisms and Internationalisms.* London: Blackwell Publishers.

Sklar, M. J. [1988] 1991. *The Corporate Reconstruction of American Capitalism, 1890–1916.* New York: Cambridge University Press. Reprinted 1991.

Skolnick, J., and J. Fyfe. 1993. *Above the Law: Police and the Excessive Use of Force.* New York: Free Press.

Sloan, A., and J. L. Roberts. 2002. *Newsweek,* July 22.

Slomanson, W. 2003. *Fundamental Perspectives on International Law.* 4th edition. Belmont, CA: Thomson/West.

Snider, L. 1987. "Towards a Political Economy of Reform, Regulation, and Corporate Crime." *Law and Policy* 9: 37–68.

Solomon, N., and R. Erlich. 2003. *Target Iraq: What the News Media Didn't Tell You.* New York: Context Books.

Soulliere, D. 2003. "Prime-Time Murder: Presentations of Murder on Popular Television Justice Programs." *Journal of Criminal Justice and Popular Culture* 10(1): 12–38.

Southern Studies. 2003/2004. Winter Report 2003/2004. http://www.southernstudies.org/.

Southern Women's Employment Coalition (SWEC). 1986. *Women of the Rural South: Economic Status and Prospects.* Lexington, KY: SWEC.

Spector, M., and J. I. Kitsuse. 2000. *Constructing Social Problems.* New Brunswick, NJ: Transaction Publishers.

Staudt, K. 1997. *Women, International Development, and Politics: The Bureaucratic Mire.* Philadelphia: Temple University Press.

Staudt, K., and K. Timothy. 1997. "Strategies for the Future." In *Women, International Development, and Politics: The Bureaucratic Mire,* ed. K. Staudt, 333–351. Philadelphia: Temple University Press.

Steady, F. C. 1996. "Gender Equality and Ecosystem Balance: Women and Sustainable Development in Developing Countries." *Race, Class and Gender* 6, no. 1: 13–32.

Steele, K. D. 1989. "Hanford: America's Nuclear Graveyard." *Bulletin of Atomic Scientists* (October): 15–23.

Sterba, J. P. 2001. *Three Challenges to Ethics: Environmentalism, Feminism, Multiculturalism.* New York: Oxford University Press.

Sterling, T. G. 2002. "Arthur Andersen and the Baptists." *Salon,* February 7. http://www.salon.com/tech/feature/2002/02/07/arthur_andersen/.

Stern, W. 1996. "Has the FAA Been Coming Clean?" *Business Week,* June 17, 37.

Stockwell, J. 1991. *The Praetorian Guard: The U.S. Role in the New World Order.* Boston: South End Press.

Stone, C. D. 1975. *Where The Law Ends: The Social Control of Corporate Behavior.* New York: Harper and Row.

Strategic Safety. 2001. Firestone Tire Tread Separation: Firestone ATX, ATX II and Wilderness. June 26. http://www.strategicsafety.com/library/si003.htm.

Sturdevant, M. 1992. "Remarks." *A Watershed Conference on Mining and Treaty Rights.* Tomahawk, WI. October 31.

Surette, Ray. 1992. *Media, Crime, and Criminal Justice.* Berkeley, CA: Brooks/Cole.

Suskind, R. 2004. *The Price of Loyalty: George W. Bush, the White House, and the Education of Paul O'Neill.* New York: Simon and Schuster.

Sutherland, E. H. 1940. "White-Collar Criminality." *American Sociological Review* 5: 1–12.

———. 1945. "Is 'White-Collar Crime' Crime?" *American Sociological Review* 10: 132–139.

———. 1949. *White Collar Crime.* New York: Dryden Press. Reissued, New York: Holt, Rinehart and Winston, 1961.

———. 1985. *White Collar Crime: The Uncut Version.* New Haven, CT: Yale University Press.

SWEC. *See* Southern Women's Employment Coalition.

Sykes, G., and D. Matza. 1957. "Techniques of Neutralization: A Theory of Delinquency." *American Sociological Review* 22: 664–670.

Taft, W. H., and T. Buchwald. 2003. "Preemption, Iraq, and International Law." *American Journal of International Law* 97: 557–563.

Taguba, A. 2003. Taguba Report: Investigation of the 800th Military Police Brigade. Joint Interrogation and Debriefing Center [JIDC], U.S. Military Occupation Facilities, Abu Ghraib Prison, Iraq. http://globalsecurity.org/intell/world/iraq/abu-ghurayb-prison-abuse.htm.

Tappan, P. 1947. "Who Is the Criminal?" *American Sociological Review* 12: 96–102.

Thomas, H. 1971. *Cuba: The Pursuit of Freedom.* New York: Harper and Row.

Thompkins, P. 1977. "Management Quo Communication in Rocket Research and Development." *Communication Monographs* 44: 1–26.

———. 1978. "Organizational Metamorphosis in Space Research and Development." *Communication Monographs* 45: 110–118.

Thompson, R. 1989. Statement Before the U.S. Congress, House of Representatives. Committee on Energy and Commerce. Subcommittee on Transportation and Hazardous Materials. Environmental Crimes at DOE's Nuclear Weapons Facilities. 101st Cong., 1st sess. Washington, DC: U.S. Government Printing Office.

Thornton, R. 1987. *American Indian Holocaust and Survival: A Population History since 1492.* Norman: University of Oklahoma Press.

Thurber, J. 2004. The *Progress Report* Archive. American Progress Report. http://www.americanprogress.org/site/pp.asp?c=biJRJ8OVF&b=9328 (accessed November 17, 2004).

Tillman, R., and M. Indergaard. 2005. *Pump and Dump: The Rancid Rules of the New Economy.* New Brunswick, NJ: Rutgers University Press.

Tilly, C. 1985. "War Making and State Making as Organized Crime." In *Bringing the State Back In,* ed. P. Evans, D. Rueschemeyer, and T. Skocpol, 169–191. Cambridge: Cambridge University Press.

Time. 2004. "The Paper Trail: Did Cheney Okay a Deal?" May 30, 1.

Tirman, J. 1997. *Spoils of War: The Human Cost of America's Arms Trade.* Collingdale: PA: Diane Publishing Company.

Tomaševski, K. 1993. *Women and Human Rights.* London: Zed.

Tomaskovic-Devey, D. 1991. *Sundown on the Sunbelt? Growth without Development in the Rural South.* A Report to the Ford Foundation. Raleigh: North Carolina State University Press.

Toombs, S., and D. Whyte. 2002. "Unmasking the Crimes of the Powerful." *Critical Criminology* 11: 217–236.

———. 2003. "Scrutinizing the Powerful." In *Unmasking the Crimes of the Powerful,* ed. S. Toombs and D. Whyte, 3–45. New York: Peter Lang.

Traverso, E. 2003. *The Origins of Nazi Violence*. New York: New Press.

Trento, J. J. 1987. *Prescription for Disaster: From the Glory Days of Apollo to the Betrayal of the Shuttle*. New York: Crown Publishing.

Trevor, G. 1991. "Work-Safety Advocates Buck Anti-Union Sentiment." *Charlotte Observer*, October 27, B1, 4.

Trevor, G., and D. Perlmutt. 1991. "Worker to Testify of Order to Rush Repair." *Charlotte Observer*, September 12, A1, 10.

Trevor, G., and P. Williams. 1991. "Worker: Repairers Left Fryer On." *Charlotte Observer*, September 10, A1, 9.

Tunnell, K. ed. 1993a. *Political Crime in Contemporary America*. New York: Garland.

———. 1993b. "Political Crime and Pedagogy: A Content Analysis of Criminology and Criminal Justice Texts." *Journal of Criminal Justice Education* 4: 101–114.

Turk, A. 1969. *Criminality and the Legal Order*. Chicago: Rand McNally.

Turner, J. H. 1991. *The Structure of Sociological Theory*. 5th ed. Belmont, CA: Wadsworth.

Turpin, J., and L. A. Lorentzen. 1996. *The Gendered New World Order: Militarism, Development, and the Environment*. New York: Routledge.

United Nations. 2001. [Online]. http://www.un.org/ (accessed February 24, 2005).

United Nations Development Programme. 1996. *Human Development Report, 1996*. New York: Oxford University Press.

United States v. Arthur Andersen, LLP. 2003. (T. 18, U.S.C., et. seq).

United States v. Ford Motor Company. 1973. 522 F.2d 962 (6th Cir.).

U.S. Army Corps of Engineers. 2003. Iraq Facts and Question. http://www.hq.usace.army.mil/. Also available at http://www.constructionweblinks.com/Resources/Industry_Reports__Newsletters/April_21_2003/iraq_reconstruction.htm

U.S. Coast Guard. 2000. *Oil Pollution Act of 1990 (OPA 90): An overview* [abstract]. http://www.uscg.mil/d13/dpa/news/oil_pollution_act_of_1990.htm (accessed April 10, 2001).

U.S. Department of Defense. 2004. *Contracts*. http://www.defenselink.mil/contracts/ (accessed February 24, 2005).

U.S. Department of Energy. 1979. *DOE Research and Development and Field Facilities*. Oak Ridge Files. Washington, DC.

———. 1995a. *Human Radiation Experiments: The Department of Energy Roadmap to the Story and Records*. Washington, DC: U.S. Government Printing Office.

———. 1995b. *Human Radiation Studies: Remembering the Early Years: Oral History of Dr. Bain*. Washington, DC: U.S. Government Printing Office.

———. 1995c. *Human Radiation Studies: Remembering the Early Years: Oral History of Dr. Totter*. Washington, DC: U.S. Government Printing Office.

———. 1995d. *Closing the Circle on the Splitting of the Atom*. Washington, DC: U.S. Government Printing Office.

U.S. General Accounting Office. 1985. *Environment, Safety, and Health: Environment and Workers Could Be Better Protected at Ohio Defense Plants*. Washington, DC: GAO.

———. 1986. *Nuclear Energy: Environmental Issues at DOE's Nuclear Defense Facilities*. Washington, DC: GAO.

———. 1989. *Dealing with Enormous Problems in the Nuclear Weapons Complex*. Washington, DC: GAO.

U.S. House of Representatives. 1973a. *Oil and Natural Gas Pipeline Rights-of-Way*. Part I. Washington, DC: U.S. Government Printing Office.

———. 1973b. *Oil and Natural Gas Pipeline Rights-of-Way*. Part II. Washington, DC: U.S. Government Printing Office.

———. 1976. *Alyeska Oil Pipeline Oversight.* Washington, DC: U.S. Government Printing Office.

———. 1986. *Committee on Science and Technology Investigation of the Challenger Accident.* Washington, DC: U.S. Government Printing Office.

———. 1987. *Coast Guard Authorization Act of 1987.* Washington, DC: U.S. Government Printing Office.

———. 1989. Hearing before the Subcommittee on Coast Guard and Navigation of the Committee on Merchant Marine and Fisheries. 101st Cong.

———. 1991a. Committee on Education and Labor. *Hearing on H.R. 3160, Comprehensive OSHA Reform Act, and the Fire at the Imperial Food Products Plant in Hamlet, North Carolina,* Serial no. 102–47. Washington, DC: U.S. Government Printing Office. September 12.

———. 1991b. *Negotiated Settlement from the Exxon Valdez Oil Spill.* Washington, DC: U.S. Government Printing Office.

———. 1993. Committee on Science, Space and Technology. *Environmental Crimes at the Rocky Flats Nuclear Weapons Facility.* 103rd Cong., 1st sess.

———. 2000a. Committee on Energy and Commerce. "Tire Recall Timeline." http://www.house.gov/commerce_democrats/tirerecall/summ.htm. (accessed November 2, 2001).

———. 2000b. House Resolution 5164. The TREAD Act, 106th Congress.

———. 2001. *Hearings before the Committee on Energy and Commerce, Subcommittee on Commerce, Trade and Consumer Protection, Joint with Subcommittee on Oversight and Investigations.* Washington, DC. June 19.

———. 2003. See Waxman (2003).

———. 2004. Democratic Members of the House Committee on Government Reform. Memorandum. March 10.

U.S. Senate. 1977. *Coast Guard Authorization Act of 1978.* S.1250. 95th Cong. 1st sess., no. 95–200. Washington, DC: U.S. Government Printing Office.

———. 1982. *Coast Guard Authorization Act of 1983 and 1984.* S.2252. 97th Cong. 2nd sess., no. 97-361. Washington, DC: U.S. Government Printing Office.

U.S. Senate Lobbying Disclosure Statements. 2004. http://thomas.loc.gov/home/thomas.html (accessed April 27, 2005).

Van Every, D. 1976. *The Disinherited: The Lost Birthright of the American Indian.* New York: Morrow.

Van Horne, Winston A. 1991. *American Indians: Social Justice and Public Policy.* Volume 9 of the Ethnicity and Public Policy Series. Ed. Donald E. Green and Thomas V. Tonnesen. University of Wisconsin System Institute on Race and Ethnicity.

Vaughan, D. 1982. "Toward Understanding Unlawful Organizational Behavior." *Michigan Law Review* 80 (June): 1377–1402.

———. 1983. *Controlling Unlawful Organizational Behavior: Social Structure and Corporate Misconduct.* Chicago: University of Chicago Press.

———. 1988. "Autonomy, Interdependence, and Social Control: NASA and the Space Shuttle Challenger." Department of Sociology, Boston College.

———. 1992. "The Macro-Micro Connection in 'White-Collar Crime' Theory." In *White Collar Crime Reconsidered,* ed. K. Schlegel and D. Weisburd, 124–145. Boston: Northeastern University Press.

———. 1996. *The Challenger Launch Decision: Risky Technology, Culture, and Deviance at NASA.* Chicago: University of Chicago Press.

Verderey, K. 1991. "Theorizing Socialism: A Prologue to the Transition." *American Ethnologist* 18, no. 3: 419–439.

Walker, D. 1986. Statement before the U.S. Congress, House. Committee on Government Operations. Subcommittee on Environment, Energy, and Natural Resources. Review of DOE's Compliance with Environmental Laws in Managing Its Hazardous and Mixed Radioactive-hazardous Waste. 99th cong., 2nd sess. Washington, DC: U.S. Government Printing Office.

Wallach, L., and M. Sforza. 1999. *The WTO: Five Reasons to Resist Corporate Globalization.* New York: Seven Stories Press.

Wall Street Journal. 2004. "Halliburton Overcharged on Troops' Food." February 2.

Wallerstein, I. 1989. *The Modern World System.* New York: Academic Press.

Ward, T., and P. Green. 2000. "Legitimacy, Civil Society, and State Crime" *Social Justice* 27: 76–93.

Washington Post. 2004. News Archive. January 21.

Waxman, H. 2004a. *Iraq on the Record: The Bush Administration's Public Statements on Iraq.* Committee on Government Reform, Minority Staff, Special Investigative Division. Washington, DC: U.S. House of Representatives.

———. 2004b. Memorandum: Congress of the United States, to Committee on Government Reform. March 10. http://www.house.gov/waxman/.

———. 2003. House of Representatives. Letter to General Robert Flowers. October 20. http://www.house.gov/waxman/.

———. 2005. U.S. House of Representatives. http://www.house.gov/waxman (accessed February 2005).

Weeramantry, C. G. 2003. *Armageddon or Brave New World? Reflections on the Hostilities in Iraq.* Ratmalana, Sri Lanka: Sarvodaya Vishva Lekha.

Weiner, T. 1990. *Blank Checks: The Pentagon's Black Budget.* New York: Warner Books.

Weisbrot, M. 2002. "Economists in Denial." *Washington Post Weekly Edition,* August 18, 27.

Weisman, J. 2002. "Sarbannes-Oxley Debated." *Washington Post,* August 7: E1.

West, Mike. 2003. Whistleblower testimony. Online at Henry Waxman, http://www.house.gov/waxman.

Western, J. 2005. *Selling Intervention: The Presidency, the Media, and the American Public.* Baltimore: John Hopkins University Press.

White House. 2003. News Release. http://www.whitehouse.gov/news/releases/2003/04/print/20030411-8.html (accessed April 12, 2003).

———. 2004. News Release. http://www.whitehouse.gov/news/releases/2004/04/print/20040413-5.html (accessed April 14, 2004).

Whyte, D. 2003. "Lethal Regulation: State-Corporate Crime and the United Kingdom Government's New Mercenaries." *Journal of Law and Society* 30: 575–600.

Wickman, P., and T. Daily. 1982. *White-collar and Economic Crime.* Lexington, MA: Lexington Books.

Wilkinson, M. 2004. "Corruption Stench as Company Loses Contract." *Herald Correspondent* (DC), May 21, 2004.

Williams, R. C., and P. L. Cantelon. 1984. *The American Atom: A Documentary History from the Discovery of Fission to the Present.* Philadelphia: University of Pennsylvania Press.

Williams, P., and J. Drescher. 1991. "Plant Not Inspected as Authorized." *Charlotte Observer,* September 21, C1.

Williams, W. A. 1959. *The Tragedy of American Diplomacy.* New York: Dell. 1959. Reprinted 1988.

———. 1969. *The Roots of the Modern American Empire: A Study of the Growth and Shaping of Social Consciousness in a Marketplace Society.* New York: Random House.

Wilson, David. 2004. "New Halliburton Whistleblowers Say Millions Wasted in Iraq." Quoted in Pratap Chatterjee, Special to *CorpWatch*. June 16. www.corpwatch.org/article.php?id=11373.

Wilson, J. Q., and R. J. Herrnstein. 1985. *Crime and Human Nature*. New York: Simon and Schuster.

Wingfield, M. 2002. "Attorney General Sees Similarities in Enron's Fall and Arizona Foundation." *Baptist Standard,* January 21, 1.

Winslow, A. 1995. *Women, Politics, and the United Nations*. Westport, CT: Greenwood Press.

Wolff, E. 1995. *Top Heavy: A Study of the Increasing Inequality of Wealth in America*. New York: Twentieth Century Fund.

Wolfgang, M. E., R. Figlio, P. Tracey, and S. Singer. 1985. *The National Survey of Crime Severity*. U.S. Department of Justice, Bureau of Justice. Washington, DC: U.S. Government Printing Office.

Wonders, N., and R. J. Michalowski. 2001. "Bodies, Borders, and Sex Tourism in a Globalized World: A Tale of Two Cities, Amsterdam and Havana." *Social Problems* 48: 545–571.

Wonders, N., and F. Solop. 1993. "Understanding the Emergence of Law and Public Policy: Toward a Relational Model of the State." In *Making Law,* ed. W. Chambliss and M. Zatz, 204–225. Bloomington: Indiana University Press.

Wood, P. 1986. *Southern Capitalism: The Political Economy of North Carolina, 1880–1980*. Durham, NC: Duke University Press.

Woodward, B. 2004. *Plan of Attack*. New York: Simon and Schuster.

Yeager, P. C. 1987. "Structural Bias in Regulatory Law Enforcement: The Case of the U.S. Environmental Protection Agency." *Social Problems* 34: 330–344.

Young, G., L. Fort, and M. Danner. 1994. "Moving from 'The Status of Women' to 'Gender Inequality': Conceptualization, Social Indicators, and an Empirical Application." *International Sociology* 9: 55–85.

Young, T. R. 1981. "Corporate Crime: A Critique of the Clinard Report." *Contemporary Crises* 5: 323–336.

Zinn, H. 1980. *A People's History of the United States: 1492–Present*. New York: Harper. Reprinted 2003.

Zunes, S. 2003. Tinderbox: U.S. Middle East Policy and the Roots of Terrorism. Monroe, ME: Common Courage Press.

Contributors

TRICIA CRUCIOTTI is currently a criminal investigator for the Memphis, Tennessee, Office of the District Attorney. She earned a master's degree in sociology from Ohio University in 2001 with a research emphasis on state-corporate crime, particularly in the case of the *Exxon Valdez* oil spill.

MONA DANNER is associate professor of sociology and criminal justice at Old Dominion University. She is the author of numerous articles and book chapters in sociology and criminology focusing on issues such as social inequality, gender, and women and global development. In 1997 she was the recipient of the New Scholars Award from the American Society of Criminology Division on Women and Crime.

DAVID KAUZLARICH is associate professor and chair of the Department of Sociology and Criminal Justice Studies at Southern Illinois University Edwardsville. His published works include *Crimes of the American Nuclear State,* coauthored with Ronald C. Kramer, as well as articles and chapters on state crime, peace studies, and criminological theory.

RONALD C. KRAMER is professor of sociology and director of the Criminal Justice Program at Western Michigan University. His published works include *Crimes of the American Nuclear State,* coauthored with David Kauzlarich, and articles and chapters on corporate crime, state crime, peace studies, and social justice. In 2004 he received the Lifetime Achievement Award from the American Society of Criminology Division on Critical Criminology.

RICK A. MATTHEWS is an associate professor, chair of the Department of Sociology, and director of the Criminal Justice Program at Carthage College. His published works cover a variety of topics, including state-corporate crime, juvenile delinquency, and the effects of deindustrialization on homicide rates. He is currently researching the link between masculinities and risk-taking behavior in sport.

RAYMOND MICHALOWSKI is Arizona Regents Professor of Criminal Justice at Northern Arizona University. His published works include *Order, Law, and Crime, Radikale Kriminologie, Crime, Power, and Identity,* and *Run for the Wall: Remembering Vietnam on a Motorcycle Pilgrimage,* as well as a wide array of articles and chapters on topics including the political-economy of crime and punishment, transnational corporate crime, state corporate crime, second economies, Cuban law and justice, environmental crime, criminological theory, and the social construction of memory.

CHRISTOPHER W. MULLINS is an assistant professor of criminology in the Department of Sociology, Anthropology, and Criminology at the University of Northern Iowa. His published works include *The International Criminal Court and Masculinites, Streetlife and Violence,* as well as articles in the journals *Criminology, Critical Criminology,* and *Criminal Justice Review.*

LINDA ROBYN is member of the Anishinabe (Chippewa) nation and associate professor of criminal justice at Northern Arizona University. Her published works include articles and chapters on American Indians and the justice system, environmental justice, and state-corporate crime.

DAWN L. ROTHE is a an assistant professor of criminology in the department of sociology, anthropology, and criminology at the University of Northern Iowa. Her published works include *The International Criminal Court* as well as chapters on globalization, terrorism, and private military firms.

NANCY A. WONDERS is professor and chair, Department of Criminal Justice, Northern Arizona University. Her published works include a wide variety of articles and chapters on gender, social inequality and justice, globalization, sex work, and feminist theory. She is also past chair of the American Society of Criminology Division on Women and Crime.

Index